Small-Space
GARDENING

BOOKS BY PETER LOEWER

Author/Illustrator:

American Gardens

The Annual Garden

Bringing the Outdoors In

The Evening Garden

Evergreens: Guide for Landscape,
Lawn, and Garden

Gardens by Design

Growing and Decorating with
Grasses

The Indoor Water Gardener's
How-to Handbook

The Indoor Window Garden

The Month-by-Month
Garden Almanac

The New Small Garden

Seeds and Cuttings

Solving Deer Problems

Solving Weed Problems

The Wild Gardener

Thoreau's Garden

Tough Plants for Tough Places

Winter Gardening in the
Southeast

A Year of Flowers

Author:

Fragrant Gardens

Letters to Sarah

Pond Water Zoo (with Jean Jenkins)

The Inside-Out Stomach (with Jean
Jenkins)

The Moonflower (with Jean
Jenkins)

Secrets of the Great Gardeners

A World of Plants: The Missouri
Botanical Garden

Editor:

Garden Ornaments

Ornamental Grasses

Taylor's Guide to Annuals

Illustrator Only:

Growing Unusual Fruit by Alan E. Simmons

Wildflower Perennials for Your Garden by Bebe Miles

Small-Space
GARDENING

How to Successfully Grow
Flowers and Fruits in
Containers and Pots

PETER LOEWER

The Lyons Press
Guilford, Connecticut
An imprint of The Globe Pequot Press

The Lyons Press is an imprint of The Globe Pequot Press.

Interior design by M. A. Dubé

10 9 8 7 6 5 4 3 2 1

Printed in the United States of America

Library of Congress Cataloging-in-Publication Data

Loewer, H. Peter.
  Small-space gardening : how to successfully grow flowers and
vegetables in containers and pots / Peter Loewer.
      p. cm.
Includes bibliographical references (p.   ) and index.
  ISBN 1-58574-671-1 (hc : alk. paper)
  1. Container gardening. 2. Plant containers. I. Title.
  SB418.L64 2003
  635.9'86--dc21
                        2002156059

❧ CONTENTS

FOR CENTURIES, THE IDEAL GARDEN COVERED VAST acres of land. It might feature a gigantic waterfall, dramatic tree-lined avenues, a glittering conservatory, and complicated beds of every sort of plants with every sort of blossom. The only folks who got to appreciate these vast estates were those who owned them, their friends, and the army of workers who maintained them.

Times have changed. A few large private gardens remain, but most of them are now public parks, historic sites, or botanical gardens and arboretums—although an occasional member of the *nouveau riche* will build a 10,000-square-foot house with a garden equal to the acreage of an average-sized shopping mall.

Contributing to the trend toward shrinking gardens is the typical middle-class family lifestyle. Today's job market demands mobility, which means the family gardener often begins a garden in one home at the end of March and starts another after moving anew at year's end. Older gardeners are on the move, too. They don't want the fuss and expense of home maintenance and move into smaller houses on smaller lots. Social trends like these point to the benefits of a smaller, more easily managed garden that offers a continually changing picture that doesn't outgrow its frame.

In the 1970s and 1980s, my garden covered most of three acres. Today, we have less than one acre to plant (and sometimes taking care of that seems equal to the energy needed to clean the Augean

Stables—twice). Hence, many of the ideas suggested in this book have found a home in our own backyard. Our smaller garden is just as pleasant as the large one, but it takes much less energy to maintain it.

Special thanks, as always, go to my wife, Jean, my good garden friend Peter Gentling (and his wife, Jasmin), Ann Armstrong in Charlotte, North Carolina, and all those great garden writers like Jim Wilson, Anne Halpin White, and Linda Yang who keep the ideas coming down the garden path.

❧ INTRODUCTION

I NTRODUCTIONS ARE WRITTEN TO BE IGNORED, SCANNED, or—on rare occasions—read. The following text is kind of a wrap-up on plants, from the individual cells to the final production number. It contains a bit of botany that most books written today skip, but it's useful information. Sometimes a little understanding helps to avoid a lot of future problems.

The Life Processes of a Plant Cell

Most plants can transform simple chemical substances into food, both for them and for us. The most important of these chemicals, taken from the soil and atmosphere, are carbon dioxide and water. When chlorophyll (manufactured by special cells in the plant's leaf) is triggered by sunlight or artificial light, carbon dioxide and water combine to produce carbohydrates in the form of dextrose, the staple form of energy for a plant. At the same time, pure oxygen is produced as a by-product. This chemical process, called "photosynthesis," while it sounds complex, is really simple.

Plants we associate with dark, dank, and gloomy places, such as molds, mildews, and mushrooms, lack chlorophyll and are unable to photosynthesize their own food. Instead, they live on the remains of other plants and animals. (Or, thriving in our kitchens, they exist on stale pieces of bread.)

Photosynthesis is, without doubt, Earth's most important chemical process. The oxygen that all living things require to convert food into energy is a direct result of photosynthesis. The green plant is the only significant source of free oxygen in our atmosphere. And directly or indirectly, all of our food comes from plants. I cringe at the sight of rich farmland, ripped up and coated with layers of blacktop—for this is dead land.

In most plants (the exceptions are the cacti and other succulents), the leaf is the center of the photosynthetic process. The exchanges of oxygen, carbon dioxide, and water vapor occur in small openings on the leaf's undersurface. These openings, called stomata, are easily visible under a hand lens as minute pores.

By day, water pressure builds up within the stomata walls, forcing them open. At night they lose water and collapse inward, more or less closing. The water evaporated through these pores will be replaced by water drawn up from the roots. This little-understood process is called "transpiration." Botanists assume that, since the stomata must be open during the day to take in air, the loss of water is a side effect, beyond the plant's control.

One of the major problems that plants have in today's well-heated homes (most plants welcomed the Energy Crisis with open leaves!) is maintaining a balance between the water lost from the stomata and the overly dry conditions surrounding them. The humidity in an average heated home hovers at about 15 percent, but even the vast sandy and parched Sahara Desert enjoys an annual average of 25 percent humidity. So you can see why houseplants, especially tropicals, appreciate a frequent misting of water.

Of the four major methods of home heating (hot-air, hot-water, steam, and electric), electric is the best for plants because the heat is relatively constant and doesn't rely on fans or forced-air equipment to move the heat around. Hot-water heating is the next best; the changes in temperature are always gradual. Steam heat causes rapid fluctuations in temperature, however, and plants must be kept away from pipes. Hot-air heating has a definite drying effect, especially if a plant is placed in front of a heating duct; the steady blast of hot air quickly dries out its leaves, and the roots will need additional waterings because the soil will become rapidly depleted of water.

By liberal placement of gravel and pans filled with water, favorable humidity can be re-established. You might also consider adding a humidifier to the furnace system. They are relatively inexpensive, and the additional humidity they provide benefits plants, furniture, and people.

Since the stomata close at night, in the morning you'll occasionally find drops of water at the tips of your plant's leaves, especially those of the tropicals. Don't worry about it. When the stomata are closed, roots continue to absorb water. Any excess is released as droplets through special pores in the leaf tips. This allows the plant to maintain a proper internal water pressure. It's called "guttation" and sounds a great deal worse than it is.

Making Sense of Plant Names

Throughout this book I have used both the common and the scientific (Latinized) names for various plants. This is not to confuse, but to ensure that author and readers are dealing with the same plants, and to be certain that any plants readers may decide to buy are the same plants that they receive from the nursery.

Although it's true that many plants can be recognized by their common names, many more cannot. For example there are five plant genera that use "mother-in-law" in their appellations: mother-in-law or *Kalanchoe pinnata*; mother-in-law plant or *Caladium* spp. and *Dieffenbachia Seguine*; and mother-in-law's tongue or *Gasteria* spp., *Sansevieria trifasciata*, and *Dieffenbachia* spp. All of these names are in general use. Now imagine the local variations across the fifty states and Canada. Then picture the additional confusion when one mother-in-law plant is confused with another by someone in a nursery order department who is suffering from allergies or hates plants to begin with.

To prevent confusion, all known plants have been given scientific names—each one unique—that are easily understood throughout the world, whatever native language is in use. Carl Linnaeus (1707–78) is the man primarily thought of as the founder of the system. In the 1700s, when the system was first adopted into general use, Latin was the international language of scholars and seemed the obvious choice to educated botanists. Therefore, plant names are derived from Renaissance Latin with a great many appropriated from Ancient Greek. To show that many of these botanical names have a reasonable and often delightful history behind their creation, I have, whenever possible, included the translations of the original words used in creating this fascinating nomenclature.

If you are concerned about pronunciation, don't be. Very few people can pronounce these names with alacrity. The English, for example, have rules for Latin pronunciation that are at odds with most of the rest of the world (remember, the English pronounce a migraine headache as a "meegraine" and Don Juan as "Don Jooan"). Besides, you will probably only use them in writing.

A Guide to Names

Scientific names may contain four terms that are in general use: *genus, species, variety,* and *cultivar* (there are others but they are beyond the scope of this book). All reference books, most gardening books, nearly all responsible catalogs and nurseries, and even the majority of seed packets list the scientific name along with the common. In many cases, the common names of popular plants are also their scientific names, and people use them every day without realizing it. Delphinium, geranium, sedum, and gladiolus immediately come to mind.

Genus refers to a group of plants that are closely related, while *species* suggests an individual plant's unique quality, color, or even habit of growth. Either genus or species names may honor the person who discovered the plant. For example, the spiderworts are called *Tradescantia* after John Tradescant, one of the greatest and most adventurous of the English plant collectors.

Genus and species names can also be descriptive. The botanical name given to the popular spring bulb the milky white snowdrop is *Galanthus*, from the Greek *gala*, milk, and *anthos*, flower. The species include *byzantinus* for a type from southeast Europe, *caucasicus* for another from the Caucasus, and *grandiflora* for one with extra large flowers.

The third term, *variety*, is often abbreviated to "var." A variety represents a noticeable change in a plant that naturally develops by chance and breeds true from generation to generation.

The fourth term, *cultivar*, was introduced in 1923 by world-famous botanist and horticulturalist Liberty Hyde Bailey and derived from the words "*culti*vated *vari*ety." Cultivar represents a desirable variation that appears on a plant while it is in cultivation and could result either by chance or design.

It should be noted that many plants listed in catalogs have scientific names that are woefully out of date. This is because the catalog writers know that the public recognize, for example, the name *Lisianthus* but will be unfamiliar with the current and correct name of *Eustoma*, so they use the old. I've indicated both names when possible.

1

THE IMPORTANCE OF AND REASONS FOR CONTAINER GARDENING, INCLUDING A BRIEF HISTORY OF POTS AND POTTING.

YOU WILL BE AMAZED AT WHAT WILL HOLD A PLANT. There are vases and jardinières, urns and pots, troughs and tubs, window boxes for window ledges, pots to hang on walls or from trees, and plain hanging baskets, not to mention discarded sinks, old wheelbarrows, abandoned tires, abandoned supermarket carts, old milk cartons, tomato cans, and even a toilet (or two).

Believe it or not, an antique toilet bowl (especially from the nineteenth century), in good condition, makes a very effective pot. And while purists bemoan the use of old car and truck tires (especially at the entrances to trailer courts), I do not. Anything that helps to relieve the increasing monotony of both our urban and suburban scenery is welcome—at least to me.

These days, considering the demands made upon my time and my energy, if given a choice between having the backyard become an ample garden or a terrace filled with a grand collection of pots, I'd take the pots, hands down.

Why? A variety of pots provides many choices for gardeners. Dress up the front entrance to your home, transform a bare deck from a lineup of uninteresting wooden planks to a lush platform garden, or hide an ugly foundation without digging up the existing soil. Want to change the look of your garden? Bring in new pots with new plants and take the old to a secret place on your property—well screened by a fence or hedge—and replant them at your

One of the new 'Red Flower Carpet' roses in a blue pot dresses up the entrance to this home.

ease. Tired of the general look of your perennial border but not willing to take the time to redesign or replant? Move in some great containers holding, for example, a small Japanese maple or an artfully planted mix of perennials and annuals that will bloom all summer, and well into the fall. Want to experiment with plants that usually give in to the extremes of your climate? Try growing these beauties in pots. You'll have ample control of their environment, using portability to your best advantage as you move them from place to place, providing weather protection where you find can it. Thinking of a new color combo that even the trendiest magazines say is a bit too much? It might look fabulous, but by using a pot, you can try it out without digging everything up if your scheme proves garish after all.

These containers can also offer a short-term solution to growing a number of plants, such as many bulbs that come into bloom and then fade, leaving behind a clump of uninteresting foliage that must ripen before the bulbs go into storage. When the plants become unsightly, you simply move them out of sight.

Finally, if you're not as young as you once were, and either your garden or your physical prowess is limited, pots can be placed at any level and can be moved about with ease—larger pots can go on wheels or be lugged about on a dolly.

✤ A BRIEF HISTORY OF CONTAINERS

Every few years, newspapers feature a sunken-treasure story, where a ship of old is found buried at the bottom of the sea, and when its cargo is unearthed, among the treasures are marvelous pots once used to hold olive oil, wine, or water.

Since civilization's beginnings men and women (usually women) have made earthenware pottery. The Greeks were masters of the craft, as were the Romans. Even earlier, however, the kings of Crete decorated their terraces with marvelous pots, as did the Egyptians. Tomb paintings of Ancient Egypt show men digging up palm trees and planting them in great pots. And Egyptian wall paintings portray gardens with beds of annuals in groups of solid colors; the containers are made of pottery or wood, and placed as edging on garden walkways. One particular fresco is a depiction of early gardeners moving plants. Incense trees that were collected in Somalia, their roots tightly held by roped balls of earth, are hauled aboard a ship bound for Cairo.

In *The Story of Gardening*, Richardson Wright (the most famous editor of the original *House & Garden* magazine) noted the Egyptian love of garden motifs: "The walls of the bedroom of Amenhotep IV were painted with flowers, and the floor was made to simulate a lily pool with its flower beds, from which sprang flower stalks that formed the pillars of the room."

The tomb of Sen-nofer, one of Amenhotep's honored garden directors was a simulated grape arbor, complete with a full display of fruits. Such decorating concepts were so fashionable that the upper classes would attempt to create the same kind of looks on a much smaller scale.

According to ancient garden records, the Egyptians loved roses and actually grew them to supply other Mediterranean countries, even shipping them as far away as Rome. Cut flowers were also beloved, and anemones, thistles, papyrus leaves, reeds, and cornflowers were all available at bazaars and could be taken home to brighten a room or two. In fact, like the later Greek order of columns known as the Corinthian, the Egyptians had three column designs that were derived from plants: the Palm column, the Lotus, and the Papyrus. The first resembled a palm trunk topped with nine leaves, the second was formed by a stem for the shaft and a lotus flower for the capital, and the third was modeled after a wrapped bundle of papyrus stems.

The Ancient Greeks were forced by geography to become container gardeners. As Mary Grant White points out in *Pots and Pot Gardens*:

> . . . Greeks do not seem to have made gardens as we understand them, being hampered, no doubt, by the rocky nature of their soil. Such ornamental gardening as did exist had great religious significance, often taking the form of sacred groves dedicated to some god or goddess. Among their religious practices, none makes more delightful reading than the cult of Adonis, which was thought to have originated in Phoenicia, and spread to Greece by way of Cyprus. In these particular rites, Adonis, a beautiful youth beloved by Aphrodite, was worshipped as the spirit of Nature and plant life. In the autumn, he was believed to die and disappear into the underworld, to be rescued by Aphrodite and brought back to earth again in the spring. The Greeks made great play of this myth and each midsummer held festivals during which they would place a number of earthenware pots around a figure of the god. These were sown with quick-growing seeds such as fennel, lettuce, and barley, and when they sprouted, the people rejoiced to think that Adonis had come back to them.

Soon the pots planted for the Adonis festivals were in every home and became such a popular item of outdoor decoration that, although Adonis faded, pot gardening continued. Flowerpots from Ancient Greece were amazingly similar to many of today's elegant designs and held everything from rooted tree cuttings to bunches of blooming poppies.

The Adonis festivals spread until the Greeks developed the roof garden and, later, Roman gardeners planted flowers and bushes in tubs and set them in courtyards and along garden pathways. In fact, it was Rome that began the custom of the window box.

Today, throughout Europe and the Mediterranean, earthenware pots remain in vogue. By the early 1900s they had made their way to the Mediterranean-style gardens found in Florida and California. Any fashionable house in a Hollywood movie of the 1930s sported pots of flowers carefully positioned on the tops of walls, adorning terraces, around tiled swimming pools, and here and there along the perennial border.

2

AESTHETICS OF POTS

THERE ARE TWO WORDS ASSOCIATED WITH THE POTS of today: clay and plastic. Clay is a time-honored material with a long horticultural history, while plastic is a Frankenstein monster, conceived in the 1930s and now out of control. Oh, sure, there are well-designed plastic pots out there, but at the dawn of the twenty-first century, they remain few and far between.

When archaeologists of the future search through our long-forgotten rubbish piles, not only will they unearth a plethora of beer cans and disposable diapers, but also millions of non-disintegrating plastic flowerpots (some with golden edges).

These plastic and Styrofoam pots work well for commercial growers who must balance continually rising costs and deadlines for seasonal markets (as hectic as the fashion industry) with demands for cheap transportation. They have an excuse to use such pots because they're lighter and less expensive. But you, the buyer, upon reaching home can easily remove the plant from its artificial housing and give it a new, more functional home.

There are more than aesthetic reasons for using clay containers. Clay breathes, allowing air and water to pass through its walls; therefore, it's much more difficult to over-water when using clay. (I'm convinced that more damage is done by the lethal use of water than any other mistreatment.) Furthermore, clay is much heavier and keeps larger plants from toppling over in a mild breeze or crashing to the floor when the cat bumps into it on its way to the water dish.

Clay pots will also last much longer (as long as you don't drop them) than plastic, which becomes brittle with age. Finally, by looking at the algae and salt deposits forming on the clay, you have an early warning sign that predicts problems long before the plant itself shows symptoms of trouble.

⚜ CLAY POTS

Clay pots are made in many different sizes and shapes. They start at 2 inches, measured by the diameter across the top, and go up to 16 inches or more. Their height is about the same as their diameter. Many have names long associated with English gardens. The 2-inch pot is called a "thimble," the 2½-inch pot a "thumb."

When the height exceeds the diameter, pots are called "long Toms"; when shorter than they are wide they're called "dwarfs." You'll also find azalea pots that are three quarters of the standard depth, allowing for their shallow root systems.

I rarely find a use for the thimble or thumb pots because they're so small the soil dries out too quickly, but they're fun to have around for an extra small cactus or a tiny vine seedling.

Before peat pots and Jiffy-7s (compressed peat blocks enclosed in fine mesh) were developed, these small pots were extensively used for seedlings. These days, you can transplant beginning seedlings and their peat pots into 3-inch clay pots when the plants are large enough to move. Depending on the age of the pot and its manufacturing process, you will find minor variations in the thickness of the clay walls and the top measurements.

New clay pots should be soaked in water before use, or they'll quickly draw most of the water from the soil. Old and reused pots must be cleaned and scrubbed with steel wool, which will easily remove an accumulation of mineral salts.

You'll find drainage holes in the bottom, and these should be covered with a few shards of a broken pot to keep soil from escaping and, if your plants are outside or in a greenhouse, a small piece of screen to guard against wandering slugs and other undesirables.

Unless you have the talent of Picasso, however, never paint pots. If you want to make an attractive display for a beautiful plant, find a suitable jardinière or other container and place the clay pot inside it.

✦ LEARNING FROM THE EXPERTS

When gardening with containers, I temporarily push aside my predilection for native plants (although I often use them as subjects), and turn to English gardeners and those glorious photographs in English garden magazines.

High on my list of authorities is Gertrude Jekyll, the author of numerous books on home garden design (not to mention grand estates), who found that plants growing in pots were noteworthy additions to any garden scheme. Miss Jekyll often wrote about the beauty of Italian gardens, where most views include quantities of plants in pots standing at various levels and in interesting groupings. These are usually in addition to larger pots with small trees such as oranges, lemons, or oleanders that, in their immense and often richly decorated earthenware receptacles, form an important part of the garden design.

In our mountain climate of North Carolina, citrus fruits are out, but even here we can grow Japanese maples, conifers, most native shrubs, and many plants with winter interest, as long as their pots are more than a foot in diameter.

In her classic book, *Colour Schemes for the Flower Garden*, Miss Jekyll describes how she makes use of the Italian-style grouping in her own English garden:

> Good groupings of smaller plants in pots is a form of ornament that might be made more use of in our own gardens, especially where there are paved spaces near a house or in connection with a tank or fountain, so that there is convenient access to means of daily watering. I have such a space in a cool court nearly square in shape. A middle circle is paved, and all next the house is paved, on

The autumn-flowering hosta (Hosta plantaginea), *with attractive leaves and very fragrant white flowers, was a Gertrude Jekyll favorite. No other plant beats its late-season bloom.*

a level of one shallow step higher. It is on the sides of this raised step that the pot plants are grouped, leaving free access to a wooden seat in the middle, and a clear way to a door on the left.

She goes on to describe terracotta pots lush with hostas, particularly *Hosta plantaginea* and *H. sieboldii,* situated in front of, and hiding from view, more common pots full of blooming annuals. Early in June, *Clematis montana* is still in bloom and pots of cast-iron plants (*Aspidistra elatior*) sit near the side of the house, not to mention all sorts of ferns. And, of course, there are pots of lilies (*Lilium longiflorum, L. candidum, L. superbum*), and Spanish irises and various cultivars of the gladiolus tribe, backed up by a trellis of the tropical cup-and-saucer vine (*Cobaea scandens*), either in the traditional purple or pure white.

"There are seldom more," she continues, "than two kinds of flowering plants placed here at a time; the two or three sorts of beautiful foliage are in themselves delightful to the eye; often there is nothing with them but Lilies, and one hardly desires to have more. There is an ample filling of the green plants, so that no pots are seen."

She chooses geraniums for their color, linking white and soft pink in one area, while elsewhere she has many pots of rosy scarlets or salmon reds. She takes great pleasure in grouping the palest salmon pink next to a good and pure scarlet cultivar.

She suggests that, when designing gardens that include areas of flagstones, many of the pots look their best standing slightly above ground level, perhaps having the pots on clay feet, which are now available at most garden centers.

One of her favorites is the maiden's wreath (*Francoa racemosa*), a plant with many uses. The distinctive foliage is quite attractive, and the long flower stems are flung out in all directions, much like the tapestry strands thrown out in Pre-Raphaelite artist Holman Hunt's marvelous painting, *The Lady of Shalott*, which hearkens from the same era in which Miss Jekyll was designing top gardens in England. At summer's end the flowering stems become so heavy that in a stiff breeze, there's a danger that the stems will snap off or that some of the plant's roots will be pulled right out of the pots. She suggests that short pieces of wood be used to strengthen the stems.

She also espouses the use of potted plants, noting that a well-blooming plant will give life and interest to even the dreariest corner. After all, the bloom is long lasting, and the fall colors of many blooms and leaves are beautiful to see.

As a final note, she points out that it's rare to see, at least in England, plant tubs that are painted a pleasant color. In nearly every garden she describes, the tubs are painted a strong, raw green with hoops of contrasting black, whereas any green that is not bright and raw would be much better. And, I might add, it's much the same in twenty-first-century America.

Miss Jekyll advises that the matter of coloring most garden accessories deserves more attention than it commonly receives. Doors in garden walls, trellises, wooden railings—these and any other items of woodwork that stand out in the garden and are noticeable among its flowers and foliage should, if painted green, be a green that is not so bright so that it detracts from the natural greens of the surrounding plants. It's the plant that should be in the limelight, not the tub.

An appropriate, quiet green paint can be mixed from black and chrome green with enough white added to give the depth or lightness desired.

3

THE CARE AND FEEDING OF
THE PLANTS

PLANTS ARE ALIVE. THEY TAKE IN FOOD, PRODUCE WASTE, and, like people, reproduce sexually with male and female gametophytes (although some species reproduce asexually). Plant cells and animal cells contain many of the same cellular parts, such as mitochondria, DNA, and RNA.

To keep a plant alive and healthy, you need to know its light requirements, its proper soil mix, when and how to water, when to fertilize, and how to propagate it.

⋇ LIGHT

Light intensity is measured in foot-candles (FC). One FC is the amount of light cast on a white surface by one candle, one foot away, in an otherwise dark room. You can measure FCs with a photo exposure meter using the simple FC conversion tables found in a camera instruction manual. (If you've lost your camera's manual, as I have mine, you'll find the information on the Web.)

Plants that need full sun, such as cacti and most flowering annuals, generally require about 6,000 to 8,000 FC. Plants such as ferns and most begonias prefer partial shade or an average of 2,000 FC. And other plants, such as deep jungle dwellers, require full shade, or between 100 and 500 FC. Many plants will survive in 20 FC of light, but 100 FC seems to be the minimum for growth.

Windows immediately cut down on light intensity. Outside, the glass refracts the light, and some is actually absorbed by the glass. Add architectural details, such as eaves and cornices, and even more light is lost. A west-facing window in mid-morning, for instance, may read 400 FC at the inside sill, but only 10 FC six feet into the room, while the outside reading is over 10,000 FC. If windows are lightly curtained, screened, or dirty (a major problem for city dwellers) more light is lost. Add a layer of dust to the leaf tops, and the amount of light received by the leaves is dim indeed. Plants should be dusted right along with books, tabletops, and everything else. A comfortable light for reading is 50 FC but that's hardly enough to keep a plant alive, much less healthy.

You can get an idea of the light intensity your plants are receiving by using measurements from the exposure meter on a regular camera. Set the film speed to ASA 200, and the shutter speed to $\frac{1}{500}$ of a second, and adjust the f-stop. Take the reading using a piece of white cardboard until the meter gives the OK.

$$f\ 22\ = 5{,}000\ FC$$
$$f\ 16\ = 2{,}500\ FC$$
$$f\ 11\ = 1{,}200\ FC$$
$$f\ 8\ \ \ = \ \ \ 550\ FC$$
$$f\ 6.3 = \ \ \ 300\ FC$$
$$f\ 4.5 = \ \ \ 150\ FC$$

❧ PLANTS UNDER LIGHTS

A new world has opened up for the plant lover who is denied adequate natural light for good plant growth. Plants can be grown under artificial light using a combination of fluorescent and tungsten lighting. The process can require a whole volume in itself, and the bibliography lists two excellent books available on the subject. Yet, all the plants mentioned in this book may be grown under lights, even in a closet, if the intensities are high enough.

⚜ SOIL MIXES FOR POTTING THE PLANTS

Most of the plants in this book are also very tolerant of soil conditions, with only a few preferring specialized mixes (which are so noted). I use packaged potting soils or mix my own using a good commercial potting soil, composted manure, and sharp sand.

Commercial potting soil is usually sold in 10- and 20-pound bags at nursery centers and variety stores. If it's not labeled "sterilized," don't buy it—the eventual germination of the weed seeds in an unsterilized mix will drive you mad. Composted manure (either sheep or cow) is usually sold in 20- and 40-pound bags, and it is easier (and neater) to use than regular animal manure. Sand is also one of the main components of a good soil, since it makes a heavy soil more porous. Use builder's sand or sharp sand, and be sure to wash it before use. "Sharp" simply means that the sand grains are rough to the touch, as opposed to soft sand which is generally too fine to be of use. Beach sand, for instance, is too soft and it is also too full of salt.

⚜ FERTILIZERS

The composted manure added to the various soil mixes will usually provide sufficient nutrients for most plants if they are repotted annually. But if a plant is a heavy feeder and is submitted to repeated waterings, important nutrients and soluble salts will soon be leached from the soil and the plants will suffer. Therefore, feeding potted plants with a good, soluble fertilizer is very important. It doesn't matter what brand you use, as long as the ratio of usable nitrogen, phosphorus, and potash is about 10:10:10 or 20:30:20. For example, 5:5:5 contains 5 percent nitrogen, 5 percent phosphorus, and 5 percent potash; the rest of the solution consists of inert ingredients.

Plants need nitrogen for strong stems and healthy foliage, but too much leads to rampant growth at the expense of flower, fruit, or seed production. Phosphorus helps plant tissue ripen and mature, but a phosphorous deficiency can cause stunted growth. Potash also helps plants in early growth stages by strengthening tissue and making them more resistant to cold; too little potash, however, results in poorly developed root systems and stunted plants.

Don't start fertilizing until the plants are really growing. Even then I dilute the formula by half, never using it more than once every two or three weeks. Remember: Less is more.

If you are in an organic frame of mind, you can use one of the fish emulsion concentrates. These are natural, non-burning formulas derived from seagoing fish. Be sure to buy the deodorized products, though—especially if you plan to use them indoors.

Other liquid fertilizers can also be used without any worry on the gardener's part. Some come in a concentrate with a medicine-stopper top for easy mixing, and still others are in powder form, which must be dissolved in tepid water. Just follow package directions.

✺ PLANTING AND WATERING CONTAINERS

To make things simpler, I've used variations on the same soil mix for years. I buy large bags of sterilized potting soil, builder's sand, and composted sheep or cow manure, mixing the three together in equal amounts. Except for alpines, which require more grit for drainage, this mix seems to work well for almost any potted plant.

Once the plants are potted, watering begins. The soil in pots and troughs will dry out faster than garden soil, so it's a good idea to check your pots every day, especially during hot summers. Be prepared to water every day.

Always use tepid water for watering plants, especially if they are growing in the hot summer sun. Cold water is a shock to their root systems in the same way that cold water can shock you in the shower.

A watering can is the most common device for delivering water, but there are other ways to get water to the plant. For example, you can shallowly set a small custard cup into the soil, and then place a wick (of fiberglass or the kind used for kerosene lamps) with one end in the water and the other end in the soil, and the roots will absorb what they need. In very hot weather, you can leave ice cubes on the soil surface; the ice will slowly melt, quenching the plant's thirst.

❧ DORMANCY

Everything in life must come to rest at one time or another and plants are no exception. Once they finish flowering, and their leaves have manufactured adequate food for the coming season of growth, most plants enter a period of dormancy.

This quiet time in a plant's life is governed by a natural cycle that revolves around a combination of shorter days and a drop in temperature. Dormancy is particularly noticeable with plants from the temperate regions of the world, especially those growing in areas with extreme seasonal weather variations. It's not as noticeable with tropical plants because the closer you get to the Equator, days and nights become equally balanced, and seasonal temperatures stay about the same. Even tropicals, however, must have periods of rest—no plant will flower, fruit, and continue to sprout new leaves on a year-round basis. If forced to overwork for long periods of time, plants will ultimately die, literally worn out from exhaustion.

In the northern part of the United States, native plants brought in from out-of-doors will still slow down their growth during the darker days of winter, and most will not only refuse to flower but will also eventually die if not given a periodic rest in combination with cooler temperatures.

Trees give ample evidence of the value of dormancy by dropping their leaves in the fall. Even those small northern trees used as bonsai subjects have leaves that turn colors and drop—even when kept indoors. If not given a period of cool rest, they will also die.

Nobody really knows the exact temperatures that constitute what horticulturalists call "chilling temperatures," but from years of observation, most scientists conclude that such temperatures need not reach freezing. For about six weeks, 45°F is all that's necessary for most plants to start new growth in the spring.

✹ THREE KEYS TO HEALTHY PLANTS

For your plants to flourish, you must ensure that they can photosynthesize efficiently, meaning they must get the proper amount of light, air, and water. Carbon dioxide, which contains both carbon and oxygen in the only source readily available to a plant, is of primary importance to the process of photosynthesis and healthy plant growth. I've always thought that the success of many "green-thumbers" might be due to not only the constant attention they give to their plants but also the exhalations they make in the plant area, giving the plants an extra shot of carbon dioxide with every breath—they literally grow with every word. I don't advocate hyperventilating for your plants every morning, but there just might be something to talking to your plants!

Generally, enough carbon dioxide is available in the surrounding air to provide for a plant's needs, but many experiments in horticulture today are trying to increase plant growth by releasing measured amounts of this gas in greenhouse atmospheres. The resulting increased growth rate can be startling. The more sophisticated garden and plant catalogs even sell automatic equipment for this purpose.

✹ WATER

Plants need water in order to pull minerals from the earth, to provide the basic ingredient for cytoplasm, and as a supply of hydrogen for the photosynthetic process. Therefore, the side effects of wilting can be disastrous. When a leaf wilts, the stomata close to prevent further water loss. This cuts down on the intake of carbon dioxide. As a result, the plant cannot use the carbon and oxygen necessary to produce the dextrose required for energy on the cellular level, and it must rely on its reserves. If a plant has not wilted too badly, it will generally snap back, but successive wiltings damage cells, as well as cause the loss of potential food energy.

✿ RESPIRATION AROUND THE CLOCK

All plant and animal cells respire. Breathing is a purely mechanical activity developed by many animals in which large amounts of oxygen are transported to the cells deep inside the body. Most animals need this additional oxygen to provide the amount of energy required for movement. In plants, however, respiration is the process that supplies cells with the oxygen they need to convert the food produced by photosynthesis into energy. A plant does not breathe the way animals do, but absorbs oxygen through its roots, stems, and stomata. So, while plants and animals respire, only animals breathe.

Respiration occurs twenty-four hours a day in every living plant cell. Each cell absorbs oxygen through the stomata, or by diffusion through the roots and stems, releasing carbon dioxide as a waste product. Photosynthesis, however, occurs only during daylight, and only in those cells that have chloroplasts (generally in the plant's leaves), which take in carbon dioxide and hydrogen from water, producing food and releasing oxygen as a by-product. If the two processes proceeded at an equal rate, with respiration using the oxygen and food as quickly as photosynthesis produced it, there would be nothing left for growth and repair. Fortunately, photosynthesis occurs at a faster rate, producing a surplus of food and oxygen. Thus, a plant in a sealed container, given an initially adequate supply of water, soil, and ample light, may exist for years without outside help. This is why a sealed terrarium works so well.

Yet, temperature also plays an integral role in plant respiration. As temperatures fall, respiration decreases. Generally a 10-degree drop from the average temperature a plant enjoys is considered the best. If your plant does best at 70°F during the day, try to give it 60°F at night; if it likes 60°F during the day, give it 50°F at night. Most plant growth occurs at night. In fact, that 10-degree drop helps the plant digest the sugars it produced during the day.

Once we understand the effect temperature has on a plant, we can prolong the life of a favorite flower. Blossoms on azaleas, orchids, lilies, and tulips, for instance, will last longer if given a cool night. Much like leaves, flowers are made of individual cells that continue to respire and grow, even if cut. Dropping the temperature nightly slows everything down. When we go on vacation, I always move the plants to a cooler part of the house to slow down their activity. This also cuts down on their water intake, which should prevent them from drying out in our absence.

Not too long ago, people were so worried about plant and flower respiration that they removed them from bedrooms and hospital rooms at night, believing the carbon dioxide levels would become so high that human life would be in danger of suffocation. Experiments have shown, however, that the carbon dioxide level in a greenhouse in the early morning increases by only one half of one percent. A crowded room at a cocktail party, however, can raise the concentration fully one percent!

✳ POTTING ON!

When a plant needs repotting, it's only moved up one size, two at the most. A small plant in a large pot not only looks rather strange, it usually doesn't last too long either. Unless plant roots extend throughout the soil, the excess becomes soggy and compacted, leading to sickly growth.

Repotting becomes necessary when the roots completely occupy all the soil and the root ball assumes the shape of the pot. Roots working their way through drainage holes are the first sign that you need to repot. The best time for repotting is early spring when plants begin active root growth after a winter's rest. The worst time is during winter, because broken roots have a smaller chance of healing quickly before disease sets in. An actively growing plant, however, can be repotted at any time.

If you are worried about a plant being pot-bound you can easily check without hurting it. Place two fingers, one on either side of the stem to hold the soil and flip the pot over. Rap it on a hard edge and the soil ball should slide out. Wait until the plant's soil is fairly dry for this routine; soaking wet soil will fight you all the way.

If all looks okay, and the roots are not massed on the outside, pop the plant back in the pot. If not, move it up to the next size.

Take a larger pot, crock it, sprinkle some new soil on the bottom, and place the root ball on top. Sprinkle new soil around the sides and give the pot a sharp thump on a table or the floor to help settle the soil. Firm the edges with your thumbs and the job's done.

One important thing to remember: Leave enough room at the top of the pot for watering. With a 5-inch pot, there should be at least a ¾-inch clearance between the rim and the soil. Nothing is quite so annoying as watering a plant, dribbling mud down the pot sides, and then having to go at it again because during the first attempt the plant got half of the water and the floor got the rest.

After potting, water the plant well because it helps to settle the soil. If it is packed a little too loosely, you'll notice a few depressions, so sprinkle in some more soil to level the surface. I always drop a small shard or flat stone on top to break the force of water when it leaves the watering can.

When watering a plant, you should sit the pot in a saucer to catch the excess water. If there is no room between the water and the bottom of the pot, the water will seep back in. This is fine with many plants, but some resent it. In that case, set the pot on a few pebbles, or large pieces of gravel, and make sure the saucer is large enough to catch the water without overflowing. Slow evaporation from the saucer will add to humidity and save the time devoted to emptying saucers after watering.

❦ ROOT PRUNING

Plants need fresh new root growth in order to adequately absorb nutrients from soil. Root pruning and repotting a root-bound plant will invigorate it and cause a flush of new growth. To prune the roots, remove the root ball and set it on your work surface. Take a large, sharp knife and slice off about half an inch of soil and roots. Then repot as before, adding new soil around the edges and at the bottom. Next, lightly prune the plant itself. Don't overdo it. The plant just lost some roots, and you'll make its job easier by giving it less top growth to supply with water.

⚶ TOP DRESSING

Suppose you have a truly root-bound plant but no extra pots and no time to become overly involved with potting on. Remove about an inch of the surface soil and replace it with new potting mix. As you water, the freshened soil will help the roots along and stave off the inevitable for a while. Occasionally, the pot will break from the pressures of the roots, and you'll be forced to repot it.

4

PROPAGATION AND PESTS

I F BUYERS HAD TO WAIT FOR SUPPLIERS TO GROW ALL THE plants people want from seed, there would never be enough plants to go around. Luckily, nature has accomplished an alternate method called asexual or vegetative reproduction, which leads to the manufacture of thousands of clones to meet consumer demand. There are several methods to promote propagation, each with its own unique advantages.

PROPAGATION

Softwood Cuttings

The term "softwood" refers to the soft, green stem tissues found in houseplant annuals or the first season's growth of perennials before the stem matures into woody tissue.

Late spring or early summer is the best time to propagate by taking softwood cuttings. If you only want a few plants, I've found the best method uses a combination of peat pots or Jiffy-7s and small plastic food bags. First, choose a plant that needs pruning. Cut the healthy stems, which are about 3 to 6 inches long, with a sharp knife or razor blade slightly below the point where a leaf petiole (or stalk) joins the stem. Remove any damaged leaves and flowers and neatly slice off any bottom leaves close to the stem.

Take an expanded Jiffy pot (or any small container will do) and make a hole with a pencil or similar object, three-quarters of the pot's depth. Insert the cutting, making sure that the base of the stem touches the bottom of the hole. Firm the medium back into place around the stem. Now put the whole affair in a baggie, leaving the opening at the top.

If the air is very dry, seal the bag with a twist; the baggie will hold in the moisture that the leaves throw off but cannot replace until new roots form. The medium should be moist at all times, but never soggy. Open the plastic bags every few days and check for mold—stagnant air and damp conditions will give mold and fungus a helping hand.

In about two weeks, give the cuttings a slight tug to check if rooting has commenced. If not, pull out the cuttings and see if the end has started to rot. If all looks well, try again, perhaps dusting it with a hormone powder. Make doubly sure that the base of the cutting is touching the rooting medium; it needs the stimulus of this contact to start new roots.

Hormones

Both plant and animal cells use hormones to regulate and stimulate growth and development. Often, a cutting that refuses to respond to the rooting process simply needs the additional stimulation of a plant-growth hormone. These are sold in powdered form. Dip cuttings from vigorous plants in the powder using pieces between 3 and 6 inches long. Remove any flowers or leaves at the base of the cutting. Make sure there are no air pockets around the stem end. Hormone powders should be used with care since they can irritate the skin.

Sectioned Leaf Cuttings

Sanserieria and other common houseplants can also be reproduced by sectioning a leaf. Cut a healthy leaf into pieces, each 3 or 4 inches long. This process will not work if the leaf is upside down, so cut the bottom at a slant just to keep directions straight. Plant 3 inches of the cutting in a rooting medium, such as moist sphagnum or sand. A new plant will develop to one side of the mother leaf.

Single Leaf Cuttings

Streptocarpus, gloxinias, African violets, hoyas, and many other plants can be reproduced by cutting, using variations of a single leaf, a leaf with petiole, or of a leaf, a petiole, and a section of the stem, including the bud. Plant as you would a sectioned leaf cutting.

When using leaves that are thick, waxy, and of a succulent character, the cuttings need not be covered, but be sure the medium stays moist.

Cuttings in Water

Rooting cuttings in a glass of water is an old-time method that works for ivies, begonias, inch plants, and many others. Snip a new shoot from the mother plant that is about 3 inches long, and place it in a jar of water. Change the water every few days, to give the plant new oxygen. If you allow the water to become cloudy or sludgy, the rooting will usually occur near the water's surface, where oxygen is more plentiful, and there won't be enough new growth to support the plant.

After roots have shown healthy growth, add small amounts of sand or soil to the water every few days. You won't have a tangled mass of roots to sort out during transplanting, and the earth will stimulate the roots to grow new root hairs, which are the plant's true providers of food and water.

Plants by Division

Another easy way to produce new plants is by dividing the rootstock. Early spring is the best time, before new growth begins for the coming season. Dig all the way around the plant and gently lift it out of the pot, keeping as much of the root system intact as possible. Shake off loose soil and wash until you can clearly see roots and crowns. Each division should have two to five strong shoots with ample roots attached. Next, divide the plant into smaller clumps, removing any dead areas. Cut back remaining foliage to half the height of the original clump. Replant the divisions promptly so the roots don't dry out. Water thoroughly. You need to keep the soil moist until the new plant becomes established. This process works best with plants that form multiple crowns, and will not work for single-stemmed plants.

Runners

Any houseplant that grows runners that have tiny plants at their tips will reproduce if the tips are allowed to root. The easiest way to help this along is to anchor the small plant to a 3-inch pot of soil using a bobby pin or a paper clip. Make sure that adequate roots have formed by giving a slight tug before you cut the runner from the mother plant.

❧ PESTS IN THE OUTBACK

Once aphids have established a beachhead in your indoor garden they tend to appear with the regularity of bubbles in a lava lamp. But bad as they are, at least you can spot an aphid as it sluggishly sucks the sap from fresh young leaves and stems. In my gardening world, however, spider mites are far worse: They are such tiny creepers that I miss their presence until their numbers and the webs they produce multiply to the point where my plant's leaves turn brown and shrivel up, looking as if each one is wrapped in the most delicate webbing. By this stage, it's usually too late to save it.

The only person who could ever conquer either of these creatures is the incredible shrinking man, that hero of an existential sci-fi movie of the 1950s. But the script writers (knowing how much an audience can take) confronted our hero with a cat when he was 2-feet tall and an average house spider when he had shrunk to an inch—aphids and mites were left out of the cast completely.

I have had infestations of both these pests, aphids usually in the spring, and spider mites generally during the dog days of August when the heat is high and the humidity low—they love desert conditions. They take advantage of the times I am so busy out-of-doors that I've neglected my houseplants, or when those plants that have been outside are once again brought indoors.

Aphids

Aphids usually time their arrival to those days in the spring when your crops of seedlings start to stretch new leaves to the lights above or to the sun shining through a window. The perfection of an aphid's reproductive system is such that a female aphid will mate in the fall, laying eggs on a houseplant vacationing outdoors that you later bring indoors, where the eggs spend a cozy winter only to hatch in the spring. The hatched insects are all females, known by the wonderful term of "stem mothers." These ladies of the stem then produce several generations of offspring asexually—this time, though, they don't bother with the egg business and bear live off-spring. These children of the stem are either born without wings and just hang around the neighborhood eating, or they sprout wings and fly off to greener pastures—in this case, your emergent seedlings. Soon both the stay-at-homes and the fly-by-nights produce an ever-increasing number of aphids. Don't underestimate this insect's reproductive capabilities. Ten days after an aphid is born, this virgin daughter is not only chomping away at your plants, but also at the same time producing her own little aphids, who are, once again, born live rather than hatched from an egg.

Not only do these insects weaken a plant, their feeding can also distort both leaves and flower petals, and their excrement (which has a high sugar content) can give rise to mildew as well as attract ants.

Spider Mites

Aphids are in the minor leagues when compared to the spider mite, truly one of nature's most awesome and awful creatures. Spider mites love heat and, as cold weather arrives, they invade your home either by migration or hitching a ride on a houseplant that has been outside for the summer. All the time they are engaged in this search for heat they are laying eggs, so that the plants in your garden are already harboring next year's plague.

If your house is relatively warm and dry—as most houses are—the mites soon show up as tiny specks wandering the under-surface of a leaf. There the females spin loose webs to hold their eggs, while the males actually protect the unmated females from other male competitors by shooting silk in an attempt to tie them down—there is no spirit of parthenogenesis here. Imagine such drama where the combatants are less than ½ of an inch long! Once they become established, the females lay about one hundred eggs each during a two-week cycle. Each of these eggs will soon hatch and produce another hundred spider mites, all of them hungry.

As they suck the life juices of a plant, the mites, like the aphids, are motionless. If disturbed, however, they scurry about their web-bing, looking for a port in the storm. If you place a piece of white paper under the infected leaves and shake them, the mites will fall and you can easily see them rushing about on the paper's surface.

Of the two, I'd much rather fight an aphid infestation. You can—if the invasion is limited—wallow in your rage and crush them by rubbing the infected leaf or stem between your index fin-ger and thumb and relish the visible results. Spider mites, however, are more difficult because they are so small; you're never sure you've gotten them all. But by the time the indoor gardener can actually see the problem, it's usually on its way to being out of con-trol, so other measures are needed.

The first step is to remove your plant from the company of others, keeping it apart until there is no more evidence of infec-tion, whatever the pest involved. When the problem is aphids and the weather is still clement, take the plant outside. During the win-ter, move it to a sink or tub. Using an outside hose, faucet, or a shower hose—and humming a tune from South Pacific—wash those aphids right out of your hair. They have but a tenuous grasp on plant stems and can easily be dislodged. I don't own a leaf-blower, but it would be interesting to find out if a blast of air dis-lodges them as easily as a blast of water.

COMMONSENSE RULES

Finally, here are five commonsense rules that will go a long way in protecting your plants.

❀ Always quarantine new plants for at least two weeks. Most pests will show up in that time.

❀ Pick up all plant debris. Don't allow piles of organic litter to accumulate and become a potential breeding ground for trouble.

❀ Keep leaves clean and dust-free, examining the plants while cleaning to spot potential troublemakers.

❀ No matter how fond you are of your plant, if the infestation is too far-gone, destroy both the plant and the soil.

❀ Give all plants a thorough inspection after their summer outside before they join others in your collection.

For a light infestation of spider mites, first cover the pot's soil with a sheet of aluminum foil, so none of it will spill out. Using a bar of white hand soap or one of the new insecticidal soaps, lather up and completely cover both sides of the leaves and the stems with soapsuds. If the leaves are tender, use your fingers; if the leaves are tougher, a small brush will do no harm. After the suds sit on the leaves for a few minutes, carefully rinse them off and return the plant to isolation, renewing the attack in a week. Wash the plant a second time, even if you see no immediate sign of mites; there is still the possibility of hatching eggs. And be patient—perseverance pays off.

Insecticidal Soaps

If infestations are light, you can spray the plant with insecticidal soaps, making sure you read the label directions first (a few plants such as palms or some members of the euphorbia family will be damaged by the soap). If ferns are infected, increase the recommended dilution. With soap in your arsenal, there is no need to resort to chemical sprays, bombs, or whatever—the potential health risk to you, your family, and your pets is not worth the effort. Always beware of any pesticide that gives you a toll-free number to call in case of accident.

Scale and Mealybugs

Believe it or not, shellac is made from a scale insect found in India, which is the only good thing I've ever heard about this group of insects. When young, they are too tiny and colorless to notice as they walk up a stem while searching for a juicy leaf to feed on. Once they've settled down, they develop a thick, armored hide, literally glue themselves to the leaf surface, and begin to eat. You can flick them off with your fingernail, but a cleaner method is swabbing them off with a cotton Q-tip soaked in alcohol.

Mealybugs are other common pests, closely related to scale, that resemble small mounds of cotton fluff. Use the Q-tip and alcohol solution for control. If they attack the roots of succulents, remove the plants from the infected soil, then dip the roots in alcohol, rinse well, and replant in fresh soil.

5

FLOWERING PLANTS

I'VE SAID IT BEFORE, BUT IT BEARS REPEATING: THE NUMBER of plants that can be grown in containers is only limited by what's available at your garden center or just how far afield your imagination wanders when ordering from seed and plant catalogs. With foliage, it's enormous, and the same applies to flowering plants.

You've been to garden centers and have seen hanging pots and standing containers filled with geraniums, fuchsias, lobelias, myrtle, petunias, and marigolds. The following list—by no means exhaustive—gives the scientific and common name of a host of flowering annuals, biennials, and perennials that are perfectly at home growing in pots and containers.

HELLEBORUS

The Lenten rose (*Helleborus orientalis*) is a wonderful plant for small-space gardens. Use a 12-inch clay pot and set a well-grown hellebore in the center. Around the edge, plant three specimens of *Bergenia cordifolia* 'Purpurea' (a cultivar Gertrude Jekyll admired for its marvelous winter color). The deeply cut, glossy, dark green leaves of the hellebores are a sharp contrast to the rounded leaves of the bergenias. Be sure to water often since hellebores like damp soil. They are temperate perennials, so store Lenten roses in a garage or other chilly spot for the winter.

The white blooms of the Christmas rose (Helleborus niger) brighten the dark days of winter.

H. Niger, the Christmas rose, is another easy-to-grow member of the family. As its name implies, its bloom will brighten the darkest month of the year.

THE FLOWERING MAPLE

We've had a flowering maple in our window since the days that we lived in a 5-flight walk-up in Manhattan back in the late 1960s. The plants are extremely popular for pots because they flower over a long period of time and can spend many productive summers in a garden as splendid bedding plants.

Their generic name is *Abutilon,* an Arabic name for a species of mallow, which these flowers closely resemble. The common name, however, refers to the shape of its leaf, for it closely resembles a maple leaf both in size and shape.

One species, *A. theophrasti,* known variously as the velvet leaf, the butter-print, the pie-marker, or the China jute, is a naturalized wildflower—often called weedy—that is found growing across the United States and is considered an important fiber plant in northern China. The whole plant is velvety with single inch-wide yellow flowers and an odd-shaped fruit that is often used in dried flower arrangements.

But the flowering maple usually grown in windows is the *A. hybridum,* a species that has given rise to an unusual number of hybrids of many colors and various qualities, including bloom for most of the year. Its flower colors include coral pink, deep red, deep rose, pure white, lemon yellow, and orange.

These plants can be set outside after the danger of frost has passed, and they will bloom throughout the summer, requiring only a spot in full or partial sun and plenty of water. As fall approaches, they can be dug up, put into pots, and pruned back by at least two-thirds. They'll proceed to bloom in a sunny window for most of the winter. At least five hours of sun and night temperatures of between 50°F and 60°F are needed for the best winter flowers. When plants are not flowering during the winter, it's best to keep the soil almost dry; water just enough to prevent wilting of the leaves.

Seeds may be started in February or March with a soil temperature of 60°F. Repot the seedlings when four to six leaves have appeared, using a mix of potting soil, peat moss, and sand, at a ratio of one-third each. A mature plant is perfectly happy in a 7-inch pot. Since it can get scraggly, however, remember to pinch it back in the early spring. Cuttings from old wood can be taken in September. They should be fertilized every two or three weeks throughout the summer, benefiting particularly from fish emulsions.

A. metgapotamicum, or the trailing abutilon, is from Brazil and will survive outdoors in the far South and southern California. 'Variegata' is an especially fine cultivar with yellow and green mottled foliage and yellow flowers with a red calyx, perfectly suited for hanging baskets.

A. pictum 'Thompsonii' is also a Brazilian native and bears bright orange flowers with mottled yellow and green foliage. A transmittable virus in this case causes the mottled leaf colors, for if a variegated shoot is grafted on a green-leafed stock, the whole plant soon becomes variegated. This particular plant is also a good subject for becoming a standard tree. Start with a small plant of only one shoot and nestle it in a 3-inch pot, tying the stem to a foot-long bamboo cane or stick inserted in the dirt at the pot's edge. Use one loop of soft cord around the stem and one loop on the stake so that the stem is never crushed. When the flowering maple grows to about 10 inches, move it to a 6-inch pot, adding a longer length of stake. Remove all the side shoots, leaving just one at the tip of the stem.

As the plant approaches 2 feet, move it to an 8-inch pot— remember, as you have been forcing the plant upward, the roots have been growing, too. Pinch off the terminal bud to force the plant into bushy growth. The stem will develop a woody look and you will have a beautiful flowering tree.

❧ THE WILLOW-LEAFED ACACIA

I completely forgot to water my willow-leafed acacia during a spell of hot weather earlier this summer. The pot hangs on a runner, and the runner is overhead with the plant's branches arching out more than a foot on either side of the edge. When I saw browning leaves, I realized my error and ran for the watering can. Within two weeks, however, new leaves were appearing and I never lost a blossom.

Acacias are tough plants, numbering some 800 species, with most coming from Australia, where they are called "wattles." The botanical name is from the Greek *akakia* and originally referred to a thorny tree found in the deserts of Egypt.

My plant is *Acacia retinodes*, known in Australia as the wirilda, or sometimes the monthly mimosa, so named because the small flowers are produced from early March right through to November. In its natural habitat, the plant becomes a small tree reaching a height of 20 feet. It is hardy in the south of England, and many trees are grown for decoration along the French Riviera.

In their marvelous book, *Flowers: A Guide for Your Garden,* Pizzetti and Cocker report that the wirilda was introduced from the Australian state of Victoria to Europe in 1656. Mine arrived only last year and began as a rooted cutting—acacia cuttings of half-ripened shoots are slow to root but not difficult. It bloomed right away, bearing dozens of tiny fragrant yellow balls of gold, each beginning at a diameter of $\frac{1}{16}$ of an inch and ending up about $\frac{1}{4}$-inch across. Other acacias found on the market are known for bigger flowers but this particular plant is among the toughest around. It's often used as grafting stock for less hardy varieties.

Propagation is usually by seed. Germination is accelerated by softening the hard seed coats, either by placing them in hot ashes and allowing them to cool or dropping seeds in boiling water and leaving them to soak in the cooling water until the seed coats are inflated, a process that takes about four days.

Use a mix of half potting soil and half peat moss. Keep the soil on the dry side and try for a winter temperature of 50°F to 55°F. Indoors, give them as much light as possible and let them spend the summer outdoors in full sun. Fertilize once a month during the warmer part of the year.

❧ GARDEN CANNAS

The common garden cannas (*Canna* x *generalis)* are attractive in pots, especially when combined with *Tagetes patula,* the French marigold. For an effective summer display, plant a ring of marigolds around two cannas in a 12-inch terracotta pot. French marigolds range in height from 8 to 14 inches and come in orange, yellow, gold, or mahogany red. For smaller pots, there are also dwarf cannas that reach a height of 30 inches and bear regular-sized pink blossoms, blooming in ninety days from seed.

Cannas are among the easiest plants to grow, being prolific bloomers and sporting large tropical-looking leaves. Plant the rhizomes directly in the garden or in pots but never before the soil is above 60°F. Use a good garden soil, well-laced with composted manure, either sheep or cow. While in active growth, cannas require a good deal of water and, except in the Deep South, as much sun as possible.

They are often hardy in Zone 7, and will sometimes winter over in a shelter spot in Zone 6.

❧ THE CHENILLE PLANT

Everblooming is a term that is thrown about with great abandon by many members of the horticultural world, especially those who sell flowering plants. But few plants actually produce flowers for months—not to mention years—on end. Among those plants that will perform is the chenille plant, or as it's sometimes called, red hot cattails, foxtail, or Philippine Medusa. First introduced from New Guinea in the late 1800s, this tropical shrub is so proficient a bloomer that even a rooted cutting will soon produce flowers.

The botanical name is *Acalypha hispida.* The genus was first used by Hippocrates to describe the nettle, which the flowers of this plant somewhat resemble, and *hispida* is from the Latin for "bristly."

I never thought it would number among my favorite plants, as the blossoms do resemble chenille (from the French for caterpillar), a type of bedspread fabric often found in very cheap motels. But its vigorous bloom was so irresistible, and I succumbed to its charms.

Give the chenille plant a sunny window (except in mid-summer), keep the soil evenly moist—this plant is a good candidate for a self-watering pot—and never allow temperatures to fall below 60°F. Your plant will soon develop red flowers that can be up to a foot long. Soil should be a good potting soil with plenty of composted manure and sand, one-third each. Feed the plant every month during warm weather. In the spring, propagate by stem cuttings with a heel to have plants blooming for fall.

Chenille plants are subject to spider mites so make sure you mist the leaves every day and check under the leaves on occasion just to be sure you haven't been invaded.

There is also a cultivar called 'Alba' that bears creamy-white flowers with a flush of pink that intensifies during the summer months.

If happy, plants can grow quite large (they are shrubs in the tropics).

✵ THE AMARYLLIS OR HIPPEASTRUM

During my years as a garden writer, I've been asked more questions on how to keep amaryllis in bloom from year to year than about any other single houseplant problem. And the biggest hurdle that I see is the mistaken belief that this plant is a bulb that should be allowed to go dormant for at least half of the year.

To begin with, the amaryllis is a more or less evergreen plant that arises from a bulb. Nursery suppliers, and many growers as well, allow the bulbs to dry off after flowering, both for convenience in the greenhouse and for the ease of shipping dormant bulbs to market. Seedling plants, however, should never be dried off until they reach flowering size. If properly cared for, your amaryllis will become larger every year and will continue to flower with increasing vigor and blatant display.

There is some confusion, however, even with botanical nomenclature. Many people still believe that *Amaryllis* is the correct generic name for this popular winter houseplant. Well, it is a name for a genus, but one with only one species, an entirely different bulbous plant known as the belladonna lily or *A. belladonna.* The confusion arose in the United States because growers did not want to confuse the American consumer with the correct name, *Hippeastrum.*

The genus *Hippeastrum* contains some seventy-five species, mostly native to tropical America (although one hails from Africa). It is sometimes called the equestrian starflower, a name derived from *Hippeus,* or knight on horseback, and *astron,* a star. Why? Nobody really knows. As with many names in the botanical world, the initial reasoning is lost in the mists of time.

The bulbs can be left out-of-doors in the southern tip of Florida, in a bit of southern Texas (where it touches Mexico and the Gulf), and in a few small areas of California. Elsewhere, this is a potted houseplant that can sojourn to the backyard only during the heat of summer.

Hippeastrum vittatum was first introduced from the Chilean Andes in 1769, bearing strap-shaped leaves and up to six 6-inch-wide flowers of magenta-striped white. Arthur Johnson, a watchmaker in England, crossed this plant with *H. reginae*—the one species from Africa—and produced the first hybrid, now called *H. x Johnsonii,* or St. Joseph's lily, a bulb that produces three or four tubular flowers of brilliant scarlet, streaked with white.

Using this plant as a starter, Dutch hybridizers have produced the 'Leopoldii Hybrid'—bulbs that bear flowers of almost every color except blue. Today when you see an amaryllis advertised for home or greenhouse, it's usually a descendant of one of these plants.

Sometimes, however, an entirely new bulb appears on the plant horizon. The butterfly amaryllis (*H. papilion*), for instance, is described as having a blossom 5½ inches high and 3½ inches wide. The blossoms have a background color of white lightly touched with soft green and with crimson-maroon markings radiating from the throat.

As for the lack of a blue flower, for years horticulturists and nurserymen have touted the fabulous blue amaryllis, *H. procerum,* but this turns out to be *Worsleya rayneri*, a one-species genus from Brazil. This long-necked bulb was named after Arthington Worsley (1861–1943), a mining engineer who traveled extensively in South America.

To plant an amaryllis, fill ⅔ of a pot with equal parts of potting soil, composted manure, and sand. Choose a pot no larger than 2 inches greater than the bulb's diameter. Bury the bulb in the soil but leave the top part (about ¼) uncovered. Keep the soil moist but not wet and set the pot in a warm spot.

After the leaves appear, feed the plant every month during active growth, and allow at least four hours of full sun at 50°F at night and 70°F during the day. Every summer after the first year, replace the top inch of old soil with fresh, and repot every three years. In time, a healthy bulb can produce many flowers and attain a circumference of some 14 inches. After the nights are warm and frost danger is past, you can place the potted bulbs out in the garden for the summer.

From late October to mid-December, keep the bulb slightly drier and allow it a rest. When you wish to start the bloom, bring the pot to a warm place. When the flower stalk is about 6 inches high, place the plant in a sunny window.

If you wish to store the bulbs, in September, withhold water completely and allow the leaves to turn yellow and die back. When they are completely brown, cut them off at the top of the bulb. Dormant bulbs and pots are best stored on their sides in a spot with temperatures no lower than 40°F. To start flowering add water and bring to a warm room.

Remove the flowers after blossoming is complete unless you wish to set seed. Don't worry about the water that seeps out of the sheared stalk. It will soon stop.

Amaryllis from Seed

Cross-pollinating your own amaryllis hybrids is a fascinating hobby. Try to pick two parents of pure color—a red with another shade of red or bright orange with a dark orange. Hybridizers claim this achieves the best results. Using a small, clean watercolor brush, take pollen from the anthers of one flower and brush some on the stigma of the second. Separate the recipient plant and remove its anthers so no other pollen becomes involved.

When the pods ripen and burst, black seeds will appear, stacked like slices of bread. Sow these seeds in sphagnum moss or a prepared soil mix, covering them lightly. Using a germination temperature of 60°F to 65°F, seeds should germinate within ten to fifteen days. When seedlings are old enough to handle, place ten in a 6-inch pot and keep them in a warm place.

When the leaves are 6 inches long, pot each plant individually in a 4-inch pot using the recommended mix. Until they flower for the first time, however, never let them dry out. Be sure to keep accurate records of your trials and errors.

⚘ THE FLAMINGO FLOWER

J.-K. Huysmans (1848–1907), a French novelist born of a Dutch family, is today remembered for having written the book that Dorian Gray—in Oscar Wilde's masterpiece—claimed ". . . was the strangest book he had ever read."

The title was *À rebours* or, in English, *Against the Grain*. Its hero, Des Esseintes, was a young nineteenth century Parisian who spent his life trying to realize all the passions, philosophies, and modes of thought that were found in every age previous to his own.

"After such a book," wrote Barbey d'Aurevilly, the famous author of *Les Diaboliques*, "there remains nothing left for the Author but to choose between the jaw of a pistol or the foot of the Cross." Quite a statement about a book written in 1884.

But what has all this to do with flowering plants?

Des Esseintes, passionately interested in flowers, was most delighted by "rare plants of high-bred type, coming from distant lands, kept alive by skill and pains in an artificial equatorial temperature maintained by carefully regulated furnaces." And for a time his greatest joy of all was keeping an artificial flower that aped the true.

Toward the end of the book, however, he truly wished for natural flowers that imitated the false.

[The nurseryman] unloaded a tangled mass of leaves, lozenge-shaped, bottle-green in hue; from the midst rose a switch on top of which trembled a great ace of hearts, as smooth and shiny as a capsicum; then, as if to defy all the familiar aspects of plants, from the middle of this ace of hearts, of an intense vermilion, sprang a flesh tail, downy, white and yellow, upright in some case, corkscrewed above the heart, like a pig's tail, in others.

It was, of course, an anthurium.

Its botanical name is also *Anthurium,* from the Latin *anthos,* flower, and *oura,* tail. They are tropical plants from South America and number some 600 species. In most of them, a single blossom with the consistency of patent leather dyed in various shades of red—not really a petal but a spathe—wraps itself around a spadix that is made up of dozens of tiny flowers, which can only be seen clearly when examined under a lens.

Originally from the deep jungle, anthuriums require a humid and warm atmosphere at all times. Never let temperatures fall below 60°F. They enjoy the morning sun but should be protected during the hot afternoon. A mix of potting soil, peat moss, composted manure, and sand, one-quarter each, is best, and the plants do well in self-watering pots, since the soil should always be evenly moist.

These plants are climbers and will eventually lift themselves above the pot. If you wrap the new roots in moist sphagnum moss, eventually you can repot the plant up to the level of the new bottom leaf.

At present, I have *A. scherzeranum* 'Rothschildianum', an extravagant cultivar with a large spathe of creamy white, dotted with red specks and a very curly spadix of sulphur yellow. It is definitely a conversation piece, and the blooms last for weeks before they eventually expire.

Other types include: *A. radicans,* a prostrate creeping dwarf with metallic leaves; *A. scandens,* with shiny foliage and small green flowers with a little spathe and a longer spadix; and *A. andraeanum* 'Mickey Mouse', another dwarf hybrid that has shiny scarlet flowers with ear-like lobes.

Propagation is by division, but make sure each new plant has a separate crown. Many new hybrids are available by seed, and in colors that include various shades of orange, pink, white, and red. Only fresh seed will germinate, but most suppliers take orders for anthurium seed so its freshness is guaranteed. Seed should be sown in damp sphagnum moss, slightly covered, and placed in a moist propagating case with a temperature of 75°F to 85°F. Germination takes at least thirty days, but often lasts considerably longer.

⚜ THE BEEFSTEAK BEGONIA

The begonia is both the common and generic names for a large collection of mostly tropical plants. Its also the breeding ground for some of the most popular summer bedding plants—the annual *Begonia semperflorens* hybrids; the truly beautiful hanging basket plants, the tuberous begonias; and a number of fanciful cultivars with glorious leaves, including the time-honored rex begonia.

The generic name *Begonia* was verified by Linnaeus in 1724, but was first used by Charles Plumier, a Franciscan monk, in honor of Michel Bégon (1638–1710), at one time the *intendant* of the French Antilles and eventually Canada, who was an avid amateur botanist and plant collector. Even earlier, however, Georg Rumpf (1628–1702) set about describing the begonias hailing from the islands located between New Guinea and the Celebes. Fortunately, his name was not honored, or we'd be growing flowering rumpfs in our backyards.

For a number of years I tended many pots of begonias, chiefly *B.* 'Queen Mother' and *B.* 'Iron Cross' as well as a number of smaller specimens. Invariably, though, when I would forget to keep them warm they would become less than attractive. I would always wind up giving them away to various visitors over the garden year.

Sometimes I would plant *B. semperflorens* cultivars, starting the seeds in June in order to have flowering plants in December.

A pot of classic begonias (Begonia spp.) brings a spot of new color to a small garden area.

But even that activity gave way to a fascination with more exotic plants.

Yet one begonia in our plant collection has been growing and blooming—on and on and on—since my sister-in-law brought it over some thirty years ago. It's an old-fashioned beefsteak, or pondleaf, begonia (*B.* x *erythrophylla*) and was taken from a cutting provided by her own mother plant, which is at least sixty years old, having belonged to an aunt on her husband's side of the family— and the years roll by.

Now, I have it in a large self-watering pot (it measures a foot square) and the stem (or, more correctly, the rhizome) has twirled around and around itself in such a complicated configuration that I invariably hesitate to repot it, a service it sorely needs. For a house-plant companion that will go on year after year, with only a mini-mum of care, is something of a rarity.

Its leathery, rounded leaves are a highly polished green with maroon undersides and the flowers come freely in a lovely pink, usually in February. It enjoys morning or afternoon sun, with temperatures that fluctuate between 50°F and 65°F, and evenly moist soil. In the spring, the plant propagates freely from cuttings. I use the usual potting soil, peat moss, and sand mix, one-third each, and try to remember to fertilize at least once a month during the summer—but I often forget to do just that.

❧ ANOTHER GREAT BEGONIA

There is another stellar begonia in my collection. It's called a "shrub begonia," and its botanical name is *Begonia* 'Alleryi'. This is a cultivar derived from a crossing of *B. gigantea* and *B. metallica* by one Allery Aubert back in 1904.

In *The Adventurous Gardener*, there is a color illustration of a *B. haageama*, a pink-leaved begonia, in a collection of pot plants on Christopher Lloyd's front porch. Included in the group was a fall-blooming lily, *Lilium formosanum* (he notes that it's deliciously scented and the earwigs come out at night to feed on its pollen, which exemplifies the English predilection for being kind to anything, including the repulsive earwig).

It turns out, however, that *B. haageama* is also an incorrect name of a cultivar of obscure origins that was developed in 1939 from a hybridization that included one known parent, *B. Scharffii*, (now called 'Drostii'). The nursery I ordered my plant from was out of the second and instead sent me the first. I've never been sorry.

These particular begonias are also known as hirsute or hairy-leaved begonias, and are among the easiest to grow in the entire family. They need watering only when dry, prefer a shady eastern or western exposure, and a temperature above 50°F at night.

'Alleryi' can reach a height of 5 feet if grown well. The entire plant is covered with silky short white hairs. Leaves are deeply cut and pointed, with a glossy green on top and pale green with maroon veins on the bottom. The rosy-pink blossoms appear in profusion from mid-August through September.

❧ YESTERDAY, TODAY, AND TOMORROW

"What's in a name? That which we call a rose by any other name would smell as sweet," said Juliet to Romeo. But somehow the line doesn't ring quite as true when confronted with the appellation of "yesterday, today, and tomorrow." Such is the descriptive common name of a number of species in the *Brunfelsia* genus, flowers so-called because they begin their bloom a deep purple, which slowly fades over a period of days to pale blue and then finally washes out to white.

Brunfelsia was named in honor of Otto Brunfels (1489–1534), a gentleman who began his career as a Carthusian monk, and then became a Lutheran convert, before finally becoming a physician. He is remembered today for his book *Herbarum Vivae Eicones*, published from 1530 to 1536, one of the first great herbals and an important milestone in the history of botanical illustration.

The flowers that appear from January to April—frequently throughout the year—are sweetly scented and funnel-shaped, with a long tube and a flat, 5-lobed lip. They usually open in one color but slowly change with age. Other common names are morning-noon-and-night, yesterday-and-today, and Paraguay jasmine.

They are good candidates for a self-watering pot since their soil—one-third each of potting soil, composted manure, and sharp sand—must be kept evenly moist at all times. Repotting, however, should be accomplished after the plants cease blooming. Propagation is by rooted cuttings in heated sand. And since they are jungle denizens, they appreciate high humidity, so frequent misting will keep them healthy. Sunlight is necessary most of the year except the hot sun of July and August in a typical southern window.

Over time, these plants can become very shrubby and large, flowering profusely. Prune them back before the new growth appears, which leads to more compact specimens.

Three kinds of these plants are usually offered: *B. australis* bears 1½-inch wide flowers, while *B. pilosa* from Brazil, has 1¾-inch wide flowers (both change color from purple to white). Finally, *B. jamaicensis* comes from the Blue Mountains of Jamaica and has fragrant white- to cream-colored flowers that bloom throughout the summer.

❧ THE BEAUTIFUL GARDENIA

A few flakes of light snow are falling on this last night of the year. The snow will not last, however, for temperatures are too high and the thin clouds above are quickly blowing away. Though it's December, the landscape is still barren—fields and woods of brown, not white. Yet in my study, one small, white gardenia has opened, its perfume filling the room with visions of tropical nights and gentle trade winds.

This gardenia was a gift from a lady who lived down the road. She had cared for the plant for many years, since it began as a small houseplant purchased at a local supermarket. Somebody told her that gardenias needed iron to be healthy so she stuck a wire clothes hanger in the back of the pot. Whatever the reason, it quickly grew into a shrub 4 feet in diameter and 4 feet high, all while living in a 12-inch tub.

The *Gardenia* genus is named after Alexander Garden (1730–1791), a Scottish-American naturalist and physician who settled in South Carolina. Amazingly, he also discovered the amphibians known as the Congo snake or Congo eel, and the siren or mud eel. Because of his Tory sympathies during the War of Independence, he was named a Fellow of the Royal Society.

Requirements for this particular gardenia, *Gardenia jasminoides* var. *Fortuniana* (a double-flowered form), are not taxing, except for the need for warmth—60°F and up—but it will survive 50°F without damage, though its disdain for lower temperatures becomes obvious, for the plant's leaves will slowly drop or yellow. The temperature for optimum growth is between 65°F and 85°F. Amazingly enough, bud growth is initiated by temperatures below 65°F. If you especially want winter flowers, pinch off the developing buds until September.

Soil must constantly be kept evenly moist since the thin fibrous roots cannot tolerate too much dryness. Fertilize once a month with an acid-based plant food as long as there is active growth. Cuttings can be struck at any time during the year using half or fully ripened stems taken with a heel. Gardenias want as much full sun as possible, especially during the winter. If light is poor, the buds will drop.

The yellow fruit that results from fertilized flowers is said to be eaten in China, but my plant has yet to produce such fruit.

G. jasminoides, or the Cape jasmine, is often used in baskets and, as long as light is plentiful, it will produce flowers all year long. *G. thunbergia,* from South Africa, bears intensely fragrant blossoms set among small elongated diamond-shaped leaves.

⚘ THE EVERBLOOMING AFRICAN GARDENIA

According to *Hortus Third,* there are only two species in the genus *Mitriostigma* (*mitra,* Latin for a headband or hat, refers to the stigma of the cap-like flower). Of the two, *Mitriostigma axillare* is slated to be a very important addition to the houseplant fleet.

It's a gardenia relative that has everything one could wish for in an indoor plant. The evergreen leaves are glossy-green, and from the axils where they meet the stem—the species name refers to this fact—legions of 1- to 2-inch-long arbutus-shaped white flowers (with a touch of pink) are in almost constant bloom. And those blossoms are fragrant, too. Originally from Natal, for years they were known as *Gardenia citriodora,* which refers to their citrusy fragrance.

Use a soil mix of potting soil, peat moss, and sand, one-third each. Full sun or light shade is required, and temperatures should stay above 50°F. Keep the soil evenly moist, never letting it dry out. Propagate by cuttings at any time of the year. Eventually the plants can reach a height of 5 feet.

❧ THE OLEANDER

Nerium oleander, better known simply as oleander, starts blooming in early spring and continues until well into December. In areas with freezing temperatures, it must spend the winter indoors, but as soon as the days warm up again, it will bloom anew. A 3-foot-tall oleander planted in a 12-inch Eura Cotta pot, makes a beautiful display.

❧ THE SHRIMP PLANT

The shrimp plant is one of those few denizens of the plant world whose common name is so exact that it takes little imagination to see that the derivation is right on. The blossoms look exactly like a shrimp or prawn getting ready to leap out from amid the leaves. And there is another truth: It's said to be everblooming, and it is.

The genus is *Justicia,* named in honor of James Justice, a nineteenth-century Scottish gardener. The common name of the genus is water willow. Older books also include it under the genus *Beloperone, Calliaspidia,* or *Drejerella,* and in the species *guttata,* but its correct name is *Justicia brandegeana.* This is a fairly new plant to commerce, having been introduced to the European horticultural world in the 1920s, and thereafter to England and America in the 1930s.

The "shrimps" are really overlapping bracts of a reddish bronze color, and the true blossoms are two-lipped white flowers that peek out from amid the bracts, each bearing two black stamens resembling the pop-eyes of a crab and a long pistil with a bead of nectar at the tip.

Since shrimp plants are originally from Mexico, they prefer a warm spot in full sun. Make sure that surrounding temperatures never fall below 50°F. The best soil mix is potting soil, composted manure, and peat moss, one-third of each. Allow the dirt to dry completely before rewatering.

Since shrimp plants are 3-foot shrubs in nature, they can become quite large and rangy so keep them pruned back. They are also effective plants in the garden border where they can spend the summer producing. You can then take cuttings for the winter indoors. Cuttings for propagation, however, can be made at any time of the year. Simply remove the developing flower buds until the proper size is reached.

Two cultivars are available: *J. Brandegeana* 'Variegata' has leaves that are peppered with white spots and 'Yellow Queen' has bracts of a bright yellow color.

✥ THE COLORFUL KALANCHOES

The generic name for the kalanchoes is *Kalanchoe*, said to be the original Chinese term for the Christmas tree kalanchoe, or *K. laciniata* (where species name refers to the cut edge of the leaf), which is just one species of this popular group of succulent plants. There are over 125 other species mostly from Madagascar but also from tropical areas, such as South Africa, India, China, and the Malay Peninsula.

The kalanchoes are popular houseplants because of their attractive foliage and also their long-lasting flowers. For those indoor gardeners interested in forming a collection of plants based on one genus, this group could be a good choice.

The most attractive kalanchoe in my window of plants is the kitchingia or coralbell plant (*K. uniflora*), originally from Madagascar. The species name here refers to the fact that each stem bears a single flower. And what a flower it is: a coral-red, puffed-up blossom that resembles a tiny hot-air balloon. The flowers appear in spring, and last for almost a month.

Best in a hanging basket, these plants require plenty of sunlight as well as a soil that provides excellent drainage—one-third each of potting soil, peat moss, and sand works extremely well. For planting in an open-weave basket, however, line the bottom with sheets of sphagnum moss before adding the soil mix. Allow the mix to dry between waterings and be sure temperatures stay above 50°F.

Around Christmas time, florists always display pots of the Christmas tree kalanchoe or *K. blossfeldiana* (named in honor of

Robert Blossfeld, a seed and cactus dealer of Potsdam). Also from Madagascar, this plant and its popular cultivar 'Tom Thumb', will provide flowers from Thanksgiving to May. Although the natural flowering period comes during January, plants can be grown in all parts of the world and flower at any time of the year by regulating the day length. Plants with as few as two leaves, for instance, will flower under short-day conditions. Seeds sown in January (using bottom heat) will bloom for the following Christmas, however, as long as they are shaded with black cloth or black paper, or put into a dark place for about four weeks at the beginning of September. Make sure they receive no more than nine hours of daylight. Cuttings can be taken at any time of the year. Fertilize only during active growth.

The 'Selma Hybrids' are attractive Christmas kalanchoes that grow easily from seed. They provide a mass of flowers in a color mix of orange, yellow, and red. Like others in the clan, they need full sun, and warm temperatures, and the soil should be allowed to dry out between waterings.

A number of the kalanchoes are especially interesting because they are viviparous and produce young plants at the tips of their leaves. *K. gastonis-bonnieri* (named for Gaston Bonnier), or the life plant, is always a conversation piece. These 2-foot-high plants have attractive 5- to 7-inch succulent, toothed leaves of a pale copper-green dusted with white that produce perfect little plants at the leaf ends, complete with little white roots.

The famous air plant that was once advertised on the back cover of every comic book published in the 1930s and 1940s, is *K. pinnata* (*pinnata* means feathery). Other common names include: life plant, floppers, Mexican love plant, curtain plant, miracle plant, and good-luck leaf. And, of course, that time-honored term of endearment, the mother-in-law plant.

Nobody really knows the origin of this particular species since it gives of itself with such abandon. An erect plant that stands up to 3 feet high, its leathery leaves are a green tinged with red and are divided into three to five scalloped leaflets that produce endless clones in between the notches. Individual leaves can be removed, pinned to a curtain, and they will continue to produce plantlets until they eventually dry up.

The previous soil mix is fine for these last two plants. Provide full sun and never overwater. The plantlets will root with ease.

✿ THE CHARMING OXALIS

According to *Hortus Third*, there are over 850 species of oxalis, most of them from South Africa and South America. One of the most beautiful wildflowers of a northern forest is the wood sorrel, *Oxalis montana*. Yet, one of the most pernicious weeds, especially to greenhouse owners, is the pesky yellow wood sorrel, *O. stricta* because their seedpods split open with an explosive charge that sends seeds flying for great distances. *Oxalis* is from a Greek word for sharp, which refers to the acidic taste of the leaves. The chemical involved is called oxalic acid and is poisonous in large quantities, but the leaves of the European *O. acetosella* has been used to flavor soups and salads for years.

A number of these make suitable houseplants, but I find two especially delightful. One is everblooming, and the other blooms in spring with bulbs that fall dormant during summer.

O. regnellii originally came from Brazil. It has beautiful white flowers and attractive shamrock-shaped foliage—somewhat square cut, not rounded, and purple underneath—blooming most of the time. I've had a pot in continual flower since the spring of 1986, and it shows no sign of slowing down. I used a soil mix of potting soil, peat moss, composted manure, and sand, one-quarter each. Temperatures should always be above 50°F, and full to partial sun should be provided for the fullest flowering and best leaf color.

Amazingly enough, *O. regnellii* will bloom in a north window. One of my good gardening friends has a small plant set in an attractive basket on her kitchen table, 5 feet away from an east window, and it has bloomed for five years.

O. braziliensis blooms during the spring over a period of two months. Its flower petals are wine red on top—about the hue of a good burgundy—and paler beneath. By summer, however, the leaves disappear and the plant goes into dormancy only to resume growing in the late fall.

✵ THE SMELL OF SERISSA

According to the *RHS Dictionary of Gardening*, only one member can be found in the genus *Serissa*—the species *foetida*, originally from southeast Asia and introduced to the horticultural world in 1787. *Hortus Third* reports one species, perhaps three, but only mentions *Serissa foetida*. *Serissa* is the old Native American term for the plant, and you should know what *foetida* means.

I think we have another case of a plant getting a bad rap from a simple overstatement. Both tomes say the bark is fetid when bruised, and *Hortus* claims that the leaves, too, have an odor that leaves much to be desired. But what truly represents a bad smell?

Now, I know plants that have a bad smell. When in bloom, the Devil's tongue (*Amorphophyllus rivieri*) has an odor so powerfully putrid that people clasp handkerchiefs over their noses and run, not walk, from any room where the blossom meets open air. And a number of the larger species of the stapeliad clan smell like a combination of dirty sneakers mixed with 3-day-old hamburger that was left out last July. And what of the aroma from the seeds of the female Ginkgo tree? It's much like rancid butter, and should never be planted close to any segment of refined society. But pity the poor serissa. At worst, the smell is slightly foxy, and at best, it isn't there at all. Yet, the moniker of fetid has been forever attached to it.

I first saw this plant in the temperate greenhouse of the Brooklyn Botanic Gardens. It was an attractive bush about 2 feet high, covered with tiny shiny green leaves, each edged with a thin line of creamy white and boasting dozens of single ½-inch long, pink flowers. The name was *S. foetida variegata*, also called the yellow-rim serissa, because the variegations have a slight yellow tone when new.

They make excellent plants for dish gardens and indoor bonsai since they respond well to pruning and shaping. Use potting soil, peat moss, and sand, one-third each and fertilize every few months when the plants are in active growth. Serissa likes a place in partial sun with evenly moist soil.

But keep an eye out for a number of cultivars. *S. foetida* 'Flora Plena', for instance, is called the snow rose and bears double white flowers that resemble tiny roses. *S. foetida* 'Kyoto', on the other hand, is said to be excellent for topiary and bears single white flowers, while *S. foetida* 'Mt. Fuji' has variegated foliage with each leaf edged with bands of pure white. Finally, *S. foetida* 'Sapporo' is a fastigate form—its branches turn upward and lie close to the main stem—and it has tiny white flowers and very dense foliage.

❧ THE SOPHISTICATED CALLA LILIES

Back in the Manhattan of the 1930s, when displaced members of the middle class tried to earn a living by selling apples on the corner of Seventh Avenue and Forty-second Street, the movies presented a different world, a world of sophistication and pizzazz, a world of martinis in crystal glasses, evening dresses trimmed with ostrich feathers, and elegant dining tables standing upon black marble floors—all set before floor-to-ceiling windows that looked out upon a city bathed in a combination of searchlights and theater lights, but the feeling was more of fairy lights. And in the center of every table, in a tall bud vase, was one calla lily, its organic shape echoed in wall standards of white frosted glass and plaster anaglypta high in the ceilings. Fred and Ginger danced and Katharine Hepburn announced, "the calla lilies are in bloom again." They were the flowers of the decade—at least on the silver screen.

In fact, it's an African plant of the genus *Zantedeschia*, named in honor of Francesco Zantedeschi (1773-1846), an Italian physician and botanist. Originally it belonged to the genus *Calla* (from the Greek *kallos*, for beauty) but this name was transferred to the water arum or *Calla palustris* (the species is a Latin term for marshloving). So the calla had to find new nomenclature. A French botanist, L. C. Richard (1754-1821) was summoned, but he eventually lost out

In my garden, calla lilies (Zantedeschia spp.) are grown in pots set directly in the border for the length of the summer.

to Francesco. The species is *aethiopica,* named for the peoples of northeast Africa, and the plant was introduced into Europe in 1687.

Once upon a time, I grew calla lilies the time-honored way: in a pot until late summer when the foliage was allowed to die down and yellow, then water was withheld and the rhizomes allowed to rest until being repotted in spring. Then I saw a reference by William Robinson in *The English Flower Garden,* which said that callas were basically aquatic evergreen plants that grew freely in the ditches and swamps of South Africa.

In the fall of 1988, I planted the rhizomes in an 8-inch plastic pot mixing potting soil, peat moss, composted manure, and sand, one-quarter each. First I watered well, then placed the pot in a waterproof crock and filled it with water up to the level of the soil. The temperature never fell below 55°F, and the plants always received full sun. In addition, since callas are heavy feeders, I fertilized every month while in active growth.

Within a few weeks, the first green leaves pushed up and soon grew into handsome spear-shaped, glossy-green leaves between 2 and 3 feet high. The first flowers appeared in January. And what flowers they were: a pure, pure white (though calla haters always say "deadwhite") folded spathe that surrounded a bright yellow spadix and soon gave off a lovely sweet fragrance that delighted my winter's day.

These tiny true flowers surround the spadix, with the males on the upper part of the column and the females below. If left alone, they will set seed. In about two months, the flowers stopped and I cut them off, but new leaves continued to appear. Then in April, the growth stopped and the leaves yellowed and fell away. I continued to water but left the pot alone until mid-May when I set it out in the garden pond. Soon, in the heat of June and July, new leaves appeared and the cycle began again.

There are probably a number of combinations that can be used to grow this lovely plant, so experimentation is in order. Since they are winter hardy in Zone 8 they could be lovely in an outdoor garden where the winters are mild.

Watch out for spider mites, though. They have a predilection for the taste of calla leaves.

❧ ROSES IN POTS

The love of roses has a venerable tradition (at least in Europe and America), and there are more than eighty references to the rose in the fifteenth edition of *Familiar Quotations*. That doesn't include the thirty-three references to roses when plural. They are also the national flower of America (showing that Congress has little horticultural sense but knows what the public wants).

The selection of roses you can grow in containers is vast. Hybrid teas, miniature roses, tree roses (of *Alice in Wonderland* fame)—in fact, almost all roses are suitable for small-space gardens. Imagine how a pot of blooming roses would add sparkle to a barren deck, empty balcony, forlorn doorway, lonesome patio, or along a naked driveway.

Today's large selection of pots, made of not only terracotta, cast iron, and stone, but also of much lighter high-tech composites and fiberglass, open up a new world to rose horticulture. Mixing and matching containers, when roses are the plants of choice, open another garden door.

Technically, just about any rose a gardener can handle can be grown in containers. But remember, as with gardening in general, much depends on the effort a gardener is willing to expend. Traditional roses often grow too fast for most pots. And sometimes these might weaken just a bit due to the stress of container planting, and they'll become more vulnerable to common rose problems such as black spot or mildew. One solution is to use a very large container, put the classic rose in the center then under-plant with perennials and annuals to hide the less-than-attractive bush-bottoms.

Another option would be to use the emerging category of the so-called "garden" roses. These are specifically bred to produce florist-type blossoms on vigorous, leaf-crowded bushes. Examples include the new series of the Dream Rose, available in yellow, orange, red, or pink, along with longtime favorites such as the classic white floribunda rose, 'Iceberg' or its coral counterpart, 'Margot Koster'.

Best Container Roses

From a practical point of view, the smaller ground cover and shrub roses, with their compact growth habits and weeping canes, are better candidates for life in a pot. They have abundant flowers, an extended period of bloom, and are easy to care for.

A white Meideland rose ('Alba') grows next to a small patch of Euonymous 'Green and Gold', the rose blooming most of the summer and the shrub starting out very bright in the spring and toning down as the days get hotter.

Any of the popular Flower Carpet ground cover roses are excellent choices and include Flower Carpet Pink, Flower Carpet Red, Flower Carpet White, Flower Carpet Apple Blossom, and the recently introduced Flower Carpet Coral. When looking for these roses don't be misled by the term ground cover—Flower Carpet roses grow about 3 feet tall and nearly as wide, making it an easy job of filling out a fairly large container.

Other shrub roses that look perfect in containers include the delightfully fragrant *Rosa* 'Flower Girl' (pastel pinks and creams) and the pale pink *R.* 'Mix 'n Match'. Don't forget Meideland's *R.* 'Bonica' with its shell-pink blossoms, *R.* 'Carefree Wonder', with flowers of violet-pink or white, *R.* 'Carefree Delight' with its vivid pink blooms, and *R.* 'Alba' with its gentle white petals.

Roses have deep and thirsty roots so shallow containers are not recommended. Instead, they should be at least 18 inches to 2 feet across. Larger pots help to insulate rose roots against excessive heat and cold, both of which can damage roots. A larger pot is also a good bet because the roots can then spread during a longer period without becoming root-bound, which adds the threat of continual repotting.

Roots need air, so the best pots are terracotta, wood, or unglazed ceramic. Be sure there are holes in the bottom for adequate drainage. To keep dirt from falling out, cover the holes with a bit of plastic screening or even a piece of paper towel, as standing water in a pot can easily add to the problem of root rot.

The planting mix should include two parts soil, one part builder's sand, and one part composted manure, compost, or other organic matter (except peat moss). Mix in about one-half cup of bonemeal at planting time.

When planting, make a small mound of soil at the bottom of the hole. Spread the roots out over the mound and cover them with dirt, so that the crown of the rose and the soil level are about 2 inches below the edge of the pot. This extra space makes watering much easier and allows room for a layer of mulch, which helps keep the roots cool. Roses need four to six hours of sunlight a day but never let the roots bake in the hot sun.

Soil in pots tends to dry out quickly so frequent watering is a must. And remember, it's important to water thoroughly. You may think you have doused a container but often you'll leave the center root ball as dry as it was when you began. Water well once, then do it again, making sure you can see the excess water draining from the pot's bottom.

Roses in containers will need frequent feeding. Every time water runs out the bottom it will take valuable nutrients along for the ride. When using a fast-release rose food, feed your plants once a week. If using a slow-release formula, however, you need only fertilize a few times during the growing season.

6

PLANTS FOR FOLIAGE

EXCEPT IN THE CASE OF MANY ANNUALS, MOST PLANTS have leaves for the long run and flowers for the short. You can have a great garden consisting of various plants with attractive or interesting leaves and nary a flower need be purchased.

Leaves come in light, medium, and dark shades of green, not to mention yellow, silver, or cream, often with streaks ranging from pink to red to white. Some leaves have colored chlorophyll, which instead of green, actually tints the leaf bright red or shocking pink. The combinations and variations are as endless as your imagination.

So forget about lilies, roses, and colorful petunias, and think about plants that have fantastic foliage as opposed to flowers. *Amaranthus* 'Tricolor Perfecta', for instance, makes a colorful display in any container garden. Last summer my next-door neighbor put a 10-inch clay pot with three of these plants in front of a trellis made of stout, dried grape vines. Then he set a second pot of cup-and-saucer vine (*Cobaea scandens*), just behind it, so that the vine's satiny purple-blue flowers were suspended in front of the yellow, green, and crimson leaves. The effect was bright and beautiful.

For years in my garden, I've grown the cabbage palm (*Cordyline australis*), which starts out as an elegant seedling tree with long, arching leaves. It's often planted in the midst of pots of geraniums. If kept in a frost-free area over the winter, in some twenty years it

59

Cup-and-saucer vine (Cobaea scandens) *winds around morning glories and ivy, blooming all summer long.*

will come to occupy a 14-inch-wide container. When it reaches an unmanageable height, however, it can be air-layered and even the shortened version is a showstopper—especially in the middle of a perennial border. This tree is hardy in London and the southern counties, so having a specimen in your garden will add a traditional English touch. Look for a cultivar called 'Super Spike', a variety that will grow to about 3 feet high.

Even though flowers have always captured the public's imagination, there is much to be said for a garden composed of foliage, and the following plants are all elegant in leaf.

❧ CHINESE EVERGREENS

The botanical name for the Chinese evergreen is *Aglaonema*, from *aglaos*, meaning bright, and *nema*, for thread, which refers perhaps to the flower's shining stamens. I've asked a number of houseplant experts if anyone knows the derivation of this name but nobody has a clue.

The Chinese evergreen's common name originated with *A. modestum*. According to the *Aglaonema Growers Notebook*, this particular plant has been in continuous cultivation by the Chinese for centuries. It can be found in the northern part of Thailand, in adjoining Laos, and in areas of both China and North Vietnam. Many Asians own at least one *A. modestum* because the plant is thought to bring good luck, and in the Philippines this particular Chinese evergreen is known as *la suerte*, again for good luck.

Although only twelve species of *Aglaonema* are in general cultivation, and fewer than twenty-four are botanically valid species, there are more than one hundred names for its varieties, forms, and cultivars.

Aglaonemas belong to the Araceae or arum family and include herbs, climbers, and a few shrubs, all with large, simple, or compound leaves, and a flower that—like the calla lily and the flamingo flower—consists of a modified leaf, called a spathe, that surrounds a spadix: a column covered with numerous tiny flowers, male on the top and female on the bottom.

Another description that is often applied to these plants is "tough." They succeed in very dim light—surviving with as little as 10 to 15 FC—but they prefer at least the light from a north window for a few days every month or additional illumination from artificial lighting.

Potting soil for these hardy plants should be well drained and should include soil, peat moss, and sand, one-third each. Keep the mix evenly moist. Chinese evergreens also respond well to self-watering pots.

Yet they'll also grow quite well in pure water. Almost any vessel that holds water will do—except for those made from copper, brass, or lead. Simply take the plant out of the pot, remove the excess earth, and then carefully wash the roots in clear, tepid water. Next, place a few small pieces of charcoal in the bottom of the container, and add the plant and give it enough water to cover the roots and part of the stem.

Never let any leaves remain under the water surface because they will rot. And don't forget the charcoal: It is important because it will keep the water clean. As the water evaporates, replace it with fresh water. Don't use chlorinated water. If that's all you have, run a sinkful of water and let it sit for thirty-six hours. Do not use water softened by a home appliance, either. Plants don't like the chemicals involved.

Temperature can be a problem since these plants must be kept warm, especially when grown in water. The roots are especially sensitive to cold. During the day, 75°F to 85°F is ideal, with a drop of ten degrees at night.

⁂ THE BIGGEST ASPIDISTRA IN THE WORLD

During World War II, the English music-hall singer and comedian Gracie Fields kept the home fires burning bright with her boisterous rendition of "It Was the Biggest Aspidistra in the World," a song urging the British to rally round the things that made England great— and that included more homes and parlors with more "blooming aspidistras" than any other country in the world.

In 1823 John Damper Parks sailed on the *Lowther Castle* from London to China and brought back, among roses, chrysanthemums, and camellias, the very first aspidistra, a plant that by 1840 suited the burgeoning Victorian generation to a capital "T." Amazingly impervious to bad air, bad light, bad smoke, and thick dust, it was a perfect plant to set among Turkish cushions in dark and dreary corners. In fact, it soon gained the popular name of the cannon-ball plant, or in some circles the cast-iron plant thanks to its ability to withstand all sorts of ill treatment.

The genus is *Aspidistra* from the Greek for a small, round shield, referring to the shape of the flower's stigma. The species was first termed *lurida* and came from the so-called lurid purple flowers that occasionally appear at ground level. The species name used today, however, is *elatior*, meaning taller, which has to do with the size of the leaf—a leathery dark green thing that can grow up to 2½ feet long.

Its flowers are more interesting than beautiful, consisting of six to eight brownish-purple sections—not really petals—that open to reveal a disk with eight stamens. In nature, wandering slugs fertilize them.

For dirt, use a mix of potting soil, peat moss, and sand, one-third each. And try to keep it evenly moist, although the plant will live up to its common name and go for weeks without water. Temperatures should always be above 50°F, but they don't take kindly to full sun so give them a spot in partial shade, especially in the hot summer months.

One very attractive variegated form, known as 'Variegata', has leaves alternating with white and green stripes, and a dwarf variety called, 'Milky Way', has leaves beautifully shaded with ivory spots.

If you are in a hurry to develop a large plant with a pot full of leaves, buy a number of smaller plants and bunch them together.

❧ THE PONYTAIL PALM

On rare occasions, the ponytail palm is listed in the genus *Nolina*, a botanical appellation that is easy to explain since it's in honor of P. C. Nolin, a Frenchman who wrote of Parisian agriculture in 1755. Unfortunately, most authorities also include it in the genus *Beaucarnea*, (which in French means "beautiful flesh-colored," but since the flowers are usually white, I have been unable to find its true meaning). The species found in cultivation is *recurvata*, and that's easy to understand since the leaves cascade to the floor in gentle curves that often curve again, making it a most attractive plant to have around. This is one of those plants that make an architectural statement, especially in a modern home or apartment with lots of glass, chrome, and white walls or in a room with American southwestern decor.

In the wilds of southern Texas and Mexico, this tree-like plant can reach a height of 30 feet, but in its more common home surroundings—where the forgetful owner can take advantage of its ability to survive in small pots and withstand sporadic waterings—

its height rarely tops 6 feet. The leaves are flat, ¾-inch wide, and often reach a length of 5 feet, giving the well-grown ponytail a Rapunzel-like quality.

Its other common name is elephant-foot-tree, after the imposing shape of the trunk's base, a shape that resembles a balloon made of rigid bark. This swollen trunk soaks up water like a sponge, allowing it to store water, in most large ponytails, for up to a year. While a potted specimen will not withstand that degree of neglect, it will survive for months without water if the basal swelling exceeds 4 or 5 inches.

There are two approaches to care. The first is to provide the ponytail with evenly moist soil and a spot in partial shade. The second is to keep the soil on the dry side and set the plant in a sunny spot. Just remember that a well-watered plant will grow twice as fast.

While ponytails can withstand temperatures in the high 40s, they prefer temperatures between 55°F and 70°F. Its earth should consist of potting soil, peat moss, composted manure, and sand, one-quarter each. Fertilize only once or twice a year.

The expanding trunks will adjust to crowded conditions but eventually they will have to be moved to a larger pot. Perform this operation in early spring before new leaves appear.

Many ponytails in cultivation have leaves about 3 feet long and belong to the variety *intermedia*.

❧ THE PEACOCK AND PRAYER PLANTS

Both the peacock plants of the genus *Calathea* and the prayer plants of the genus *Maranta* belong to the Marantaceae. Although the flowers are pretty, they are small and completely overshadowed by exceptionally beautiful leaves that appear in such luxurious colors and color combinations that they surely must rival those found in Joseph's coat. Both are native to tropical America.

Calathea is supposedly derived from the first botanical description when an unknown botanist saw the leaves of *C. lutea* used in basket weaving, hence the Greek word *calathos*, meaning basket (the leaves also produce a wax similar to carnauba). The common name of the peacock plant, however, is obvious at first sight.

My favorite is *C. makoyana*, a species originally from Brazil, which bears large oval leaves—often a foot long—that are patterned on both sides: the top with olive-green lines and ovals over a field of pale yellow-green while underneath the pattern is repeated in a rich purple-red.

Running a close second, however, is *C. Warscewiczii*, a species from Costa Rica that bears very dark green leaves feathered with paler green markings on either side of the midrib and purple underneath. The plant is named in honor of a Polish botanist, Joseph Warscewicz (1812–66). At least twelve different species and cultivars are also available, including a number of dwarf plants if space is limited.

Peacock plants prefer a humid atmosphere similar to that found in their original jungle habitat. Keep the soil evenly moist—they do well in self-watering pots—and use a mix of potting soil, composted manure, sand, peat moss, and perlite or vermiculite, one-fifth each. Prepared African violet soil is also excellent. Full sun must be avoided because the leaves will burn, so keep your plants in filtered sunlight or strong artificial light. Fertilize once a month during active growth and never feed plants until they have settled in. Never let temperatures fall below 60°F.

These plants stop growing from the end of December until February so watering should be cut back during this time. If you're using a self-watering pot, let the reservoir dry out, watering only once the soil becomes dry. Plants should be divided in early spring before new growth occurs.

❧ THE PRAYER PLANTS

Prayer plants also belong to the genus *Maranta* and were named in honor of Bartolomea Maranti, a Venetian botanist, who flourished in the mid 1500s. They're aptly named, too, because the foliage patterns strongly suggest those found in Venetian glass. The word "prayer" refers to the plant's habit of curling up its leaves at night and unfurling them in the morning.

Three varieties of M. *leuconeura* (the species names refer to the light veining or pattern of nerves) are commonly found in cultivation. Var. *erythroneura* (*erythro* is a $50 word for red) bears leaves up to 5 inches long that exhibit a herringbone design of carmine red veining that overlays a background of a velvety olive green. It is easily the most beautiful of the three. Var. *kerchoviana* (named for Oswald Charles Eugène Kerchove de Denterghem [1844–1906]) has dark brown and dark green splotches on a light green background, and var. *leuconeura* has silvery gray feathering on a black-green background.

⊁ THE FANCY CALADIUMS

For most of the year, the majority of the plants in this book produce either attractive foliage or flowers, or both. Caladiums are an exception: Their flowers are interesting rather than beautiful, and they spend part of the year in complete dormancy giving no hint of their presence. But the leaves are so spectacular they are worth a major effort to grow in the window. There are about fifteen species in the genus (named for the Malay word *kalady*), most having beautifully marked leaves and originally hailing from South America.

Their one weakness is sensitivity to cold. Never start them indoors unless the tubers can be kept warm and never plant the tubers outside until night temperatures fall no lower than 55°F to 60°F and the soil is very warm. Yet when they leaf out, keep those leaves out of direct sunlight during the hot summer months or the foliage will scorch and burn.

Caladium bicolor is usually called angel wings, sometimes mother-in-law plant (why I cannot fathom), and in tropical countries, it's called the heart of Jesus. This species is probably the chief parent of today's many exotic cultivars. It is also an important tropical food crop where the ginger-like roots are boiled and eaten under the name of cocoa roots. In addition, a purgative medicine is extracted from its fresh rhizomes.

The original plant grows to about 30 inches high and bears arrow-shaped leaves—or elongated hearts—14 inches long by 10 inches wide. The leaves are red with a broad red border on purple stems. From this humble beginning, however, hundreds of cultivars have been created. Tubers can be ordered from major nurseries and come in a bewildering variety of colors.

Caladiums arrived in 1850s Europe, and the first cultivar was 'Chantinii', which was introduced in 1857 and named for a French nursery. Basically, it resembles the original plant but with leaves flecked in various bits of white. This was followed by 'Splendens', which hailed from South America in 1773, and bears red-purple veins on a green background.

Among the newest are the following choices, each reaching a height of 2 feet: 'Carolyn Wharton' with large bright pink leaves, rose veins, and an entire leaf surface flecked with green; 'White Christmas' with white leaves and green veins; and 'Red Flash', which produces leaves with bright red centers and deep ribs surrounded with splashes of pink.

There are shorter varieties, too, growing about 18 inches high. These include: 'Rose Bud' with dark green borders that blend into white, then turn to rose-pink around the veins and 'Frieda Hemple', which bears solid red leaves bordered with green.

And finally, a new miniature has arrived on the scene. Growing about 8 inches tall, it can be used as a border for the larger types. It's called 'Little Miss Muffet' and has lime green leaves marked with splotches of wine red.

Propagation is by little tubers that grow around the edges of mature tubers and by homegrown seed (although seedlings usually vary greatly).

Plant the dormant tubers just below the soil surface—knobby side up—in 6-inch pots and keep them at 70°F until the leaves appear. Use a mix of potting soil, composted manure, and sand, one-third each, water well whenever it becomes dry, and fertilize once a month while plants are in active growth. Syringe the leaves with warm water during hot weather, and turn the pots every day to keep the leaves from growing in one direction.

In the fall, withhold water and store the pots in a warm spot—never below 60°F—until the following spring. Then replace the first inch of soil with fresh, bring into heat, and the tubers will grow again. Tubers can also be removed from the pots and stored in a bed of sphagnum or peat moss.

Often when the tubers are receptive to their environment, they will bloom. The flowers, which are members of the same family as flamingo flowers and Jack-in-the-pulpits, have a unisexual spadix. Watch out for spider mites!

☙ BEAUTIFUL DIZZY

Recently a friend asked me about the care and nurture of a fairly popular houseplant known by turns as the false aralia, spider aralia, threadleaf, splitleaf maple, or, by those in the know, Dizzy. Its botanical name is *Dizygotheca elegantissima*, the genus referring to a 2-yolk case since its anthers have double the usual number of cells. Its species name, however, is obvious because it is such an elegant and beautiful plant.

Originally discovered in the New Hebrides Islands in about 1870, this shrub will eventually grow into a small tree of up to 25 feet—but generally not in the average home.

Confusion over Dizzy's various life stages began some years ago. When young and shrubby, its leaves are compound and sit on long, dark green and white mottled stems, with seven to ten arching leaflets, toothed and graceful. As it reaches maturity, however, the leaf character changes: Leaflets become lance-shaped, generally broader, and the toothed edge becomes lobed. The leathery leaves are a copper color until they mature, when they change to a deep green that appears almost black. For a while botanists puzzled over the true identity of this plant, and it was placed in the *Aralia* genus (as were a number of other genera). It is still offered occasionally as *A. laciniata*.

These plants thrive best in filtered sun or bright, indirect light in temperatures always above 60°F. Keep the soil evenly moist, because they originally come from a jungle environment. Use a mix of potting soil, peat moss, and sand, one-third each, and fertilize every month during the spring and summer. Repot plants in early spring before new growth commences. Propagation is by stem cuttings.

Two other species are sometimes offered for sale. *D. kerchoveana* has a very pale midrib and *D. veitchii* has leaves that are green on top and coppery red beneath. This last plant was found growing on New Caledonia in 1865 by John Gould Veitch, who was unable to explore many of the islands in the South Pacific because of the savagery of the inhabitants. At one point, a native chief was held on board Veitch's ship as a hostage for his safety while he roamed swamps up to his armpits, looking for new species.

There is also a new cultivar called 'Pink Rim' where the leaflets are margined with a soft pink color when young.

✤ THE JAPANESE MEDLAR OR LOQUAT

A friend of mine who travels yearly to Florida brought back some loquat seeds for me in the spring of 1988 and assured me that, as a container plant for the home, I would be surprised both by its reasonably quick growth and the attractive look of its leaves.

I planted the seeds in late spring, using 3-inch clay pots and a mix of potting soil, peat, and sand, one-third each, and placing the pots on a heating cable. By the time autumn came around there were three leaves on each seedling.

The leaves themselves are rather strange: gray-green, soft, and covered in wooly down on both top and bottom. As the leaves mature, the topside down can be rubbed off—rather like lint—revealing a dark green leathery surface. The nether down will stay.

By the time the tree reached 8 inches it possessed ten leaves, the last three being 1-foot long. By the summer of 1989, the loquat was 14 inches tall and sported 18 leaves.

The botanical name is *Eriobotrya japonica. Erion* is the Greek for wool, and *botrys* for cluster, which refers to the 1½-inch long fruit that is covered with a soft downy skin.

Having been cultivated both in China and Japan for centuries, loquats were introduced into Britain in 1787, where they were popular in the glass houses of large and stately homes and gardens. Its common names include Japanese medlar tree, Japanese plum, and Chinese loquat.

When prepared in advance for cold weather a tree will survive in 15°F temperatures, but the new shoots will die at just a few degrees below freezing. Therefore, in most of the country, it's best used as a potted plant living in temperatures between 50°F and 65°F, with a sunny window, and lime-free soil kept evenly moist at all times. This final requirement makes the loquat a good choice for a self-watering pot, but even then the soil should be loose. The mix I used for the seedlings is also appropriate for the maturing tree.

In the spring when the loquat reaches a height of 2 to 2½ feet, it should be pruned so that the two or three main branches will develop. Its flowers will be white and fragrant, each about ½-inch wide and borne in wooly panicles up to 8 inches long. They are said to be most profuse after a long, hot summer.

✥ THE CLOWN FIG

According to horticultural tomes, the fig family includes food, fodder, natural rubber, and bark cloth. The banyan tree, which sends down aerial roots forming trunks to support the canopy, thus allowing the tree to cover several acres; the strangler figs that begin as plants that live in the open air, then strangle their host, and eventually become self-supporting trees; and the host plants for the lac insect (an insect that secretes a resinous substance that, when melted, becomes shellac) are all members of the fig family.

A number of figs make great plants for the window garden, including the edible fig; the rubber plant (yes, it's a member of the fig family); the weeping fig (one of the most common container plants in today's smart, new office buildings); and the clown fig.

The clown fig. What an apt name for a plant that has such a distinct feel of delight about it. From its winsome variegations to its striped fruit, this is a fig to lift the spirits. The botanical name is *Ficus aspera*, *Ficus* being the old Latin name for this genus, and *aspera* being either an archaic Latin word for rough (referring to the rough feel of the upper leaf) or an old Greek word for white (literally the whiteness of silver coins).

Often called *F. Parcellii* in older reference books, the clown fig is a small shrub or tree with 8-inch leaves that are dotted and splashed with ivory-white dabs against a light green background. The fig-like fruits are about 1 inch in diameter and striped with green, white, and pink.

Of the plants described in this book, this is not one of the easiest to cultivate, for its leaves will drop in response to a chill and it's very prone to spider mites. If you would rather grow an old warhorse, find a rubber plant, but if you are willing to give just a bit of extra effort, read on and adopt a clown fig.

Use a mix of potting soil, peat moss, composted manure, and sand, one-quarter each. Give the plant a spot in partial sun and be sure to keep it warm in winter, never letting the temperature fall below 60°F. Water well and let the soil dry before watering again. Propagate by cuttings.

Spider mites truly love clown fig leaves, so the price of a healthy plant is eternal vigilance, especially during the summer months. Check the underleaf of your plants at least once a week. If these horrors do appear, immediately treat the leaves with insecticidal soap, or wash them in a bathtub or sink, using Ivory soap or its equivalent.

✷ THE VELVET PLANT

The look of a velvet plant presages something out of the ordinary— it could easily be the favorite houseplant of the Wicked Queen in *Snow White* or could perhaps be found growing in the musty basement where the Spider Woman outwitted Sherlock Holmes. The genus is *Gynura,* which comes from the Greek *gyne,* for female, and *oura,* tail, referring to the long and rough stigma in the flower. Not, in fact, a very romantic name for a plant so mysterious-looking.

Its green leaves and stems are soft to the touch, completely covered with a purple plush, much like the velour that was once used to cover seats in railroad cars. If you look directly down on a leaf it seems to be green stippled with purple, but when looked at slightly askew, its hairs are all in evidence.

The flowers, immediately recognizable as members of the daisy family, are orange and really "pop" against the plushy background of the leaves. But resemblance to most daisies ends with floral construction, because they smell exactly like the contents of a dust bag in an old vacuum cleaner.

There are two species generally found in cultivation. *G. aurantiaca* is known as the royal purple plant (the species name means yellow-orange and refers to the flower). Originally from Java, this is the one usually offered by nurseries.

G. sarmentosa (*sarmentosa* means "long runners") is in reality a cultivar of *G. aurantiaca* and is properly known as 'Purple Passion'. This particular variety has narrower leaves, with stems that clamber about, and they're quite visually effective seen edging over the lip of a hanging basket.

There is another cultivar in this species called 'Aurea-Variegata'. Its creamy yellow splashes on a purple background resemble nothing more than a purple sweatshirt sprayed with liquid bleach—a most unappetizing result.

G. bicolor hails from the Moluccas, the same islands that gave birth to the green-blossomed annual flower, bells-of-Ireland, leading one to think that the typical pastoral scene thereabouts is garish to say the least. The leaves are purplish green above and purple beneath.

Velvet plants are easy to grow. The best soil mix is potting soil, peat moss, composted manure, and sand, one-quarter each. Keep temperatures above 60°F and give them a spot in partial shade, although *G. bicolor* will take more sun. All varieties prefer a soil that is evenly moist. Fertilize every month or so when in active growth. Propagation is by cuttings.

❧ THE LIGULARIAS

Ligularias are from Europe and Asia and belong to the daisy family. Most are excellent outdoor perennials for the flower garden, but one in particular, *Ligularia tussilaginea*, comes from Japan. Less hardy than the others, it makes an attractive houseplant. In anything colder than Zone 7, it does not usually survive.

Because this plant resembles coltsfoot, *Tussilago farfara*—a perennial herb whose roots are used to prepare a tonic to relieve coughing—its species name came to be *tussis*, itself an archaic Latin word for cough. Older catalogs also call it *Farfugium grande* and *Senecio kaempferi*.

Ligularia, however, comes from the Latin *ligula*, which means little tongue and refers to the tongue-like shape of the large petal on each of the ray flowers surrounding the central "eye" of the simpler disc flowers. As children, when we played "She (or he) loves me, she (or he) loves me not," we tossed away one of these ray flowers off the typical field daisy for each pronouncement and finally were left holding the button of yellow disc flowers.

To make things more interesting, the common *L. tussilaginea* is never cultivated but three cultivars are. The first, and in my mind the most attractive, is the leopard plant, *L. tussilaginea* 'Aureo-maculata', a cultivar with kidney-shaped leaves, scalloped on the edge, and each leaf covered with round, yellow spots of various sizes. Its daisy-like flowers are little and light yellow, and completely unimportant when compared to the lovely leaves.

As for the other two, 'Argentea' has leaves edged in white, and in strong light the young leaves have a pink cast. And 'Crispata' or the parsley ligularia, has green leaves that are ruffled and crisped along the edge.

Since these plants are happy outdoors in much of the Temperate Zone, they do not like too much heat—temperatures should never rise above 75°F in the summer and 60°F during the winter. They all prefer to be kept evenly moist in a mix of potting soil, peat moss, composted manure, and sand, one-quarter each. Keep them in partial shade because too much sun can burn the leaves. Fertilize only while the plant is in active growth, and even then only every other month. Propagation is by division in the early spring.

✥ THE FLAX LILIES

There are only two species of flax lilies, both from New Zealand. Their genus, *Phormium,* translates to basket or wickerwork, because baskets, floor mats, sunshades, and rope are woven from the fibers of one of it species. In their native country, they are often found on poorly drained and peaty areas of mixed tussock grassland, 4,500 feet up in the mountains, not far above the tree line. It is said that these plants reshoot quickly after burning and, as do many pines and grasses in the United States, may increase after a forest fire.

The mountain flax bears fairly stiff leaves up to 7 feet high of either a deep maroon or deep green that sometimes fades to red with age. Originally called *P. cookianum* after the famous Captain Cook, the plants are now known as *P. colensoi* after William Colenso (1811–1899), New Zealand's most famous botanist.

The second species is New Zealand hemp, or *P. tenax (tenax* is Latin for tough and tenacious), the plant used for weaving. Because the seedling plants vary a great deal in habit, it's responsible for a number of colorful and unique cultivars. The leaves are much stiffer than the first species and can reach 9 feet, growing in fans that sit on top of heavy stems, eventually attaining a height of 15 feet.

The flowers of both species are dull red or yellow and stand in erect panicles more interesting than beautiful to look at. But these plants rarely flower in pots.

Phormiums are only hardy to 20°F and must be moved inside every fall in much of our country. Rather than dig up the plants every fall for the move indoors, I grow them in self-watering pots and dot them around the perennial border for marvelous color

*The maroon leaves of a New Zealand flax (*Phormium colensoi*) are a stark contrast to the autumn leaves of a hosta, in this case the cultivar 'Frances Williams'.*

accents. At one time in England, these plants were frequently set out in large tubs in gardens and conservatories, but this decoration trend eventually fell out of fashion.

A good mix for this plant consists of potting soil, peat moss, composted manure, and sand, one-quarter each. Temperatures should be kept cool, usually between 50°F and 65°F with maximum sun. Alfred Byrd Graf, in his valuable *Exotic Plant Manual*, writes of seeing these plants growing right in the cold waters of the southern lakes, which inspired me to plant mine in self-watering pots. Fertilize once in the spring and once in late summer.

The cultivars of *P. tenax* are legion, but look for 'Variegatum', with leaves striped white and creamy yellow; 'Dazzler' bearing 2-inch-wide magenta and chocolate–striped leaves; 'Apricot Queen', with a leaf combination of yellow and cream with green stripes and red edges; and 'Surfrider', with narrow twisted leaves of orange and green. 'Bronze Baby' or the dwarf flax, has leaves of bronze-purple with coppery edges.

Propagation of the species is by seed, but it loses its viability inside of a year. Vegetative propagation—with these plants, the only way to keep a cultivar pure—is by the division of the plant into single fans or groups of two or three. Discard any with flower spikes and make sure that each fan has at least four leaves. The old roots die but new roots quickly form. This is best accomplished in early spring before new growth begins.

✈ THE INDOOR LINDEN

There are three species of the genus *Sparmannia*. All are shrubs in their native South Africa, and one makes an excellent plant for the home. The genus is named in honor of a Swedish traveler, Dr. Anders Sparrman (1748–1820) who accompanied Captain Cook on his second voyage.

The species usually grown in containers is *S. africana*, called the African hemp because it is a source of fibers used in making cloth. It's also called the indoor linden because the leaves resemble those of the linden tree (*Tilia* spp.). It's a very popular plant in Europe and can be found in many sunny window gardens.

The large, soft leaves are angled and lobed, up to 8 inches long and covered with a silky down. In fact, even the stems still retain a few silky hairs long after their surface has turned to bark.

These are fast growing plants, usually flowering when only 2 feet high but continuing to grow up to 8 feet in the home, or 15 to 20 feet outside in a Zone 9 climate. Temperatures in the winter should never fall below 50°F, with 60°F ideal. If they grow too quickly, they can be cut back and new shoots will appear. Many gardeners take 3- to 4-inch cuttings in early spring and begin new plants every two years. Seed is offered from nurseries that deal in rarer plants. If you desire a large plant, pot on each spring.

Soil should be potting soil, peat moss, and composted manure, one-third each. Provide full sun for most of the year but during July and August partial shade is best. Keep the soil evenly moist from April until October, cutting back on water during the winter months. Feed the plants every month during periods of active growth.

The white flowers appear in many-flowered umbels in mid-spring. Each blossom is about 1 inch wide with four petals and four smaller sepals surrounding a large collection of purple-tipped stamens at the center. The sensitive stamens are interesting, moving outwards when brushed by a finger or touched by a gentle breeze.

S. africana 'Flore Pleno' bears double flowers, and 'Variegata' has white areas on the leaves.

✴ THE INCH PLANTS

Up until a few years ago, many of the inch plants were generally given the name "wandering Jew." This common name came from a literary and popular legend that began some five hundred years ago and referred to the plant's habit of trailing along or cascading down from a pot, growing older with a longer and longer stem, never rooting along the way. Eventually cuttings could rejuvenate it, when it would begin to wander again.

According to *The Columbia Encyclopedia*, this myth saw its beginnings in the racial prejudice of the sixteenth century, and concerned "a Jew who mocked or mistreated Jesus while He was on His way to the cross and who was condemned therefore to a life of wandering on earth until Judgment Day. The story is common in Western Europe, but it presents marked national variations; *e.g.,* in Spanish and Portuguese the Wandering Jew . . . goes about doing good for expiation."

Benét's Reader's Encyclopedia adds that the "Jew is periodically rejuvenated to the age of thirty [but] his character changes, however; he is now extremely wise, and, in his repentance, he uses the time of his wandering to exhort other men to be mindful of their sins and avoid the wrath of God."

These various members of the Commelinaceae or spiderwort family, could well have been called the "Cain plant," since Cain was the first human being to suffer such a curse or could, perhaps, be called the "Flying Dutchman plant," but literary references to such characters ranged from Goethe, Eugène Sue (who wrote sensational romances in early-eighteenth-century France), and Shelley in *Queen Mab*. So until recently, the literary appellation was used. Today, however, there is a move to change the common name from "wandering Jew" to "inch plant" for all the plants with this growth habit.

The five plants described below are all excellent for hanging baskets or pots. Even though they flower with charming three-petaled blossoms, their beauty is in the leaves. The one fault is that, as they age, they loose their older leaves, eventually becoming all stems with just a knot of leaves at the tip. In order to cultivate the most attractive plants, frequently start them anew from cuttings since they root easily at the nodes on the stem. Most will even root in a glass of plain water.

Use any mix of potting soil, composted manure, peat moss, and sand, one-quarter each. Water well, then let the soil dry before watering again. Temperatures are best held above 50°F but individual requirements are listed below.

The first plant has always been called the inch plant and bears the botanical name *Callisia congesta variegata*, its genus from the Greek *kallos*, for beauty. Leaves arise from a sheath around the stem, the space between each lengthening with age and at the tip of the stem they grow in a tight whorl. The leaf edge is wavy and they are beautifully striped with bands of white and are suffused with a purple glow both fore and aft. They make an exceptionally fine plant for a hanging basket. Provide partial shade and keep the soil evenly moist, fertilizing every two months. Temperatures should stay above 60°F.

The bamboo spiderwort bears the botanical name *Murdannia acutifolia variegata*, *acutifolia* meaning leaves sharpened to a point. This is a new plant on the horticultural scene and I've been unable to find a reference to the derivation of the genus. Nevertheless, for the indoor garden, this plant is a must. Glossy leaves up to 12 inches long are lined with stripes of white varying from a pin's width to ¼-inch or more. Since the stems have nodes and grow upright, they resemble bamboo. As with most plants in this family, the nodes are flushed with a purple stain. When the stems become too long and bend over, it's time to start new plants from cuttings. Keep temperatures above 55°F.

The giant white inch plant or *Tradescantia albiflora* 'Albovittata' bears 3-inch lance-shaped leaves of light green vigorously striped with longitudinal bands of white. Like many inch plants, the leaves have a crystalline quality when viewed close-up in sunlight. Most of the Commelinaceae bear purple or violet flowers, hence its species name— its flowers are white, and *albi* is Latin for white. The genus name is in honor of the intrepid English plant explorer, John Tradescant.

The white velvet or gossamer plant, *T. sillamontana* comes from Mexico and gets its common name from the web-like hairs that cover the surfaces of its leaves and stems. The species name refers to mountains. This plant grows erect, but then with time it begins to hang. The 2-inch leaves are almost olive drab on top and pale purple below, with the usual sparkle of the leaf cut by the cobwebs that surround everything. The three-petaled flowers are orchid purple. Because of the protective quality of its hairy coat, the gossamer plant revels in full sun. Let the soil dry completely before watering.

Finally, there are the inch plants from the genus *Zebrina* (Latinized from the Portuguese *zebra*, here referring to the stripes on the leaves). The species is *pendula*, and all its varieties are effective in hanging baskets. The 2-inch-long leaves are fleshy and their veins sparkle in the light. They all want temperatures above 50°F.

Z. pendula is the most common. Its purple leaves are striped with silver and its stems bear rosy purple flowers. The plant is very tolerant and will grow in bright sun to filtered shade. *Z. pendula* 'Daniel's Hybrid' has all purple leaves.

⚜ THE MALLET FLOWER

A number of the plants in my collection are from the tropics, mainly because these particular specimens enjoy warm temperatures all year long and rarely drop leaves. The only sign they give to a year's passing is to slip into a dormant phase—usually in the winter if they are from the Northern Hemisphere and in the summer if their home is below the Equator.

One such plant is the mallet flower or *Tupidanthus calyptratus*. The genus name and the common name are actually the same— *tupis* means mallet in Latin and *anthos* means flower. The species, *calyptratus*, means having a calyptra or cap, again a reference to the flower structure. There is only one species in this genus, hailing from India and Cambodia. It was introduced into England in 1856.

The compound leaves consist of seven to nine leaflets, each up to 1 foot in length, which hang from the end of a 14-inch stalk. The flowers are greenish and occur in umbels.

A mallet flower can reach a height of 12 feet indoors and makes a stunning decorator plant. It can also take a great deal of punishment and still recover with a grand showing.

⚜ THE FIG TREE

The fig has a long and colorful history. "And they sewed fig leaves together, and made themselves aprons," comes from the Bible. The Greek poet Menander (342–292 B.C.) remarked, "I call a fig a fig, a spade a spade." And finally John Heywood (1497–1580), the English dramatist, said the following:

> Let the world slide, let the world go;
> a fig for care, and a fig for woe!
> If I can't pay, why I can owe,
> And death makes equal the high and low.

The genus is *Ficus*, the plant's old Latin name, and that in turn comes from the ancient Hebrew *feg*. The species *carica*, is named for an ancient city in Asia Minor. The plant is unusual since the flowers are never seen. They line the inside of the fruit, and in many varieties a tiny *blastophaga* or fig wasp enters a small opening at the base of the burgeoning fruit to pollinate the flowers. *Blastophaga* cannot live in warm climates, therefore the self-pollinating cultivars 'Adriatic' and 'Turkey' are grown in cooler climates.

This wonderful tree and its legendary fruit have been in continuous cultivation for thousands of years. Properly ripened, figs are not only sweet and delicious, but good for you as well. From Zone 7 and farther south, the common fig can remain outdoors, weathering the winter during its dormant period. It can even withstand temperatures of 10°F. But remember that when it's sprouting, temperatures at freezing or below can severely damage new growth.

As far north as New York City, and in particular Brooklyn, fig trees will grow outdoors if provided with adequate winter protection, which usually means wrapping the trees in layers of burlap, building little wooden sheds—much like the Japanese wrap palm trees in Tokyo—or by bending the trees down to the ground and then covering them with earth.

Figs also make great pot plants, using 9- to 12-inch pots and planting them in a soil made up of good potting soil, peat moss, composted manure, and sand, one-quarter each. Repot the fig every fall, removing some of the old soil and adding new, or at least top-dressing the existing soil. Once in a pot, they require plenty of water, but let the soil dry between waterings.

Fertilize with plant food every month during active growth. Figs also want as much sun as possible and if kept indoors give them a sunny window and remember to spritz the leaves every day. Figs often harbor red spider mites and this pest resents water in any form.

Many gardeners who have no greenhouse or sun porch will expose the tree to a few early frosts to induce dormancy, then put it in a cool basement until spring, or bring it into a temperature of 65°F and start growth again.

Look for the self-fertile cultivar 'Brown Turkey', which produces fruit the first year it's planted. Ripened fruit is soft to the touch.

❧ HARRY ABEL AND THE BONSAIED HOSTA

Harry Abel lives in Smyrna, Georgia. He's been experimenting with bonsai techniques since the early 1970s, and he explained this gardening technique to me. "Bonsai," said Mr. Abel, "is pronounced bone-sigh—with a long a—and not to be confused with *banzai* which is a Japanese war cry! Bonsai translates as 'tray planting' or 'planted in a container.'

"When I began, I followed the time-honored tradition of growing trees but soon found that I needed more for an artistic statement so I turned to grasses, perennials, and bog pitcher plants. Then in 1981 I was asked to exhibit at the Bonsai Club's International Convention held in Atlanta, and most of the visitors thought that my creations were visionary and beautiful, but not bonsai because 'it's not trees.' Now these approaches to bonsai are considered, [and they] are called *Kusamono* or 'grass plantings.'

"And," continued Mr. Abel with a smile, "it didn't hurt to have bonsai masters like Kyuzo Murata, official bonsai gardener to the Imperial Household of Japan for some sixty years, come out with bonsaied grasses, perennials, even a water lily, in his marvelous book *Four Seasons of Bonsai*."

When asked if there were any more Japanese movements devoted to growing plants in containers, Mr. Abel told me about *Saikei*, an interpretation of bonsai that allows greater freedom in composition. This approach uses ordinary stones and seedlings, even grasses, in addition to shrubs and trees, but are meant to give a naturalness to the shape; a *saikei* tree looks like its form has been determined by the weather and not by the trained hand of its grower.

Mr. Abel has always been fascinated with miniatures, and he's been collecting and growing them for more than twenty-five years. "The rule today is smaller gardens," he said, "including gardening in containers. With bonsai techniques you can raise several varieties in a small space. And if you get tired of the color scheme you've chosen, it's very easy to change it."

The first thing to do is choose a container, but Mr. Abel quickly pointed out that it's a personal choice. "I like cobalt blue containers," he said, "and I probably have over fifty of them in all shapes and sizes. I plant blues or white variegated plant varieties in these blue pots. Sometimes maybe a gold- or a chartreuse-leafed variety—you can't put a hosta in a cobalt container and go wrong (even if you don't like cobalt).

"Lately, I've been using very unusually shaped containers for my hostas. Using a truly spectacular container somehow gives the little guys an extra little kick. Handmade pinch pots are favorites, but I also like squat, round bowls."

❧ FIRST THINGS FIRST

Mr. Abel suggests that you start with a hosta that is in active growth, but admits that it's easier to begin with a dormant plant. Either way, to begin, lift the crown from the garden with a fork (or from a pot if it's nursery grown), then wash the roots with plenty of water. Cut back all the thin, white roots to within an inch of the rhizome.

Now look for next year's growth buds (the tiny white bumps at the base of last year's growth), divide the rhizome to whatever size you wish: Multi-eyed roots are Mr. Abel's favorites, as they send up a number of tiny shoots. A single-eyed plant will produce a larger single plant, but this is not really what bonsai hosta gardeners are after.

With plants in active growth, cut the foliage down to the level of the rhizome. This will result in the forced growth of next season's buds. Do this early in the year so the buds have time to form.

At this point, you should have a rhizome with short stubby roots. Now choose a container, covering the drain holes with screening to retain your soil mix. Don't use screen door mesh because it's much too fine. Instead, use a needlepoint canvas available at any sewing notions or arts and crafts store.

❧ SOIL MIXES

Planting mixtures should be coarse and promote quick drainage. A good soil mix may contain fir bark, granite grit, crushed lava, perlite, baked clay, or leaf mould.

"The goal," said Mr. Abel, "is to provide a medium that guarantees optimum conditions for root growth. The result of using such well-drained soil means more watering is necessary but, after all, if you want to get out of watering, you can always use a drip irrigation hookup—but I really think that destroys the fun. It's a trade-off: There's a greater need for watering when using porous mixes, but the healthy root growth is worth it.

"My personal favorite," he continued, "is one-quarter granite or lava, one-quarter high-fired clay (terra green, turface, or unscented kitty litter), one-quarter ground pine or fir bark, and one-quarter compost. To this I add about one pound of an organic fertilizer per wheelbarrow-load of mix. Sieve the fines from the pine bark and save, but discard the fines from clay products."

✣ PLANTING

Mr. Abel then explained the best way to plant bonsai: "In Japan, the way to grow perennials as bonsai is to place the ball of soil, usually a clay/moss mixture, in a *suiban* with gravel on the bottom. A *suiban* is a wide, shallow tray, usually no deeper than a half-inch. Watering must be done carefully to avoid erosion. If you live where the soil is mostly clay, you can use that. One way of accomplishing this is to mix some of your wonderful gummy clay into the ball to hold the roots together. Eventually the rhizome will spread to cover the soil mass, much as a rabbit foot fern. A container of tree fern root may also be used as a pot. This is a very porous material used to grow epiphytic ferns. Another dramatic effect results from placing two or more pieces of very similar rock together in a container, and then planting between the rocks. For an instant effect, use several pieces of multi-eyed root. Find out which hostas are rock dwellers, and use these to achieve a more realistic look."

Although Mr. Abel strives for realism in his microscopic creations, he's not above tying a rhizome to a rock and burying the whole thing in a container of soil until roots and shoots have entirely covered it.

You can begin this with a fully-grown potted plant. Drape the roots over the side of the rock, and tie on with twine. Leave the rock buried until roots have grown down the sides of the rock. Retrieve the rock, dust off the outer edges, and carefully moss in them. Sit the whole mess in a shallow container where the roots can be in soil at the base of the rock. This is a technique taught to me to make "root over rock"-style bonsai.

"One of my favorite tricks," said Mr. Abel, "is to plant identical cultivars in three different sizes of container. I'll use a 1½-inch, a 3-inch, or a 6-inch bowl with the leaf size being proportional to the size of the container. Everyone thinks they are three different cultivars, but the only difference is the soil mass. The top growth is a reflection of what the roots are 'allowed' to do. A small root system means a small plant on top."

⚘ WATER AND FERTILIZER

Water carefully until growth commences. Stabilizing the new soil is difficult at first, so try growing some little mosses or selaginellas as ground cover, thus preventing soil wash.

"A good rose nozzle," explained Mr. Abel, "especially with fine holes is very helpful. I've seen them made of brass at the bonsai specialty stores for $50 and I've seen them at the department stores for $5.99.

"Fertilize with whatever water soluble plant food you use for other things (Peter's, Schultz's, Miracle-Gro, etc). Grow these container hostas in as much sun as you can without burning foliage. If foliar burn does occur, remove the petiole all the way down to the root. Similarly, if leaves should grow too large for your pot simply remove them down to the ground. This forces next year's leaves into service and the new leaves will be smaller. The size of the leaves is also determined by the size of the container and how much soil they have to grow in. Although the leaves will reduce nicely, flower size will not, so remember this when you plan to display the blooms."

Mr. Abel often uses multi-level stands for displaying his bonsais. Remember that flowering requires an incredible amount of energy, so a major floral display will deplete the plant. But at the same time watch carefully for foliar wilting.

HOSTAS FOR BONSAI

Recommended small cultivars:

'Kabitan'	'Allen P. McConnell'
'Groundmaster'	'Butter Rum'
'Blue Cadet'	'Feather Boa'
'Ginko Ciaig'	'Gold Drop'
'Sugar Plum'	'Vera Verde'

Hosta lancifolia varieties

Recommended large cultivars:

'Halcyon'	'August Moon'
'Francee'	'Wide Brim'

'Gold Standard'

Spent blooms that produce seed are interesting features but they will put a drain on any plant with such a confined and limited root area. For added interest, Mr. Abel likes to leave a few scapes with ripening seedpods.

When he gives his illustrated lectures, Mr. Abel has a couple of beautifully made open shelves that he uses to show off smaller potted hostas.

As the leaves begin to yellow in the fall, leave your hosta bonsai out in the weather. When temperatures approach freezing on a regular basis, heel in the plants in your garden, buried up to the rim in sawdust, decomposed pine needles, or garden soil. Roots are incredibly hardy, but heeling in helps to control temperature fluctuations.

The idea here is that once the soil is frozen it should remain frozen until the following spring. If you have a cold frame, use that. Dormant hostas need no light at all, so they may be "bagged" like they do in Minnesota, where black bags of fall leaves completely cover and insulate the plants. This is not done to keep them from freezing, but to keep them in a frozen state.

Gardeners with prolonged winters may want to plant out the hostas over the winter by removing the plant from the pot and burying the roots. If you store them in an unheated garage, remember to check the moisture levels every week or so.

Ignore your hostas until late winter or early spring. Then, whenever you have time (and when the weather is dry), repot your hostas, if necessary. This may be done any time while they are dormant.

❧ JAPANESE MAPLES IN POTS

Many Japanese maples (*Acer* spp.) can be grown in containers with only an occasional pruning to keep their size within bounds. Not all Japanese maples are large or tall, however. Some of the most beautiful are less than 7 feet high, and at least six that I'm familiar with stop at 3 feet. In a neighbor's garden, a beautiful specimen of the red lace-leaf maple (*A. palmatum dissectum atropurpurum*), is planted in a redwood tub that measures about 16 inches across and 12 inches deep; around the edges lay an assortment of houseleeks (*Sempervivum* spp.), mostly *S. tectorum*.

One of the most graceful of the smaller Japanese maples is *A. palmatum* 'Kamagata', which bears 2-inch, five-lobed leaves that are lightly toothed at the margins. In the spring the leaves are a rusty red, turning bright green in the summer; when autumn arrives, they are flushed light orange with sparks of red. *A. palmatum* 'Hoshi kuzu' has unusual light green leaves that look more like those of a fig than a maple. They are about 2 inches long and 2 inches wide, and turn golden yellow in the fall. *A. palmatum* 'Goshiki kotohime' has a variegated leaf that resembles a Jackson Pollack painting—its green leaves are splashed with red, pink, white, cream, and a touch of yellow.

The only problem with potted Japanese maples occurs when winter temperatures fall below 14°F at the roots; at this temperature the roots are severely damaged. If you live in winters where temperatures rarely fall below zero, the container can be enclosed in layers of bubble insulation or set within a larger box that is then filled with insulation such as polystyrene peanuts or some other insulation. If there are many days of below-freezing temperatures, it's a good idea to bury the pots in a belowground container or a box within a box. Mulch the pot heavily on top, or store it in a shed or a porch where it stays cold (about 40°F) but above freezing.

7

GROUND COVERS

IN AMERICA, GROUND COVERS ARE BIG BUSINESS. STATE highway authorities have backed away from spraying defoliants and weed killers along roadsides and have turned to plants that require little maintenance. Some states have successfully used mass plantings of wild flowers, with both annuals and perennials in great drifts of color. Others have planted ornamental grasses. Unfortunately, though, some efforts have proved disastrous. For example, the Commonwealth of Pennsylvania let loose the invasive crown vetch (*Coronilla varia*), which promises to cover everything in sight.

The ground covers I have chosen to describe (with one exception) are better behaved than crown vetch and are more suitable for plots smaller than a highway right-of-way. In fact, you can create a charming small garden using nothing more than various ground covers. The following ground covers are also perfect for underplantings in larger pots and permanent containers.

PLANTING OUT AND SPACING GROUND COVERS

Fall is a great time to plant perennials, but in most areas of the country, spring is the best time for planting out ground covers. At that time of the year, the plants are geared up for growth after having spent the last six months on hiatus.

Before planting, make sure the soil is properly prepared. Remove existing weeds and till the soil or at least spade it up by hand. If you have heavy clay, make sure you add compost. Dig to a depth of six inches.

Today almost everyone wants instant gratification, but when it comes to ground covers, that could be expensive—to fill 100 square feet with large pachysandra, for instance, would require about eighty plants. Most rooted cuttings are packed four or six to a unit and will fill in an area when planted on 6- to 10-inch centers. If you're purchasing plants in 4-inch pots, increase the distance to 12 to 14 inches. Instead of planting out in a haphazard manner, plant in staggered rows. Always allow at least two years of growth before a particular bed is filled. Next, mulch the bed with shredded bark, shredded leaves, or a commercial product, such as Nature's Helper. (Do not use peat moss; its tends to dry out and repel moisture.) And before planting, keep new ground covers in the shade and be sure they are well watered.

⚜ GOUTWEED

Goutweed (*Aegopodium podagraria*) is an aggressive spreader. In England it's known as ground elder, and Christopher Lloyd, the great English gardener, said that, if you describe this plant as a gift horse, remember that it belongs to the Trojan breed. Luckily, there is a cultivar called 'Variegatum' that spreads at a fast crawl rather than running rampant.

A good garden friend once gave us a clump of the variegated ground elder (also known as bishop's weed). We used it on an inhospitable slope in full sun, so it never took, but I take great exception with nurseries that describe this plant as "carefree and vigorous"— it's more like "raping and pillaging."

One day—in a fit of pique—I threw a clump into the nearby white pine woods, where the soil is poor and light is filtered all year by needles. The leaves seemed to glow in the shade, and over the next few years, the plant slowed it spread. So my advice is to eschew the sunny side with goutweed and plant it in the shade.

🌿 LADY'S-MANTLE

Lady's-Mantle (*Alchemilla vulgaris*) sometimes masquerades under the species name of *A. mollis* because many gardeners (and nurserymen) think *vulgaris* means "vulgar"; rather, it means "common to many places." Use lady's-mantle along the front of the border and as a ground cover. The cupped leaves are covered with tiny, silken hairs that catch drops of dew, which reflect sunlight and roll about like drops of mercury. The chartreuse flower sprays are also attractive. While hardy to Zone 4, provide shade and moist soil south of Zone 7.

🌿 WILD GINGER

The best wild ginger for most American gardens is known as *Asarum shuttleworthi*. It's a native plant from Virginia and south, to Georgia. Unlike the hardier species, *A. canadense*, this plant is evergreen and hardy in the warmer regions of Zone 5, especially when protected by snow. The shiny green heart-shaped leaves make an excellent ground cover, especially in good, acid soil with plenty of shade. The odd flowers look like little brown jugs and lie directly on the ground where they are seldom noticed. Beetles pollinate them as they scurry across the earth, and seedling plants often naturalize. The rootstocks have a ginger odor and a hot, spicy taste. In winter the leaves turn a lovely shade of purple.

🌿 THE HAY-SCENTED FERN

The hay-scented fern (*Athyrium filix-femina*) is said to be an aggressive and invasive plant. I would never introduce it to a perennial border or a rock garden full of precious alpine plants, but it's perfect for carpeting a small bank where little else will grow or at the edge of a woodland glade where other plants are out of character. Its true beauty comes in the fall, when frost turns the sensitive fronds a wonderful shade of light brown with a golden glow. Add to this its delicious scent of fresh-mown hay, and it will always be welcome in your garden.

BERGENIA

Bergenia cordifolia hails from Siberia and Mongolia where it tolerates temperatures of -30°F. When exposed to chilly winds below 0°F, however, the leaves will turn brown and burn at the edges; in winters above 0°F, however, they turn a reddish bronze. Bergenias prefer partial shade in the summer and moist, well-drained soil with humus or leaf mold. Their large overlapped leaves are a perfect foil for ferns. As a bonus, bergenias bear rose pink, waxy blossoms in early spring.

HEATHER

Calluna vulgaris is the only species of heather. Called "lings" in England, this evergreen grows to about 18 inches high, forming a small mound of foliage. The scale-like leaves overlap each other, lying closely along the stem. Heathers bloom between late June and November.

There are a surprising number of cultivars. 'Foxii Nana' blooms between August and September, bearing mauve flowers on 4-inch-high plants; 'H. E. Beale' reaches a height of 24 inches and is covered with large double pink flowers from August to November; and the pink flowers of 'Mullion' start to bloom in late July and persist through September. Some varieties of *C. vulgaris* are known for the unusual colors of their foliage, including 'Aurea', with chartreuse leaves; 'Blazeaway', with beautiful copper-colored foliage; 'Gold Haze', with leaves of gold; and 'Silver Queen', with silvery leaves.

BUNCHBERRY

Bunchberry (*Cornus canadensis*), or creeping dogwood, is ideal for northern gardeners who tire of hearing about plants that will only thrive in the South. This beauty loves colder weather and actually languishes where the summers are hot. In the spring, creamy white bracts hover above a whorl of oval leaves a few inches high. The blossoms closely resemble typical dogwood flowers and are followed by clusters of red berries in autumn. The plants need a moist, humus-rich, acid soil. Bunchberries spread slowly by underground runners.

✤ BARRENWORTS

The barrenworts (*Epimedium* spp.), or bishop's-hats, are marvelous plants to grow along walls or the edges of pathways. Both its leaves and flowers (which resemble a bishop's miter) sit on strong, wiry stems. While not truly evergreen, its leaves have a papery texture that lasts well into winter, especially where temperatures usually stay above 20°F. They are hardy to Zone 5 and thrive in partial shade. *E. grandiflorum* is about 1 foot tall, with heart-shaped leaves that are bronzy when young, then turn green. Its flowers are yellow. 'Alba' is a white form, and 'Rose Queen' bears rose-colored flowers on 10-inch stems.

✤ THE HEATHS

The heaths (*Erica* spp.), like heathers, are small evergreen shrubs bearing hundreds of pink, red, lavender, or white flowers. Unlike heathers, however, heaths have slightly urn-shaped flowers and tiny leaves that stick out from the stems like pine needles. They require an acid soil and excellent drainage. They also grow poorly where summers are too hot and dry.

   E. carnea, or the spring heath, is usually hardy to Zone 6, but will survive in Zone 5 with adequate protection. Like heather, it is acid-loving and thrives under cool, moist conditions. The flowers appear from late fall to early spring, depending on winter temperatures. In my southern climate the cultivar 'Springwood White' has been in bloom since the beginning of December and will continue at least until mid-April. The two other cultivars of *E. carnea* are 'King George', blooming with crimson flowers from January to May, and 'Springwood Pink', with pink flowers that bloom from February to

April. Probably the hardiest heath, however, is *E. tetralix*, which has gray foliage and rosy flowers that bloom from late June to October and can survive a Zone 4 winter.

❦ THE IVIES

The ivies (*Hedera* spp.), are great ground covers if kept under strict supervision. In Zone 7 or in warmer parts of Zone 6, ivy—when left to its own devices—will spread like an oil spill on calm water and must be cut back periodically.

In Zone 5, the winter cold tempers ivy's aggression, especially if there is no snow cover and plants are exposed to the chill winds. Except for Persian ivy (*H. colchica*), common English ivy (*H. helix*), and *H. pastuchovii* from Russia—as well as two of its cultivars, '288th Street' and 'Thornedale', originally from an area north of Chicago—most ivies are not reliably hardy under those conditions.

For warmer climes (Zone 6), there is 'Buttercup', whose leaves are yellow in the sunshine but turn dull green in the shade. This fast grower makes for superb ground cover and is especially attractive when allowed to grow on a wall. 'Deltoidea', often called sweetheart ivy, bears heart-shaped leaves of dark green that turn purple-bronze in the winter. A slow-growing ground cover, it is especially suited for rock gardens. For a variegated form, look for 'Stardust'. The leaves have a slim edge of white and are blotched with two tones of green.

❦ PERENNIAL CANDYTUFT

Perennial candytuft (*Iberis sempervirens*), needs well-drained soil in full sun. The 1-foot-high woody stems bear thin, glossy leaves that are evergreen even in the colder sections of Zone 5. In spring, clusters of white four-petaled fragrant flowers appear. Crawling over the ground, candytuft will tumble over the edge of a wall and slowly root in clefts and crevices. To keep plants blooming, deadhead old flowers; if they are cut back, they will bloom twice.

✻ CARPET JUNIPERS

The carpet junipers (*Juniperus* spp.) are actually conifers that make great ground covers. *J. communis* var. *depressa*, the ground juniper, is a low evergreen shrub about 3 feet high with sharp blue-green needles. Plants will artfully spread about and are especially grand when tumbling over walls. 'Aurea' has vivid golden yellow foliage that slowly turns to bronze as the summer passes, and *J. horizontalis* 'Bar Harbor' follows the contours of the land, weaving its way between various rocks. It's also attractive when hanging over the edge of a wall, and in the winter, its blue-green foliage turns a lovely purple-blue.

But my favorite ground hugger is *J. chinensis* var. *procumbens* 'Nana', an ornamental conifer discovered in the mountains of Japan about one hundred years ago. The foliage is a fresh green in spring, turning blue-green in summer, and bronzes in winter. The needles are sharp, but unfortunately not sharp enough to keep deer from devouring the rest of the plant. This conifer will eventually cover an area approximately 10 to 12 feet in diameter. If you put an obstacle in its path, the branches will work themselves up and over it. In our northern garden, one plant circled part of our scree bed. Today, in our southern garden, one specimen hangs over the ledge of a stone wall and another sits in a pot.

✻ THE YELLOW ARCHANGEL

The yellow archangel (*Lamiastrum galeobdolon* 'Variegatum') is still called *Lamium* in most nurseries and books. The evergreen leaves are attractive during the summer but turn into something special during winter, when they are liberally splashed with silver then edged with maroon. Some nurseries call this plant a "vigorous grower," which means it will spread if left uncut. Planted beneath trees, however, it's great for covering ground. Spikes of small, yellow, snapdragon-like flowers appear in spring.

❧ PACHYSANDRA

Pachysandra terminalis and *P. procumbens* are the two garden species of pachysandra. Unfortunately, most garden centers stock the first, a Japanese native, and ignore the second, a beautiful American species. It's true that in shady places, nothing beats Japanese pachysandra for covering ground. ('Green Carpet' is hardier than the species and has glossy, deep green, slightly larger foliage; 'Silveredge' is variegated.) But compared to its American relative, *P. terminalis* seems course and pushy. *P. procumbens*, commonly called the Allegheny spurge, has a far subtler leaf color, and the individual plants seem to meld, like perfectly matched pieces of a puzzle. The 1-foot-high plants bear oval gently toothed leaves with light areas of green touched with silver on a regular dark green surface. The flowers have a purplish cast and consist mainly of stamens making a mass of sparkling bloom. They are evergreen in areas south of Zone 6.

❧ THE CREEPERS

Parthenocissus quinquefolia or Virgina creeper, is usually considered a vine. One year, however, I cut down a white pine that was home to a creeper. Not wanting to lose the vine, I carefully pulled the tendrils away from the bark and laid it on the ground. Later I returned to find the vine wandering over the ground and taking root. In this case, either full sun or partial shade will do, and the leaves will turn a glorious shade of red in autumn.

   Rubus calycinoides is known as the crinkle-leafed creeper. Its attractive leaves are round and puckered, green in the summer and a bronzed maroon during the winter. Unlike most members of the rose family, it has inconspicuous flowers and no thorns. It is another ground cover given to rampant growth, sending out arching branches that soon root at the nodes and spread out again from there. For covering a bank or an enclosed area where escape is impossible, nothing is better. Give this creeper full sun or partial shade. 'Emerald Carpet' is a third cultivar that has a deep green summer color. Unfortunately, it is only reliably hardy from Zone 7 southward.

COLTSFOOT

Coltsfoot (*Tussilago farfara*), is one of the toughest ground covers known. It shouldn't even be mentioned in the same breath as plants that are termed delicate, demure, or dainty. The small golden, daisy-like flowers of early spring are always welcome, but the leaves are large and extremely insistent. Use it to carpet poor-quality soil and areas of shaded ground but keep it within bounds by planting it between concrete walkways and house foundations.

MYRTLE OR COMMON PERIWINKLE

Myrtle (*Vinca minor*), or common periwinkle, is a trailing evergreen with shiny leaves and lovely five-petaled flowers of periwinkle blue that appear in both spring and fall. Throughout the Northeast, especially in old cemeteries, myrtle has been growing for centuries. It sprouts in all but the worst soil, rooting wherever a node touches the ground. Though tolerating some sun, this plant is happier in partial shade, growing at the edges of woods or spilling over the edge of a large container with other (taller) plants in its center. In our northern garden, the myrtle grows under a tall white pine tree. In early spring, its first flowers appear, opening on and off for weeks.

There are a number of cultivars, including 'Alba', with white flowers, and 'Atropurpurea', bearing blossoms of dusty rose. 'Bowles Variety' has deep lavender-blue flowers and 'Multiplex' has double flowers of purple-blue.

8

JAPANESE GARDENS AND
MOSS GARDENS

TO UNDERSTAND THE POPULARITY OF JAPANESE GARDENS is to realize that the science fiction television series *Babylon 5* (still in re-runs, today), included in its gigantic 8-mile-long outer-space platform, a Japanese stone garden in which Earthlings and Aliens could seek spiritual enlightenment and relax from the chores of navigating deep space. Here on Earth, however, there are dozens of Japanese gardens in arboretums across the United States—not bad for an Asian garden style that has to compete with British and European designs, including cottage gardens, herb knots, and grottoes.

Japanese gardens are special places and should reside in the mind's eye of every gardener who wants a small garden. By its very philosophical definition, they are small. Very few large Japanese gardens exist today—and those are usually found in arboretums and botanical gardens.

Yet, the elements of Japanese gardens are easily incorporated into small backyard or terrace gardens. Courtyard gardens also come to mind, and such small-scale plans can be easily adapted to balconies, decks, patios, or even rooftops.

With containers, a cobalt-blue jardinière with a russet Japanese maple, next to a few smaller pots full of understated annuals and perennials, can perfectly express a feeling of peace and serenity—two hallmarks of the Japanese garden.

A lovely moss garden fills a 6-by-8-foot area and includes locally (and carefully) collected mosses and lichens.

While they are beautiful any time of the year, at winter's end, the flush of new growth brings a watercolor subtlety to shrubs, small trees, and spring flowers. By early summer, when evergreens are a vibrant green and flowers are blooming, such a garden resembles an oil sketch. But when fall arrives, the sketch becomes a full-blooded oil painting, with the colors of autumn almost flung at the canvas. When winter finally rolls in again, the garden becomes a stark etching, all the colors reduced to beiges and browns, blacks and whites.

In fact, I remember visiting the Brooklyn Botanic Garden's Japanese Garden one day in mid-December. The air was cold (about 22°F) and the pond was half frozen. Yet one small section close to the Torii (a gateway to heaven usually built near a shrine) remained clear of ice. A number of ducks had crammed themselves into the open water like commuters on a rush-hour train. Underneath the cover of ice, the hazy forms of bright orange, spotted goldfish made slow serpentine curves.

There were other colors, too: the light browns of the ducks, the diluted greens of the pine needles glowing through the snow, and the lacquered red of the Torii. Everything else was white on the canvas. The garden was beautiful, yet not one flower was in bloom.

✤ THE THEORY OF JAPANESE GARDENS

The Japanese islands have been crowded for centuries, and the stresses of such population are reflected in three religious philosophies: Shinto, Buddhism, and Zen.

Shinto, which appeared before the seventh century, teaches that humans are a part of nature along with the animals of the woods and the foundations of nature itself: rocks, water, and plants. Later, Japan adopted many elements of Chinese culture, including Buddhism, a philosophy that not only embraces nature but also teaches that the spirits of the departed can join with it.

Finally Zen, a form of Buddhism that arose in India and came to Japan in the fourteenth century, teaches that only by self-knowledge and introspection can humankind find truth. It was the Zen monk and artist Sesshu (1420–1506) who brought Buddhism to the garden. He withdrew to a rural temple, where he studied the placement of stones, especially those with flat tops, in a garden.

According to Zen, stones are endowed with the spirit of nature, representing timelessness, quietness, and stability. There are correct ways to arrange them: A large stone at the garden's center with a smaller stone in the two o'clock position is good, but if the smaller stone is at three o'clock, the arrangement is bad. One stone in the center of a bed of raked gravel can represent a ship at sea, but if there are more than two stones, they should be arranged in odd-numbered groups of three, five, or seven.

Even stepping-stones have their own history. They were developed by sixteenth century tea-ceremony masters to pave the way to the teahouse without damaging a silken slipper, grass-staining a kimono, or injuring the surrounding moss gardens.

And in every Japanese garden, artificial light is very important, since they are meant to be enjoyed at night. Tea-masters introduced stone lanterns to light the paths to their ceremonies, and the most popular were those designed to illuminate the snow as it fell upon the garden. In our northern garden, we had an inexpensive snow lantern made of concrete, and I wired the interior with a low-voltage lamp so that falling snow would reflect its glow.

Bamboo fences are another important feature of Japanese gardens. Every fence pattern has a name of its own. *Koetsu sode-gaki* is a long low-sloped fence that divides various parts of a garden. *Shiorido* uses shaved bamboo in long strips to make a diagonal latticework design.

Yet, water is sublime in the Japanese garden. The reflections of water and the sounds it makes are as important as the plants. If water is not available at a garden site, lakes are built to contain it. If space is limited, ponds are dug instead. If the garden is small, stone basins are used. And if water is unavailable, streambeds can be constructed from a serpentine pathway of dry stones. Even the outline of the lake has meaning—an irregular design gives visitors the impression that the view is constantly changing.

✤ PLANTS FOR A JAPANESE GARDEN

"Less is more," said architect Ludwig Mies van der Rohe (who actually borrowed the phrase from Robert Browning). Never has the phrase been more apt, however, than in the act of choosing plants for the Japanese garden. Most of the following plants are small and consist of shrubs, small trees, and a few special perennials.

Rhododendrons, azaleas, and small conifers are very popular in this country, and there is usually a good selection of small trees at nursery centers. Yet, American gardeners often have a surprisingly easier time finding plants for Japanese-style gardens than for their English counterparts. In addition to the plants listed below, others in the chapters on ground covers (such as the small grasses and dwarf conifers) will fit into a Japanese garden scheme. Unless noted in the descriptions, all of these plants are hardy in Zone 5.

Abelia chinensis, an attractive shrub from China, grows to about five feet high and has small toothed, oval leaves. Terminal clusters of small white fragrant flowers appear in early summer. *A.* x *grandiflora*, the most vigorous of the species, bears pink and white flowers. 'Francis Mason', a small rounded cultivar measuring about 4 feet high and 4 feet wide, bears light pink flowers and green foliage that turns yellow as the summer advances. All abelias need full sun and well-drained soil rich in organic matter. They are not hardy north of Zone 6 or 7.

Acer japonicum, the full moon maple, will reach a height of 25 feet when planted in open ground. It's a deciduous tree or shrub with a rounded bushy broad form. Its many-lobed leaves are green in summer and red in autumn; clusters of small purple-red flowers appear in mid-spring. There are many cultivars, each with a distinctive leaf pattern or unusual colors, both during summer and in the fall. Japanese maples will grow in full sun or open shade. Soil should be moist, of reasonable fertility, and well drained. Prune trees regularly for small gardens.

Aucuba japonica, or the Japanese laurel, is evergreen and attractive throughout the winter. Mature specimens can reach 10 feet; the shrub in our garden is some twenty years old and only 4 feet high— but what a splendid 4 feet! Clusters of small, purple flowers appear in early spring, followed by red berries if a male plant is present. (The flowers are dioecious, with male and female flowers on separate shrubs.) 'Variegata' is a lovely cultivar with golden-spattered evergreen leaves. 'Crotonifolia' leaves are splashed with various shades of yellow. The Japanese laurel requires partial shade, especially in the South, and its soil must be well drained and rich in organic matter. These shrubs also require protection from the wind in Zone 6 and are not hardy in the North.

Berberis thunbergii, the Japanese barberry, can reach 7 feet. This deciduous arching densely packed shrub has thorns and small, shiny leaves that turn red in autumn. In warmer climates these shrubs are

A 'Golden-nugget' barberry (Berberis spp.) shares a glazed blue pot with begonias (Begonia 'Red Dragon').

evergreen. Bright red berries follow clusters of small, pale yellow flowers. Available cultivars have gold, rosy, or red leaves all season. 'Crimson Pygmy', for instance, has leaves of deep, purplish red. These bushes thrive in full sun but adapt easily to partial shade, especially in the South, and they tolerate poor, dry soil. Japanese barberry, which makes an excellent hedge, is a companion in our garden to the Japanese laurel.

Cephalotaxus harringtonia, the Japanese plum yew, can grow to 15 feet if it isn't pruned. This evergreen, spreading conifer, is similar to a yew, but has slightly larger needles that are dark green above and gray beneath. Oval red fruits follow the flowers; and male and female blossoms are on separate plants. Plum yews, adaptable to hot, dry climates, are hardy to Zone 6 in protected sites. The cultivar *C. fortunei* 'Prostata' is a somewhat hard to find prostrate spreader. This plant grows to 3 feet high and has a 6-foot spread. The 1-inch fruits are an olive-green. Plants are not hardy, however, north of Zone 7.

Chaenomeles x *superba*, the Japanese flowering quince, is a cross between *C. japonica* and *C. speciosa*. This deciduous, 4-foot-high spreading shrub has very sharp thorns and is a suitable alternative to a formal fence. Its flowers are red, pink, apricot, or white, and yellow fruits, which are excellent for making jelly, follow them. (One marvelous taste treat is quince jelly with real butter on fresh-baked French bread.) Provide shrubs with full sun to partial shade in moist but well-drained soil. Prune out any dead wood; flowers, produced on the previous year's growth, spring from new and old wood. Our Japanese quince survived a bitter cold spell that hit our garden in mid-February. The frost burned many of the blossoms, but luckily some of the buds survived.

Corylus avellana 'Contorta', or Harry Lauder's walking stick, has survived for more than thirty-five years in our side garden. It's one of the plants that originally attracted me to my house. In summer the large, floppy leaves are often attacked by Japanese beetles, and as a shrub or small tree, it fades easily into the background. But come autumn, when the tattered leaves fall and the corkscrew stems are visible, there's nothing else like it in the garden. Then, in late winter, when the 2-inch catkins hang like dangling earrings, every garden visitor wants that tree. It is slow to grow and often expensive, but it's well worth the wait and the cost. In a small area, it makes an attractive focal point. The only requirements for this plant are full sun (or partial shade in the South) and water during dry spells.

Ilex crenata, the Japanese holly, is a 15-foot-tall evergreen shrub or small tree with a densely branched habit. It bears small glossy evergreen leaves and dull, white flowers that are followed by small, black berries. Many cultivars are available: 'Convexa', conical in shape, reaches a height of 6 feet; and 'Stokes' always remains dwarf— a 12-year-old tree is only 3 feet tall and 4 feet wide. Provide full sun to partial shade.

Ilex serrata, the Japanese winterberry or fine-tooth holly, is a deciduous shrub that reaches 8 feet high. Leaves are glossy, green, and toothed. Many bright red berries appear in autumn; male and female flowers are borne on separate plants. Hollies do not transplant well, however, so use containerized plants. 'Xanthocarpa' has yellow fruits, while the fruit of 'Leucocarpa' is white. Provide full sun to partial shade and any good garden soil.

Juniperus chinensis, the Chinese juniper, can reach a height of 50 feet, but there are many cultivars available in a wide range of sizes. Shapes range from pyramidal or columnar to mounded or low and spreading. The young leaves are like needles; mature leaves are scale-like and medium green, blue-green, gray-green, or golden. Trees have peeling bark. 'Ames' is a broad-based pyramidal tree reaching 6 feet, and needs no trimming. 'Kaizuka', the Hollywood juniper, has a twisted form and makes an unusual hedge. These conifers need full sun but tolerate a wide range of soils. They can also survive hot, dry conditions, even in cities.

Juniperus horizontalis, or the creeping juniper, is not only a good ground cover and excellent in a conifer garden, but it's also a suitable candidate for the Japanese garden. These prostrate, evergreen conifers have a low, spreading or creeping habit. Leaves are scale-like and typically bluish green. Prune these shrubs to promote bushy growth. 'Bar Harbor', a popular cultivar, hugs the ground and weaves between rocks; its leaves are steel blue. 'Glauca' covers an area with a dense carpet of blue-green foliage. Both are beautiful hanging over the ledge of a wall.

Kalmia latifolia, or mountain laurel, reaches a height of 10 feet but is a slow grower. This evergreen shrub has several branches with oval, deep green, glossy leaves that measure up to 5 inches long. Clusters of complex white or pink flowers (colors on individual plants vary) bloom from late spring to early summer. Provide partial shade and moist but well-drained acid soil rich in organic matter. Mountain laurel is striking when planted at the edge of woods and can live a century or more. Even when the trees are old, they can be pruned; cutting back the bottom branches encourages new growth. The very contemplation of lichen-stained bark on an old laurel can convince a gardener that he or she is in Japan.

Pieris japonica, the lily-of-the-valley bush or Japanese pieris, is an 8-foot-high evergreen shrub with oblong, glossy, deep green leaves. Hanging clusters of small creamy-white flowers appear in spring. It does best in full sun with mid-afternoon shade or in partial shade. For best results, provide a somewhat acid soil rich in organic matter. Remove spent flowers to prevent seeds.

Pinus mugo var. *mugo*, the mugho pine, never tops 10 feet and is an excellent landscape conifer with an attractive silhouette. This shrub-like evergreen bears many spreading branches. The needles are long and bright green, and the cones are small. Give them full sun, as they can tolerate dry, sandy soil. In four years, *P. mugo* var. *pumilo* forms a bun measuring 15 inches wide.

Pinus strobus, the eastern white pine, can reach a height of 120 feet or more. But in its fast-growing youth this evergreen conifer forms a pyramid, which if properly pruned, can become a serviceable hedge. Long soft blue-green needles grow in groups of five. Even on low-growing cultivars, 6-inch cones can appear, often white-tipped with rosin. There are many suitable cultivars for the Japanese garden. 'Horsford', a dwarf form, grows in a bun shape with smaller needles; 'Prostrata' bears normal foliage but has a completely prostrate habit, always seeking the horizontal and never sending up a vertical leader. For these, provide full sun in well-drained soil of average fertility, although this conifer will adapt to very thin, moist, and even poor soil. Transplant carefully and never let the roots dry out.

Pyracantha atalantioides, or fire thorn, is a spiny-branched evergreen shrub that can reach a height of 15 feet unless it is pruned. Glossy oblong 3-inch-long leaves surround flat clusters of white Hawthorn-like flowers in late spring. Red berries follow in autumn and persist into winter. In full sun, they'll grow more berries, but they'll also tolerate partial shade. Fire thorns prefer moist but well-drained soil, though they can withstand somewhat dry conditions, and they are hardy to Zone 6.

Rhododendron catawbiense, the mountain rhododendron, begins life as an evergreen shrub but often becomes a small tree reaching a height of 20 feet. The 6-inch-long oval green leaves are very glossy, and clusters of lilac-purple, bell-shaped flowers appear in late spring. Use this tree as a specimen plant or in a line of background shrubs. Provide partial shade and moist acid soil rich in organic matter. These plants are very shallow rooted, so use care when cultivating and make sure they get additional water during droughts. This American native is valued for its hardiness, surviving in Zone 5. *R. catawbiense* is the parent of many Catawba Hybrids. Flowers are now available in white, fuchsia-purple, magenta, violet, rosy-lilac, Persian rose, and red.

Rhododendron fortunei, the cloud brocade rhododendron, reaches a height of 12 feet. This evergreen shrub has broad leaves that are a glossy deep green above and smoky blue beneath. Clusters of fragrant pink, funnel-shaped flowers appear in the spring. Partial shade is the key to successful growth, in moist acid soil rich in organic matter. They are not hardy north of Zone 6.

Rhododendron williamsianum comes from southwestern China. It's a rounded evergreen shrub bearing round leaves about an inch long that are apple green on top and silvery beneath. A fully mature plant is only 4½ feet tall. They bloom in early spring with pink bell-shaped blossoms. They perform best in a protected place, as the new shoots are often damaged by late frosts. When frost threatens, we cover our shrub.

Rhododendron obtusum, the Hiryu azalea, is a 4-foot-tall shrub that is semi-evergreen with a few leaves persisting to the following spring. A dimorphic plant, it has two sets of leaves: 1-inch elliptical dark green leaves in spring followed in the summer by more oval-shaped leaves. Its spring flowers come in various shades of rose, magenta, red, or red-violet, depending on the cultivar. 'Amoenum' has bright wine-red double flowers, with leaves that turn red in winter. It has earned a deserving place in our garden. These shrubs require partial shade in moist soil rich in organic matter, but moderately acidic. Most hybrids are not hardy north of Zone 6.

Sophora japonica 'Pendula', the Japanese pagoda tree, is usually 12 to 15 feet tall with a spreading habit. Ferny, compound leaves surround drooping clusters of pale yellow, pea-like flowers in spring.

(Trees may not bloom until they are quite a few years old.) Provide full sun and well-drained average soil. These deciduous trees can withstand city conditions.

Taxus cuspidata, the Japanese yew, can grow to 40 feet, but it's usually an evergreen shrub or small tree. Its spreading, upright branches have soft, flat, narrow, and lustrous leaves that are dark green on top and light green below. Inconspicuous spring flowers release clouds of pollen, which are followed by scarlet-red berries (really arils) in autumn; male and female flowers are borne on separate plants. Give Japanese yews full sun to partial shade and moist but well-drained soil on the alkaline side. The cultivar 'Nana' is a low, spreading bush that grows 3 feet tall and 6 to 10 feet wide. It is often used for foundation planting. If it gets out of hand, however, it responds well to trimming.

Taxus x *media* 'Densiformis' grows about 8 feet tall and is an evergreen hybrid between *T. baccata* (the English yew) and *T. cuspidata*. Its rounded form is made up of dense, lateral branches that bear flat leaves and red berries. This plant is hardier than the English yew. Provide full sun to partial shade and moist, well-drained soil.

A JAPANESE DRY STREAM GARDEN

This garden only suggests the presence of water. Construct a small creek or stream but fill it with gravel or small stones instead of water. With the addition of a bamboo fence or a screen, it will take on a very Asian character. Many suburban lots have drainage ditches in the rear of the property. By filling the ditch with river stones and planting small conifers and ornamental grasses along the edge, it becomes an attractive addition to the garden instead of a liability. Placing flat stepping-stones that wander across the gravel "water" heightens the illusion.

For such a garden consider bamboos, including the beautiful Kamurozasa bamboo (*Arundinaria viridistriata*), with its beautiful chartreuse, yellow, and pale green colors. The striking green-and-tan Kuma bamboo (*Sasa veitchii*) is also perfect for this garden scheme. Think about larger ornamental grasses, too, including the various cultivars of *Miscanthus*; variegated prairie cordgrass (*Spartina pectinata* 'Aureomarginata') with 5- to 7-foot sweeping blades edged with a pale brownish yellow; and the common but still desirable Ohwi Japanese sedge grass (*Carex morrowii* var. *expallida*), which bears variegated leaves edged with white. The newer cultivars of Ohwi sedge—including 'Aureo-marginata', with golden-yellow striping, or 'Old Gold', with green and gold stripes—are also excellent additions.

⤥ THE JAPANESE MOSS GARDEN

Back in 1907, Nina L. Marshall wrote the following tribute to mosses in her delightful book *Mosses and Lichens*:

> The blackened embers of the picnic fire are hidden with golden cord-mosses and the roadsides in the woods and the slopes to the lake are carpeted with sturdy hairy-caps. The crumbling roofs of deserted cottages and the unused well-sweep and old oaken bucket are decorated with soft tufts of green.

I hesitate to mention this particular Japanese approach to gardening, however, because so many Americans, when confronted with moss growing either in their garden or, heaven forbid, in the lawn, immediately call the county extension agent and attempt to kill it. They should not. Instead, take a tip from nature and cut back on the work of mowing the lawn.

Next door, there is a beautiful moss garden created over many years by the late Doan Ogden. A brilliant landscape architect, he, along with his wife, Rosemary, brought moss plugs from the nearby woods and slowly turned a 30-by-50-foot area consisting of sparse grass and some large, white oaks and smaller maple trees into a garden of contemplation that inspires visitors at all times of the year. The only maintenance needed is removing fallen leaves so that the moss does not go dormant from lack of light.

But not all moss gardens have to be big; they can also be a world in miniature. Small rocks become mountains, and the mosses change from tiny plants to thickets of impenetrable green. The yellow blossom of a tiny star grass (*Hypoxis hirsuta*) assumes the proportions of the Liberty Bell.

Friends in the mountains of North Carolina created such a garden by collecting all the rocks from nearby walking tours and the mosses from an area that would eventually be cleared for a pond and small botanical garden. There are a number of small hostas and wildflowers there, including pinks (*Dianthus* spp.) and bluets (*Hedyotis purpurea*). But by far, the largest number of plants in the garden are the mosses.

Most mosses require shade because they have poorly developed water distribution systems and the hot sun can dry them out before water reaches their thirsty cells. Haircap moss (*Polytrichum commune*) will grow in open fields, but in that environment the grass provides some protection, helping to collect and channel morning dew to the mosses below. When mosses become dry, they fold up their leaves, markedly changing their appearance. Once the plants have water again, however, the individual cells quickly swell and the mosses revert to their normal size.

Mosses reproduce by releasing spores from little sacs called peristomes. Examining different peristomes—for each genus has a design all its own—is like looking at a Paul Klee etching of Turkish minarets. These fanciful capsules are edged with teeth that vary in number from four to sixty-four, although always in multiples of four. When the weather is damp, the teeth close tightly together; when it is dry, they open up and the spores are shaken to the winds like salt cast from a saltcellar.

Mosses can easily exist on bare rock. By threading their rhizoids, or tiny roots, into microscopic pores in the rock's surface, they can remove the necessary nutritional elements and will eventually create soil. Even airborne dust is trapped by moss leaves, and it eventually combines with pieces of old and dehydrated plants to form dirt.

❧ WOODLAND MOSSES FOR THE GARDEN

The following mosses are common to most temperate woods and are not in any danger of extinction.

Andreaea petrophila, or the stone-loving andreaea, was named in honor of the German botanist, G. R. Andreae. The species is from *petra*, or rock. This moss grows best on granite or slate rocks in shady, damp places. They are among the first colonizers to settle on such inhospitable surfaces.

Bartramia pomiformis, or apple moss, gets its species name, *pomum* (apple) and *form* (form), from the plant's tiny spore cases, which look like little apples. The genus was named in honor of John Bartram, the great Pennsylvania botanist. There are thirteen known species of apple moss in North America, most of which are found growing in rock clefts.

Dicranum longifolium, or the fork moss, gets its generic name from the Greek word for flesh-hook or fork, referring to the teeth's unusual formation on its spore sac. The species, however, refers to its very long leaves. It is among sixty-five species found in North America; at the turn of the century, six were discovered within the limits of New York City. The plants grow only in high-altitude rocky regions and are sometimes found at the base of trees.

Hylocomnium triquetrum, the triangular wood-reveler, makes an excellent plant for a moss garden. Its common name is an English translation of the Greek generic name. The use of triangular in its species name refers to the shape of its stems. This particular moss grows only on wood with a luxuriant delight.

Hypnum crista-castrensis, or the ostrich-plume feather moss, is so called because the plants are plume-like and a bright yellow-green. The Greek term *hypnum* suggests that these mosses were once used to promote sleep; the species name refers to the shape of the branches. Its spore capsules are large, curved, and held horizontally. Common in mountainous regions, this moss grows on soil or rotten wood.

Hypnum splendens, the arched feather moss, is a beautiful combination of gold and green leaves on reddish stems. This splendid plant can commonly be found on rocks in the deep woods and on nearby fallen stumps or rotten logs. In *Moss and Lichens,* Miss Marshall writes of them:

Glittering with yellow, red and green,
As o'er the moss, with playful glide,
The sunbeams dance from side to side.

Leucobryum longifolium, or the pincushion moss, so closely resembles a pincushion that its name required little imagination. The generic name is Greek for white moss, which refers to its unusual pallid green color. The plants are pale because the cells with green chlorophyll are surrounded by larger, transparent cells that carry water and protect smaller cells from heat.

Polytrichum commune, or the haircap moss, gets its generic name from *poly,* many, and *trichum,* hair. Pliny, the Roman naturalist and writer, called this plant "golden maiden-hair" because of the golden gloss the leaves exhibit when dry. The fringed edge of its spore caps are said to resemble a lady's tresses—hence its common name. Hair-cap moss has also been used in lieu of expensive feathers to stuff pillows. It was the first plant to be recognized by early botanists as not having true flowers.

Thuidium delicatulum, the tiny cedar moss, was named for its close resemblance to a miniature cedar tree. (*Thuidium* is an ancient name for a resinous-bearing evergreen.) This moss was well known to Linnaeus, who, because of its dainty appearance, called it *delicatulum.* The tiny cedar moss enjoys damp shady places and runs over stones, earth, and rotten logs.

Despite the rich panoply of mosses, these gardens are not for everyone. Besides a shady spot beneath some tall trees, they require a gardener who delights in the small, in fact, one who completely shuns bravado. But for a gardener inclined to create a world in miniature, the moss garden is the ideal answer.

A patio is decked out with begonias, hydrangeas, oxalis, and elephant ears, all doing well in full sun as long as they are watered on a regular basis.

Potted plants along the walkway to my garden include a variegated hosta (Hosta *spp.*), a flamboyant geranium (Pelargonium *spp.*), and a New Guinea impatiens (Impatiens *spp.*).

Subtly shaded coralbell leaves (Heuchera spp.) provide a rich setting for these jewel-toned tulips, which have been planted in a clay pot with contrasting mixed perennials. ▶

One of Christopher Mello's "industrial" pots, here filled with various succulents (Sedum spp.). ▼

Pots of Persian cyclamen (Cyclamen persicum) *bloom in a winter greenhouse, their fragrant blossoms lasting for weeks.*

*A container garden on a backyard patio includes ivies, sedums, sempervivums, and at left, a whisk fern (*Psilotum nudum*).*

The common horsetails ▶
(Equisetum *spp.*) grow
in front of an iron pot
full of maroon coleus
(Coleus *spp.*).

The saffron crocus ▼
(Crocus sativus) *is the*
source of that expensive
condiment, saffron.
Hardy only to USDA
Zone 7, it can be easily
grown in pots.

*A hand-thrown pottery bowl is home to a showy Mexican member of the hens-and-chicks family (*Echeveria gibbiflora*), needing only good drainage, full sun, and protection from frost.*

*A lovely hybrid of the Lenten rose (*Helleborus orientalis*), blooms in Peter Gentling's Asheville garden.*

A large ceramic pot is ▶
stuffed to the brim
with a combination of
summer annuals,
including cannas,
caladiums, lantanas,
and petunias.

In northeast ▼
Pennsylvania,
Budd Myers has a
stunning display of rock
garden plants and dwarf
conifers grown in
decorative concrete pots.
The controlled soil mix
in the pots guarantees
perfect drainage

Whether set out in pots or planted directly in the border, caladiums (Caladium *spp.*) are spectacular plants with marvelous leaves that last from spring until frost hits the garden.

A faux terracotta pot holds one of the new coleus cultivars (Coleus *spp.*) and brightens up the greens of the hostas and the ivies.

The Spanish iris (Iris xiphium) can be brought in the garden when in bloom, and then planted out when flowering is finished.

Coltsfoot (Tussilago farfara) came over to this country with early settlers, likes perfect drainage, and is one of the first flowers of spring.

A patch of a cultivar of spotted dead nettle (Lamium maculatum) has silver markings on the leaves and is an effective, lightly invasive ground cover.

Autumn crocuses (Colchicum 'Waterlily') brighten up the fall with their glorious blooms, but remember, if in a pot, they must be allowed to produce foliage the following spring.

The intricate and lovely blossoms of a passion flower (Passiflora edulis), easily blooming the first year from seed, is great in a pot.

The deep magenta species tulip (Tulipa pulchella 'Persian') delights in full sun and well-drained soil.

9

ALPINE PLANTS IN POTS
AND SCREE

JUST BEFORE WORLD WAR I, REGINALD FARRER, A MAN who had a profound influence on gardeners of the Edwardian era, did more to popularize alpine plants than any other horticulturalist of his time. It's said that at elegant and sophisticated dinners, where conversation usually dealt with scandal, everyone stopped the racy gossip when Farrer entered the room and talk swiftly turned to alpine wildflowers, drainage, and compost. Rock gardening and growing "difficult" alpines was so popular in those days, it was as if the *National Enquirer* (or any of today's supermarket tabloids), suddenly devoted their pages to veggie planting instead of celebrity vices and perfidies.

A number of plants have achieved mythical status with such gardeners, usually because they have questionable reputations based on the difficulties of cultivation. After all, if they were easy to grow, who would want them?

One such plant is the fabled blue poppy of the Himalayas, or members of the genus *Meconopsis*. These four-petaled (sometimes up to ten) poppies, with many golden stamens, sport colors that run the gamut—from sky blue to pale blue to deep purple and an occasional lavender.

Every year over the past two decades, I've tried to raise a few of these glorious flowers, which crowd English and Scottish gardens but are few and far between here in America. After a spotty germination I would lose nineteen out of twenty seedlings, then worry over the one survivor, a plant that survived one cruel winter, only to flower with one lone bloom and die.

One gardener friend of mine successfully grew these plants in her Brevard, North Carolina, garden but only after her husband constructed a small tent made of white plastic piping and covered it with polyethylene sheets, giving these beauties a brightly lit home. Then, in order to mimic their preferred climate of perfect drainage, plus a damp but cool atmosphere, she brought in four inexpensive fans and a few trays of ice cubes, which she renewed as they melted.

It worked.

But there are many other plants that are less demanding. They really are best grown in pots, where upon blooming, you can bring them out for all the world to wonder at and aspire to.

⇥ CHOOSING UNUSUAL CONTAINERS

During my past few trips to England, I've seen some wonderful containers for alpine plants. One line of clay long tom pots (long toms are deep) planted with thrifts (*Armeria maritima*) was stunning. Or how about the green plastic window box that another gardener filled with clear marbles, and then inserted plastic funnels planted with an assortment of sedums?

You can buy a large fairly inexpensive fiberglass container, fill it with grit and soil, and, keeping them in pots, plunge the alpines up to their necks in the soil, only removing them after their period of bloom has passed. One circular garden I saw, which had a diameter of only 10 feet, was ringed by carefully trimmed grass and held an amazing mix of rock plants interspersed with half-buried pots, many set in at an angle.

Where gardeners had been schooled in crafting hypertuffa pots, the pots' pocked surfaces were studded with jewel-like alpines, including a few common annuals. The most unusual I saw, however, was from a gardener in Kent who took tuffa rocks, drilled a hole through their centers, and then strung them up on a pole using garden rope.

A bed of well-drained soil enclosed by an edging of fieldstones is home to a number of conifers, rock garden plants, plants in pots, and a sculpture from the Boston Museum called "Fat Cat."

✢ BUILDING A SCREE BED

Luckily, when the impulse to install a scree bed swept over me a few years ago, it was already springtime. So by the time I strode up and down the backyard with a measuring tape, legal pad, and pencil, winter ice and snow was but a memory. Having been a rock-gardener for well over two decades—slowly changing the soil and installing rocks on a steep bank just off the terrace of our house—much of the work had already been accomplished. I had replaced the top foot or so of our red clay with buckets of pea gravel and composted soil in order to provide drainage and nutrition. Well-drained soil hastens the invasion of sheep sorrel (*Rumex Acetosella*) and wild carrot (*Daucus Carota*), and those weeds shared the site with various species of *Draba*, a grouping of white potentilla (*Potentilla repestris* 'Alba'), many cultivars of dwarf ornamental grasses, and a few small conifers.

But I wanted to try some of the more difficult mountain flowers, which demand absolutely perfect drainage to survive. Their roots are so sensitive to standing water that 1 foot of well-drained soil is usually not enough. The answer to my needs was what rock gardeners call a "scree bed"—a pile of crushed stone or gravel through which water drains before it can harm delicate roots.

Our house and garden are built on a hill, and in the bottom garden a 3-foot-high wall of well-placed stone separates the levels. Deciding to take advantage of the wall, I created a scree bed of flat fieldstones I'd taken from an abandoned wall at the far edge of our property.

I amassed enough rock to build a semicircular wall, about 2½ feet high, with the formal stone wall of the above garden forming the rear wall. It would also be a dry wall, with only the weight of the stones to hold it in place.

If the backyard had been small, or if I had been short of stone, the principles would still apply. I could have built a bed some 6 feet wide at the base, up to 3 feet high, and as long as I wanted. But the same problem that one confronts with a hobby greenhouse occurs with a scree bed: No matter how large it seems before you start, it always turns out to be too small.

The pluses of a scree bed, however, far outweigh the difficulties of installing it—as long as you are up to the initial strain of hauling and placing the rocks. Instead of merely dreaming about flowers like lewisias, wild sedums from the mountains of the West, and *Polygonum affine* (which had yet to live through a winter), I would finally have a chance not only to see such beauties thrive but also to enjoy their bloom.

After a few futile attempts to carry massive fieldstones from the walls and foundations in a small wheelbarrow over large humps of field grasses, I enlisted the aid of a helpful neighbor and a huge rubber-wheeled cart, which could carry three or four stones at a time without breaking our backs.

We made a single pile, about eight stones high, stretching a string level across the site and parallel to the bank. One of the tricky requirements in laying a stone wall is keeping it level with the terrain, so that one is spared the annoyance of having to look at a crooked wall for the rest of one's life. There are people who can start at one end of a plot and walk out a perfect curve, but I'm not one of them. In order to lay out the initial semicircle, we set the garden hose in place—it was like a thick piece of string that kept its position.

Next, my neighbor and I chose the largest stones, each between 14 and 18 inches wide, 18 to 24 inches long, and 3 to 4 inches thick. After laying each stone along the inside curve of the hose, we removed a bit of soil so that the back edge was about an inch lower than the front. That way, rainwater would flow into the bed along the sloping rocks and reach the roots of the plants growing along the face of the wall.

If the soil had been soft, I would have excavated at least 18 inches of it before starting the wall to give it a firm footing. As it was, the clay and shale were solid enough for us to lay stones directly on the ground.

We placed the bottom stones as close together as we could, filling all gaps with a mixture of dirt and gravel taken from a truckload of crushed stone that we had bought to make up the fill for the bed. Once the initial ring of stones was down, we put on the next layer, so that each gap in the first layer was covered by the second, and so on. We filled all the gaps in each level with the soil mix.

Piling layer upon layer, we continued until the wall reached a height of 2½ feet. The best-shaped and flattest stones finished off the top. The wall is so strong that one can step on it with nary a wiggle, and at the same time it provides a comfortable place to sit.

We then began filling in the cavity, throwing in just about every stone I had gathered during my other gardening chores, as well as broken pots, bits of broken glass, and other pieces of solid trash. Soon the first foot was full of angular pieces of rubble, but there were many open spaces in between. Only then did I add the planting mix of gravel chips (each chip half an inch or less across), peat moss, and composted cow manure. It took a good deal of material to fill the cavity the full 2½ feet: at least twenty bags of manure, most of the load of gravel, and two to three bales of peat moss.

Although impatient, I would plant nothing until the following winter was over and the mix had settled properly. Sure enough, by next spring the level of the mix had dropped some two inches, so I had to add more.

Now the real beauty of the scree bed is realized. In the layers of rock and compost near the bottom of the bed, the plants' roots can not only find air and moisture, but also enjoy perfect drainage so that rot is prevented. Plants that would be lost in bad winters if left in a typical garden's soil will survive in a scree. And in a hot summer when rain is in short supply, the garden hose will fill the bill.

I always make sure, however, that plants get enough shade during their first few days of settling in and that they get plenty of water until their roots begin to reach the bottom of the bed. Before inserting plants in the crevices of the wall, I wrap soil and roots in a paper towel. By the time the roots start to grow down into the cracks, the towel has disintegrated.

We are now entering our fourth year with our raised scree bed, and it is beginning to look as though it has been there for much longer.

⨁ THE STYROFOAM TROUGH

For a lightweight trough, nothing beats the Styrofoam carton, an invention many of my rock-gardening friends attribute to Charles Becker, Jr., of Philadelphia. Such a container may not sound appealing in your backyard, but once completed, you'll never know it's made of plastic.

First, buy a Styrofoam container of the kind that the bright young things use to carry beer to the beach. Any sturdy, Styrofoam box will do. You'll also need some asphalt roof paint and some epoxy resin (buy the epoxy in cans because the tubes are too small—and expensive). In addition, you'll need a sack of builder's sand, and something for texture—for example, aquarium gravel, pea gravel, bits of oyster shell, or marble chips.

Using a sharp wood saw, cut the sides down to a height of about 6 or 8 inches. Paint the bottom inside and out with asphalt roof paint. Then, using a brace and bit, drill at least twelve half-inch drainage holes in the bottom, each about 4 inches apart.

Next, mix together equal parts of the epoxy resin and hardener. (I suggest you wear gloves for this step.) Make just enough glue to paint one side of the trough. If you use too much glue, it will dissolve the Styrofoam. Use an aluminum pie tin as a mixing bowl, and if you have any remaining epoxy, set it on ice to inhibit the chemical reactions.

While the glue is still tacky, dribble the mix of sand and gravel over the epoxy. Use additional glue for the edges so that none of the Styrofoam shows through. Allow at least thirty minutes for the epoxy to set. Clean up excess glue with water, but be sure to do it before it hardens.

Now follow the same procedure for all the other sides of the box. The next day, shake off the excess mix and touch up any bare spots with more epoxy and more mix.

To finish the top edge, make a thick paste of epoxy and sand, and apply a quarter-inch layer with a putty knife. Score with a knife to add texture to the partially hardened material.

Wait another day, then set the finished trough in place. Place two bricks underneath it to hold it above the surface and to promote good drainage. Cover the holes with broken crockery or plastic screening, and then fill the trough with planting mix.

✢ THE HYPERTUFFA TROUGH

For a heavier trough, try hypertuffa (first named by F. H. Fisher, a past president of England's Alpine Garden Society), an artificial mix consisting of one part Portland cement, two parts builder's sand, and one part milled peat moss. You will also need wire mesh from the hardware store.

First, decide on the size of the trough you want and make a wooden form. Then blend the ingredients thoroughly. Gradually

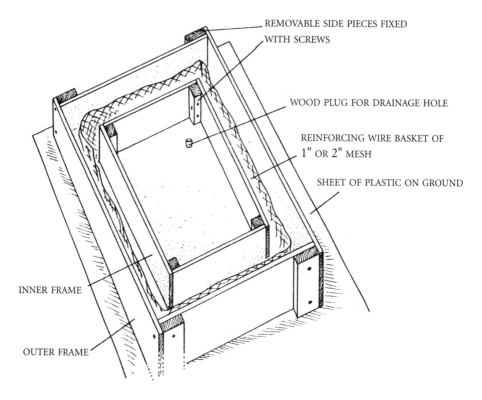

REMOVABLE SIDE PIECES FIXED WITH SCREWS

WOOD PLUG FOR DRAINAGE HOLE

REINFORCING WIRE BASKET OF 1" OR 2" MESH

SHEET OF PLASTIC ON GROUND

INNER FRAME

OUTER FRAME

Making a trough with wooden forms

add water until the mix is pliable, not runny. Let it sit for five minutes. Put a one-inch layer in the frame and set in the wire mesh an equal distance from the sides. Add more of the mix to make a 1½-inch layer all over the bottom, then set the inner frame in place. Use wooden plugs for drains. Push damp sand into the corners of the wooden frame so that, when the frame is removed, the sand will flake away, leaving worn, rounded corners rather than sharp edges.

Fill the rest of the cavity and lay plastic over the top. In twelve to eighteen hours, remove the inner frame, carefully pulling out the sidepieces, and remove the plugs. Replace the cover. Twenty-four hours later, remove the outer form. Brush the side and top to remove any large bumps, taking extra care, as the cement is still green.

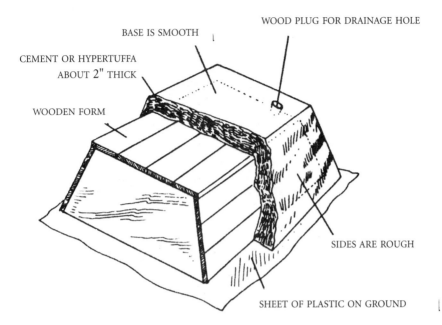

WOOD PLUG FOR DRAINAGE HOLE

BASE IS SMOOTH

CEMENT OR HYPERTUFFA
ABOUT 2" THICK

WOODEN FORM

SIDES ARE ROUGH

SHEET OF PLASTIC ON GROUND

Making a trough over a wood form

Carefully cover the trough with wet burlap or plastic and leave it for three more days. Then remove the outer framework and clean out the drainage holes. Leave the trough alone for at least another week to let it harden completely.

Cure the trough by filling it with water and adding half a teaspoon of potassium permanganate crystals (available from the local drugstore). Using a paintbrush, coat the outside with the solution. Let the trough sit for a few hours, then rinse it well and let it sit outside for two more weeks before planting.

You can make other shapes for troughs by using a wooden form set on a large piece of butcher's wrap. Use less water in the mix to make it thicker, then spread the mix over the form.

In addition to troughs, you can easily make small artificial rocks for growing tiny alpines. Dig a hole in the ground, line it with stones pushed some 2 inches into the sides and bottom of the hole, then

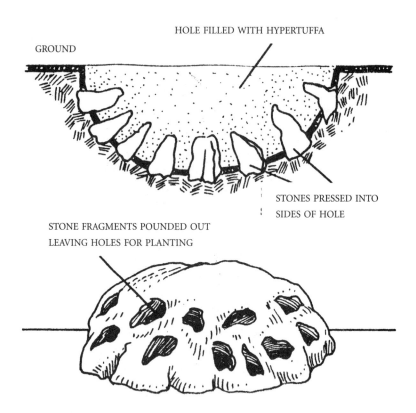

Making a hypertuffa pot.

add a mix of one part cement, one part builder's sand, and two parts moistened peat. Fill the hole with the mix, then let it cure for a week before you dig it out. Dig out the mound, then tap out the stone fragments, leaving holes for setting in plants. Cover the pot with damp burlap for another five days. Finally, soak the pot in a pail of water for a few days, and you're ready to plant.

Many creative gardeners make unusual pots by cementing pieces of stone together and experimenting with various formulas. For example, some add pre-mixed cements to sphagnum moss; others use perlite instead of sand in a hypertuffa formula. For more information on these and other methods, contact your local chapter of The American Rock Garden Society.

✵ ALPINE GARDENS FOR TROUGHS

Budd Myers introduced me to growing alpine plants in troughs. He has a wonderful collection of troughs that contain both common and rare plants, with as many as twenty-three plants in one 18-by-24-inch container. They range from dwarf conifers to tiny bushes to alpine perennials that provide a burst of color in the spring, followed by sporadic outbursts throughout the summer, and exploding in still more color in autumn.

Ruth Samotis, a rock-gardening neighbor from Hendersonville, North Carolina, made me a square trough that measures 12-by-12 inches, and it now contains one of the smallest of the dwarf conifers (*Abies balsamea* 'Nana'); a dwarf, shrubby elm tree (*Ulmus* x *elegantissima* 'Jacqueline Hillier'—originally from Birmingham, England, and named in honor of Harold Hillier's mother (of Hillier's Arboretum fame); and two small but elegant alpine snowbells (*Soldanella alpina*), which I grew from seed. The elm could grow as high as 4 feet but can be pruned to remain in scale.

✵ PLANTS FOR AN ALPINE GARDEN

The following plants are available from specialty nurseries. They are all hardy in USDA Zone 5, and all are fairly common except for *Meconopsis* spp., which I include just for the adventure.

Acer palmatum 'Red Pygmy' is a beautiful dwarf Japanese maple originally from Holland. The leaves consist of narrow strap-like lobes of a bright reddish maroon; in summer, they turn purpler. After twenty to twenty-five years, a tree will reach about 6 feet high and 6 feet wide, but can easily be pruned. 'Beni schichihenge', another striking cultivar, does well in pots, too.

Androsace villosa, or the rock jasmine, will come tumbling over the edge of a garden wall, with a jumble of rose pink, or sometimes white, four-petaled flowers. The leaves are gray and densely covered with fine hairs. As befits a plant that revels in walls, rock jasmine loves lime. This plant is easily propagated by seed.

*A beautiful cultivar of Japanese maple (Acer palmatum 'Beni schichihenge')
is planted in a foot-wide pot and in Asheville, left outdoors all winter long.*

Artemesia schmidtiana var. *nana* forms an inch-high by 12-inch-wide mound of beautiful silver-gray foliage. It also bears small yellow summer flowers, but the leaf texture and color are what make it invaluable in the rock garden. 'Silver King' is a Japanese cultivar that forms a ball of silvery white, cut leaves.

Aquilegia spp., the columbines, are at home both in the wild garden and the formal border, but there are a number of European species that excel in the rock garden. Look for the lovely yellow *A. aurea*, a native wildflower of Bulgaria that grows about 15 inches high. Or try *A. alpina* 'Alba Nana', a dwarf form hailing from the Alps that reaches about 6 inches high and bears pristine white flowers. 'Nana', the diminutive cultivar of our own native columbine, *A. canadensis*, is also perfect in a rock garden.

Bletilla striata is a reasonably hardy orchid that often surprises gardeners with its tough beauty. This terrestrial species (most orchids are epiphytes and grow high up in trees) will bloom every summer with shocking pink flowers that resemble a miniature cattleya (the corsage orchid of senior proms). Here, the flowers cluster on top of 18-inch stems. In Zone 5, the plants need a heavy winter mulch. 'Alba' is its white form.

Calceolaria 'John Innes', or the slipper flower, is only 6 inches tall by 9 inches wide. A miniature version of the popular Easter plant, this species bears yellow flowers whose lips are lightly dotted with red. Slipper flowers are so tropical in appearance, it's surprising to see them in the garden. Without adequate drainage, however, these plants soon perish, so the rock garden makes a perfect home. Provide plenty of mulch in Zone 5.

Calluna vulgaris, described in Chapter Seven, is commonly called the heather. Although it's a small shrub, I've included it with alpine plants because it's well suited to rock gardens, and there are many cultivars. I've had success with 'Blazeaway', a golden-yellow, foot-high mound of evergreen needle-like foliage that turns orange in winter and 'Golden Carpet', which becomes reddish orange when the cold arrives. Both have tiny bell-like flowers that appear in late summer, but the first has mauve flowers and the second has reddish purple blooms. They are marginally hardy in Zone 5 when given a spot protected from harsh winter winds and, of course, well-drained soil.

Chamaecyparis lawsoniana 'Minima' is one of the best dwarf conifers for the small rock garden. It reaches 20 feet high and has a 24-inch diameter after ten years. The green, fan-shaped foliage grows at the astonishingly slow rate of 1¼ inches a year. So without protection from heavy snow, its tender branches may break.

Coreopsis auriculata 'Nana' is the small version of the bluegrass daisy, an 8- by 6-inch plant that bears 1½-inch, bright orange daisies. While not truly a rock garden plant, it fits the scale of its diminutive neighbors. Eleanor Saur of Hillsboro, Ohio, introduced me to this plant, and Dr. Lucy Braun near Maysville, Kentucky, discovered it in the wild.

Cytisus spp., or the brooms, are best described as evergreen whips covered in early summer with pea-like blossoms of pink, yellow, or white. They are spectacular in bloom. *C.* x *kewensis*, 8 inches high by 8 inches wide, is one of the hardiest. Grow it close to a wall so that the stems can drape over the edge.

Dianthus spp., or the pinks, are popular spring-blooming, mat-forming perennials. The spicy-scented, five-petaled flowers are especially attractive to swallowtail butterflies. *D. petraeus* subsp. *noeanus* bears fringed white flowers, while *D. alpinus* has larger blossoms of pale pink to light purple, depending on the plant. Seeds germinate with ease and often self-sow.

Doronicum cordatum, or leopard's-bane, is a small plant measuring about 6 by 10 inches, blooming with bright yellow daisy-like flowers in late spring. Plants will bloom a second time if spent flowers are removed.

Draba spp., the Russian mustards, are tiny plants from the Arctic Circle or the steppes of Central Asia and are usually found only on rugged mountain peaks. The bright white or yellow, four-petaled blossoms will only open after their expanding buds have actually melted the surrounding snow with self-generated heat. Even on chilly days in late March, the flowers have a sweet smell; only a few flies will be attracted by the scent, however, because most self-respecting bees are still asleep in the hive.

Erica carnea, or the snow heath, requires the same care as *Calluna*. Their leaves are more needle-like than those of heathers. In addition, they usually cannot withstand winters north of Zone 6. 'King George' grows about 12 inches high and bears crimson flowers from January to May. 'Winter Beauty' is one of the best varieties, producing pink flowers from mid-February to April.

Festuca ovina var. *glauca*, or blue fescue, is one of the best ornamental grasses for the alpine garden. Its stiff blades are silvery blue in color, and the plants resemble 8-inch-tall, balled-up hedgehogs lying in wait for the gardener. Every year there are a greater number of species and cultivars available, including the 4-inch *F. alpestris*, and *F. amethystina* 'Bronzeglanz', or bronze sheep's fescue.

Heuchera spp., the coralbells, demand well-drained soil with lots of sun. Some of the smaller cultivars are perfect for the alpine garden. One of the best is the compact *H. cylindrica* 'Alpina', a native of the Northwest with greenish white flowers on 10-inch stems. The Miniature Hybrids, resulting from a cross between *H. pulchella* and *H. hallii*, bear light pink flowers on 8-inch stems.

For something new, try a bi-generic cross between *Heuchera* and *Tiarella* (foamflower). This unique plant bears leaves streaked with maroon and gray, plus 18-inch spikes of star-like flowers. First discovered in Nancy, France, in 1917, its proper name is x *Heucherella tiarelloides*.

Hemerocallis spp., the daylilies, are usually too large for rock gardens but *H.* 'Good Fairy of Oz', which measures 12 inches high and 6 inches wide, has rose-colored flowers that are in perfect scale with the alpine garden.

Hypericum olympicum, or St.-John's-wort, grows to 9 inches high by 12 inches wide and bears several 1½-inch golden blossoms, with dozens of sparkling stamens floating above satiny petals.

Hypoxis hirsuta, or star grass, grows 10 inches high by 6 inches wide. This American wildflower revels in dry soil and bears bright yellow 1½-inch-wide flowers. Members of the iris family, they have corms rather than the grass-like roots you'd expect from seeing the leaves.

Meconopsis spp. is familiar to diehard rock garden enthusiasts who are well schooled in growing difficult and demanding plants. The only species type I ever had luck with was *M. horridula*, so called because the stems are covered with spines. But *M. cambrica*, a common but still beautiful Welsh poppy, is a four-petaled charmer that comes in many shades of yellow or orange. It will seed about but is easily controlled.

Ophiopogon planiscapus 'Arabicus', or black mondo grass, is 6 inches high and 6 inches wide. Although members of the lily family, they're not grown for their small blue flowers but for the striking dark purple, almost black, color of the leaves. Unfortunately, it's not always hardy north of Zone 6, so be sure you mulch in colder areas.

Papaver burseri, often sold as *P. alpina*, is a lovely little poppy with a sweet scent that will seed around the garden. Once established, it is constant. Like most poppies, however, it resents disturbance. So start your seeds in peat pots or sow them directly in the garden. California poppies (*Eschscholzia californica*) will add striking color to a small-space garden.

Phlox subulata, or moss pink, carpets a wall or bed with bright pink, purple, and white flowers in early spring. If such floral intensity sprang forth in July, most gardeners would overlook these little flowers, but because their colors only insult a brown and barren world they will always be welcome. For the purists, one special white cultivar, called 'Sneewichen', measuring 3 inches high and 9 inches wide is covered with tiny white flowers.

Picea glauca 'Echiniformis', which grows 7 inches high by 9 inches wide, is another dwarf conifer that makes a great focal point—albeit a small one—in the corner of an alpine bed. It originated from a witches'-broom, an aberration that sometimes appears on conifers in which one branch becomes a miniature of the parent, and was thought to resemble an occult mode of travel.

Lend drama to almost any house by planting a small conifer such *Picea glauca* 'Conica', the dwarf Albert spruce, in a pot on either

A drift of California poppies (Eschscholzia californica*) brings pure gold to a narrow border in a small garden.*

side of a front stoop. Or, in smaller pots, plant *Juniperus chinensis* var. *procumbens* 'Nana', the dwarf Japanese juniper. Its fresh green sharp foliage turns blue-green in the summer and bronze in winter.

For years I've grown *Sequoia sempervirens* 'Adpressa', a dwarf sequoia, in a fancy terracotta pot that sits outdoors all summer and fall, then spends December in the living room, dressed like a Christmas tree. When we lived in the North, this tree spent most of the winter in our greenhouse. Here in the South, however, it goes to the garden room.

Platycodon spp., the balloon flower of Japan, has produced one small cultivar, *Platycodon grandiflorus* 'Mariesii' which grows to 12 inches high by 6 inches wide. Plants bear pastel blue five-pointed flowers. Before they open, the buds resemble tiny hot-air balloons.

Solidago spp., or the goldenrods, have never been criticized for being too short. But in the Rocky Mountains, Nature crossbred a few of these flowers and created one that is especially suited for alpine gardens. *S. spathulata* var. *nana* is 6 inches high by 8 inches wide and looks like one of its larger relatives seen through the wrong end of a telescope.

Teucrium chamaedrys, or germander, is an aromatic, 18-inch-high sub-shrub that produces two-lipped, pink flowers in May that frequently last until August. An ancient herb, it makes an excellent small hedge; space plants about 6 inches apart and clip frequently.

Tsuga is the genus of the hemlocks. Although these conifers are large in the forest, a number of very small cultivars have been produced by nature. At the rear of our garden, snuggled against the rising bank, I planted a group of the dwarfs: *T. canadensis* 'Cole', a creeper that will follow the outline of every rock and depression in its path; 'Jervis', a hemlock with dense foliage of deep green that grows about an inch a year; and 'Gentsch White', where the fresh growth of spring is tipped with an icy white.

❧ 10 ❧

VINES AND HANGING
GARDENS

NOT ALL PLANTS ARE CONTENT STAYING CLOSE TO THE
earth. Many invest a large share of their energies into growing their stem in order to seek out a place closer to the sun.
Vines, however, have found a different way to achieve the same goal.
Using a variety of methods that range from winding their stems
around another plant's trunk, or developing curling tendrils to grasp
a support, to simply leaning on neighboring plants, vines grow
through or over other plants, eventually pushing their way to the sky.

Nursery catalogs and garden supply stores offer a number of
gadgets to help a vine in its climb. They range from folding trellises
to bamboo stakes made from real bamboo or from plastic (including pottery caps that will hold three poles like a teepee without the
tent) to special nails that can be pounded into the mortar of walls,
giving most vines a perfect purchase.

In addition, all the basic stock of hardware stores—nails, staple's, cup-hooks, and tile hooks for bathroom walls (not to mention
vertically installed towel bars)—can serve to support vines.

Even snow fencing, when stained and attached to a wooden
frame, becomes an attractive trellis. Plastic fish line or rope can be
strung on a 1-by-3-inch frame, and the line attached to cup-hooks
to effectively screen a public window.

Another very effective support for large vines such as passion
flowers can be constructed from aluminum clothesline and a center

pole of either doweling or a 1-by-1-inch piece of wood, cup-hooks, and wire. Bend the wire frame in proportion to the size of the pot used, and paint the center pole where it is surrounded by soil. Do not use creosote, however, as this wood preservative is eventually toxic to plants—and people. If you make a movable base of plywood on furniture casters, the pot can be easily moved.

There's one thing to remember if you are planning to vine up a wall: The soil at the base of walls is generally very poor. Often, too, if it was originally quite acidic thanks to water flowing over the mortar, the entire chemical content can change. Therefore, be especially careful to test the soil. Plan to add generous amounts of organic matter to the existing soil. Finally, remember to begin plantings at least 1 foot to 18 inches away from the wall.

The following vines are quite at home in containers for standing about in a garden or climbing up a windowsill.

❧ THE CALICO FLOWERS

The birthworts (*wort* is an old English word for plant) are members of the *Aristolochia* genus. The Greek *aristos,* or best, and *lochia,* meaning childbirth, refer to this plant's use as a medicine, specifically against plague. In his 1597 version of the *Herball,* John Gerard wrote: "Dioscorides writeth that a dram weight of long birthwort drunk with wine and so applied is good against serpents and deadly things." One wonders, which ingredient was the most effective? Most are greenhouse plants and indoor vines but one, *A. durior* or Dutchman's pipe, is hardy in the north and used as a quick-covering vine for screens and porches.

The most bizarre is the pelican flower, *A. gigantea,* which arrived in England from Guatemala in 1841. A high-climbing vine that can reach 10 feet in length, it bears flat smooth heart-shaped leaves that have a rank odor when crushed. Its 6-inch flowers, off-white and veined with purple, sitting atop an inflated u-shaped greenish tube, exude an unpleasant odor. As for looks, however, they are showstoppers.

These vines grow best in pots that hang on wires, allowing plenty of room for growth. They can also be carefully unwound from one wire and rewound on another, making counterclockwise turns.

The calico flower, *A. elegans*, first exported from Brazil in 1883, is less peculiar—almost cute even. It's a free-flowering species once it has settled in. The flowers are 1½-inches long and 3 inches wide, with a yellow tube and purple flaps marked with white. As a vine it's shorter than the pelican, only stretching to 8 feet in length.

Both of these plants require warm surroundings with temperatures always above 60°F. A mix of potting soil, peat moss, composted manure, and sand, one-quarter each, should be kept evenly moist but never soggy. Give the vine a spot in partial shade because hot summer sun can burn its leaves. Propagation is by cuttings or by seed.

⚜ THE CLIMBING ONION

E. A. Bowles was a gifted English gardener who set aside an area of his garden called the Lunatic Asylum where he kept plants that had strange growth patterns, weird flowers, or just plain unsettling ways. If it were a hardier plant, I'm sure the climbing onion, or as it's often called, the Zulu potato, would have been given a front seat in Bowles' collection.

Known botanically as *Bowiea volubilis*, its genus is in honor of J. Bowie (1789–1869), a plant collector who is said to have spent much of his time in London bar-parlours telling apocryphal stories of his Brazilian and Cape Town adventures instead of working in the field. But apparently he managed to bring this unusual plant back from South Africa. *Volubilis* is Latin for twining.

Some years ago, a houseplant aficionado sent me a green ball. It was 4 inches in diameter, with a slight depression marking the top and a few dried rootlets signifying the bottom. The accompanying letter advised me to plant it in a 5-inch pot with a mix of potting soil, composted manure, and sand, one-third each, and to place the top half of the bulb above the soil line. "Water it after the growth begins," wrote my correspondent, "and let the soil dry out between waterings. Growth will die back in late spring or fall depending on when you have started the plant. Keep temperatures above 50°F and fertilize once a month while it's growing."

Following the directions, I was soon rewarded by twining stems, ⅜-inch-wide star-like green flowers, and minuscule leaves represented by tiny triangular flaps of green where the branchlets sprout from the branch.

A spot in partial sun worked best and my bulb sat for years in a clay pot that I set inside a Japanese basket so the foliage had something to cling to. A healthy bulb will eventually reach an 8-inch diameter with a corresponding increase in stem production. Propagation is by seed and sometimes by offset bulbs.

⚶ THE ROSARY VINE

There are a few plants in the window garden lexicon that live up to their reputations for toughness. The aspidistra and the sansevieria immediately come to mind, but in my experience, one of the long-distance runners is the rosary vine. In 1982, my sister-in-law gave me a plant that actually lived in the same pot for fifteen years, only fading away one bitter winter night when the heat in the greenhouse was extinguished by an ice storm.

Its botanical name is *Ceropegia woodii*. The genus comes from the Greek, *keros*, wax, and *pege*, a fountain, which supposedly refers to the flower's waxy appearance. But it's one of the more far-fetched appellation attempts that I've run across. Although it's not too obvious, they belong to the same family as the stapeliads. The species is named in honor John Medley Wood (1827–1915), who retired from the East Indian Merchant Service and began collecting native African plants. He is also the man who introduced sugar cane into Natal.

Originally from Natal and southern Rhodesia, the rosary vine has pairs of succulent heart-shaped leaves, less than 1-inch wide, running along thin, thread-like purple stems that arise from little tubers and trail or hang according to their method of planting. Because of these tubers, it can store water over long periods of time. Among its common names are: rosary vine, hearts-on-a-string, string-of-hearts, and hearts-entangled, this last because the stems easily enmesh and wind up together. It takes a great deal of patience to straighten them out.

The inch-long flowers have a round base with a tubular projection topped with a tiny parachute, whose interior is covered with a black fringe and which appears at odd times throughout the year. The little tubers that crop up at the internodes on the stems are used to start new plants.

Use a mix of potting soil, composted cow or sheep manure, and sand, one-third each. Plant the tubers with one-half sticking above the soil line. Water only when the soil is dry and give the plants a spot in partial sun. Fertilize only once or twice a year.

Propagation is by using the stem tubers, cuttings, or sometimes seeds, but the flowers are rarely fertilized when grown indoors, and if they are, a fly probably does the job.

⚘ THE WAX PLANT

Remember "Tzena, Tzena, Tzena," Gordon Jenkin's arrangement of a traditional Yiddish folk song that became one of the million-selling hits of 1950? The tune always comes to my mind when I think of the wax plant, but its title becomes "Hoya, Hoya, Hoya."

The genus *Hoya* is named in honor of Thomas Hoy, one-time gardener to the Duke of Northumberland at Sion House in England, and it represents some 200 species of root-climbing and twining plants with 3-inch-long fleshy, succulent leaves with bunches of exotic flowers. They belong to the Asclepiadaceae along with the rosary vine and the stapeliads.

What you'll usually find in unsophisticated collections are *H. carnosa* and *H. bella*. In the first, the species name means "fleshy" and refers to the color of the waxy blossoms. *Bella*, however, simply means beautiful. Many indoor gardeners become so enamored of these plants that they turn to lesser-known species. We now have a Hoya Society International, and Logee's Greenhouse keeps fifteen hoyas in their catalog, while Glasshouse Works lists thirty-three.

For years, I kept an *H. carnosa* in a large clay pot held to a chain by a wire clip. Although the silver-speckled, deep green leaves where abundant and healthy, the plant never looked quite right to me. So, two years ago I moved it and two more plants to a 12-inch wire basket lined with a sheet of sphagnum moss. After a month or so of settling in, they began to grow, sending out numerous curling and climbing stems that wound around the three chains holding the planter. One of the good things about wax plants is that you can unwind a stem if its direction doesn't please you and wind it around somewhere else—just make sure you wind them in a counterclockwise direction.

I use a mix of potting soil and sand, because these plants need perfect drainage. Temperatures should be temperate but never let them fall below 50°F (although *H. carnosa* will tolerate 45°F for a short time). Keep the soil on the dry side when plants are in growth, but remember to withhold watering during the winter months and only add water if the leaves begin to shrink and shrivel. Then make sure the water is tepid. Fertilize once in spring and only after plants have been established for at least a year. They do not do well in rich soil.

Also remember to never remove the peduncle, or flower stalk, since new buds will set on the same old spur and you can count the passing of the years by the length of that stalk. Once in bud, do not move the container; the change in light direction can impede the flower's development.

Each of the star-shaped flowers—appearing any time from May through September—are lovely, resembling flawless creations carved from wax then stamped with a red star at center. They appear in bunches of twelve to fifteen individual blossoms. At one time, when that custom was a fashion statement for men, the flowers were grown for buttonholes. They didn't last, however, because they produce crystal beads of a sweet nectar that is quite sticky.

H. carnosa 'Variegata' was introduced from Australia around 1802. Its leaves are beautifully variegated with pale pink and cream shadings and it's worthy of being in a collection even if it never flowered. Propagation is by cuttings.

THE PASSIONFLOWER

There are more than 350 members of the passionflower family, native to both the Old World and the New but most are found in tropical America. While wandering through Mexico early in the 1600s, Emmanuele Villegas, a Catholic friar, became the first European to record seeing the plant in bloom. In 1610 he presented a drawing of the blossom to the Roman theologian Giacomo Bosio, who immediately called it "the most extraordinary representation of the Cross Triumphant ever discovered in field or forest. The flower contains within itself not only the Savior's Cross but also the symbols of His Passion."

The flower described in the friar's drawing is most likely *Passiflora incarnata* (*passio*, passion and *floris*, flower), a native plant found in the southern United States and northern Mexico. It was called maypop or maracock by the Algonquin, and was thought to relieve insomnia. Its fruits are often used in jam.

Bosio was so excited by the admittedly stylized drawing, that he wrote the following:

> The filaments which surmount [the petals] resemble a fringe spattered with blood, thus seeming to represent the flail with which Christ was scourged. The column at which He was scourged rises from the center of the flower, the three nails with which He was nailed to the Cross are above it, and the column is surrounded by the Crown of Thorns. At the flower's exact center . . . there is a yellow zone bearing five blood-colored marks symbolic of the Five Wounds inflicted on Our Lord. The color of the column, the nails, and the crown is light green. Surrounding these elements is a kind of violet-colored nimbus composed of 72 filaments that correspond to the number of spines in the Crown of Thorns. The plant's numerous and attractive leaves are shaped like a lance-

head, and remind us of the Lance of Longinus which pierced the Saviour's side. Their undersurface is marked with flecks of white which symbolized Judas' thirty pieces of silver.

Bosio forgot to note that the sepals that remain on the vine after the flower falls are the Trinity, that the whips of persecution can be seen in the vine's coiling tendrils, and that its five petals and five sepals make up ten of the apostles—omitting Peter and Judas.

They are truly exotic flowers, reminiscent of the kinds usually found in a Victorian greenhouse, and are showstoppers when grown in a window, greenhouse, or outdoor summer garden.

I have a *P.* x *alatocaerulea* in a 6-inch clay pot with an attached wire hanger that I set outside in the garden every summer. I hang it from an armillary sphere, so the vine grows up among the metal circles, flowering for most of the summer.

Among the plants available from nurseries are *P. actinia,* whose 4-inch greenish white blooms with a fringed corolla of lavender and white flower in the winter and bear a sweet fragrance; *P.* x *alatocaerulea,* with large purple flowers and a delightful fragrance (the flowers are used in the manufacture of perfumes); *P. edulis,* with lavender flowers and edible fruit; *P.* 'Incense', bearing large 5-inch royal purple flowers with a corolla that entirely overlays the petals and has an intensely sweet perfume; and *P. vitifolia,* with red petals and sepals surrounding pure white filaments.

Temperatures should be kept above 55°F, though mine has lived in the greenhouse where 45°F is common. Fertilize every six weeks in summer because too much feeding produces more leaves and fewer flowers. Use a mix of potting soil, peat moss, and sand, one-third each. They need plenty of sun and evenly moist soil during the growing season.

Flowers develop on the new growth, so prune the vine once a year while it is dormant, cutting back one-third of the canes and stopping just above a lateral bud.

Sow fresh seed in the spring. Germination takes about a month and plants often flower in their first year. They can also be propagated from stem cuttings during the spring and summer months.

❧ THE HEARTLEAF PHILODENDRON

Just because a plant is thought by many to be a cliché is no reason to ignore it, especially if it works. For example, there's a roadhouse outside of Tuxedo, New York, that buses and taxi-vans use as a rest stop. Poor riders are forced to go inside, whether they want to or not. Some years ago, one of the owners brought in a heartleaf philodendron and planted it in a dull corner where the only illumination came from florescent lights in the ceiling high above. When the vine began to climb, he added strings, and it now stretches up the wall and across the ceiling of the cavernous room. At last visit, it was aiming for the woman at the cash register. Talk about a survivor.

Some years ago I saw a similar treatment in a Manhattan apartment where the only light in the room was the reflection from an airshaft window and two desk lamps. Yet, a heartleaf philodendron covered most of the ceiling, held up with staples affixed to the plasterboard that circled every three joints of the plant's stem.

The heartleaf philodendron has been around since the late 1800s and through its entire history has been used in low-light situations where few other plants will grow. In the early 1930s, the General Electric Company listed a number of plants that would do well away from the window with artificial light. Included in that list were the philodendrons. At one time this plant was more widely grown than any other houseplant in America.

Yet, these are jungle plants that begin life on dark moist spongy ground formed of layers and layers of vegetable debris. As they grow, they climb the nearest supports, striving to reach the light continually filtering through the tree branches above. The ground serves only as a holdfast and short-term feeding post until the plants have sufficient anchorage to begin their climb.

While in its juvenile stage, its leaves are between 4 and 6 inches long. On a mature plant they grow up to 12 inches long, green on both the top and bottom. Its stems produce aerial roots and, if given a moist surface such as a bark slab, a column of moss, or even a wood wall, it will cling tightly and eventually hold the plant aloft.

The botanical name of his stalwart plant is *Philodendron scandens, philodendron* being Greek for "tree loving," and *scandens* meaning "to climb." It belongs to the subspecies *oxycardium* (which means having a heart shape with a sharp point).

There are a number of cultivars, including *P. scandens* forma *micans*, or the velvet philodendron, with bronzy red-violet leaves; *P. s.* forma *miduhoi*, or jumbo velvet hearts, has larger leaves of a copper color; and *P. s. aureum*, or the limeleaf vine, has very showy chartreuse leaves.

Plant these in a mix of potting soil, peat moss, and sand, one-third each. But this particular stalwart will even do quite well growing in a jar of water. Temperatures should always be above 60°F, which explains why these vines do so well up near the ceiling. Although it will also survive in areas with only 20 FC of light, the more light available, the bigger the leaves. Heartleaf philodendrons also like to be misted on occasion, and are propagated with cuttings.

✳ THE PURPLE BELL VINE

The first mention that I read of the purple bell vine called it a "miracle plant" with an unbelievable number of beautiful flowers covering an attractive vine from head to foot. I took it with a grain of salt, having read such pronouncements many times before, but I ordered seed and thought I'd give it a try. And was I surprised, for the vine lived up to all its hype.

First registered in 1755, this fast-growing tropical beauty originally comes from Mexico. It's a perennial that will dependably bloom the first year. In fact, the earliest flowers appear about four months after seed germination. Its botanical name is *Rhodochiton atrosanguineum*, a genus name meaning "red cloak," and a species that refers to its dark blood-red color. Older books often call it *R. volubile* (here the species name means "twining").

Masses of bell-shaped blossoms soon cover the vine, with flowers the color of venous blood but not at all unattractive in spite of that imagery. The five-lobed inch-wide calyx is bell-shaped and a lighter shade of purple than the 2-inch-long tubular corolla that flares out at the bottom into five unequal-sized lobes. The leaves have long petioles and taper to a point from a heart-shaped base. A plant can climb about 10 feet in a season, and both the leaf and flower stalks will twine around a convenient support.

Many gardeners treat purple bells as a half-hardy annual, growing new plants every year since they will dependably bloom four months from germination. Seeds will sprout in about fifteen days.

Use a mix of potting soil, humus, and sand, one-third each, and fertilize once a month during summer months.

After a summer of bloom, the leaves on my plants begin to turn a deep purple and their growth ceases. Since they grow so easily from seed, however, this is never a major problem.

❧ A BLOOMING JASMINE

A rose by any other name would smell as sweet, and so would any member of the Confederate jasmine family, no matter how confusing the terminology. The genus, *Trachelospermum*, refers to the seed having a pronounced neck, a name derived from the Greek *trachelos*, neck, and *sperma*, seed.

My problem was with the species term, *mandaianum*. No matter where I looked, I could find no reference to that particular name. Then, just on a whim I checked an old copy of *Hortus Second* (revised in 1941), where under *Trachelopspermum jasminoides*, I found a reference to a yellow-flowered form, listed as *Rhynchospermum mandaianum*.

Today, plants belonging to *Rhynchospermum* are assigned either to *Chonemorpha* or back to *Trachelospermum*. *Chonemorpha* this jasmine isn't, since its flowers are decidedly pale yellow rather than white and the leaves are shiny, not slightly hairy above or pubescent beneath. The sap is white. So it must be a *Trachelospermums*—but the jury is still out as to the veracity of the species name.

For the window garden, it's a beautiful vine with shiny green leaves and those fragrant light yellow flowers appearing throughout most of the year. This year my plant bloomed in April and May, and is now blooming again in August.

The vine is a weaver, meandering back and forth and in an out as it climbs. You provide the warp and the plant will become the woof (or more properly, the weft).

A mix of potting soil, peat moss, and sand, one-third each, should be allowed to dry slightly before watering again. Fertilize every two months except in winter. Propagation is by cuttings.

HANGING GARDENS

One picture is often worth more than a thousand words, especially when it opens the mind to impressive new ways of making a garden. This story began a with a photograph of an unnamed English garden where the owner had taken clumps of tuffa and lava rocks, drilled a vertical hole through the center of each, then pulled a rope through (with a knot at the bottom). Then he hung these imaginative planters at various levels from trees in his backyard. The result was marvelous to behold, and with a water-wand attached to a hose, easy to care for. He used all sorts of alpine and succulent plants that wouldn't suffer if he forgot watering for a day or two. The ease of mowing the lawn beneath these living mini-mobiles was an added plus.

It was one step from there to another garden where the owner took a number of containers—from woven baskets to buckets to terracotta pots—and hung them from a tree on various lengths of nylon rope, and again, watered with a hose wand.

11

SOME ORNAMENTAL GRASSES
AND BAMBOOS

WHEN I BEGAN A CAREER IN HORTICULTURE, MY major driving force was a love of ornamental grasses and bamboos. One of the most imaginative garden images I'd ever seen was an Elvin McDonald photo of a balustrade on a backyard patio. There, in a row, were five pots of grasses. At the corner was the largest, a metal urn in the Grecian style planted with yellow foxtail grasses (*Setaria lutescens*) dug up directly from a nearby field. The next two were six-inch pots planted with quaking grass (*Briza maxima*), and the last two were 4-inch pots filled with some plain old lawn fescues. It was an arresting setup.

When it comes to flowers, the grasses seem to lack the same salute to beauty. The flowers, however, really are there, but they just lack petals. Because most of the grasses depend on the wind for pollination, they have no need for extensive and magnificent floral displays; garish petals and nectars attract bees, ants, beetles, birds, and the rest of nature's helpers to complete the job of pollination. With grasses, the flower parts are essentially the same as with other plants, but a few features, notably petals, have all but disappeared, and you'd need a magnifying glass to find them. Instead of flowers, botanists call grass flowers "spikelets."

When growing grasses one botanical term to keep in mind is the word "culm," which is another, more correct name for a stem. Unlike most stems, grass culms are usually hollow (although some species from arid regions, as well as corns, are solid), with stem sections joined by solid joints or nodes.

When you consider growing either annual or perennial grasses in pots, remember, if you can move it, you can probably grow it in a pot. But also remember that grasses have great masses of fibrous roots that need a lot of water, especially when under a summer sun, plus occasional feedings with plant food.

⚘ ANNUAL GRASSES

As a group, the annual grasses are rarely grown for their foliage, which, at best, usually looks weedy. But the flowers and the annual's following seeds offer so many fascinating features of form and color that one never ceases to admire their beauty. A few even demand prominent placement in a small garden or pot, because the plants themselves are often small and the flowers large.

Usually, annual grasses require a spot in full summer sun for adequate growth and flowering, but they're not too fussy about the soil used, as long as it drains well. In order to have a sequence of bloom throughout the summer and fall, I always start some seeds indoors in early spring. When planting annual grasses directly outdoors, however, remember to label them well. Seedling grasses have no individual identity of their own and easily pass as weeds.

Hardy annuals (HA) are not affected by frost and can be planted directly outdoors. Half-hardy annuals (HHA) can withstand a bit of frost, while tender annuals (TA) will succumb to it.

Cloud grass, or *Agrostis nebulosa* (HA), grows 8 to 20 inches tall. Native to the Iberian Peninsula, this lovely grass has many North American relatives, but none are quite as delicate and cloud-like. Although the plants do not last long because they dry and shatter soon after flowering, a small border of these plants, or a few pots, make a beautiful sight. This is one of the few annuals that can take a position in partial shade and still look and flower well.

Since the plants are fairly small, try a pot-full indoors while the snow is still on the ground; just give the plants plenty of light. Its panicles can be carefully picked and dried, and they'll make a valuable addition to winter arrangements.

Wild Oats, or *Avena fatua* (HA), can grow 3 to 4 feet tall. Most eastern farmers consider this a weed and it can be found along many roadsides in high summer. The plant looks straggly, even for a grass, but its flowers are most attractive and are a beautiful shade of light brown. It quickly goes to seed and dies, however, so pick the flowers early.

Animated Oats, or *Avena sterilis* (HA), will grow 3 to 4 feet tall and are a larger version of the wild oats that originally come from Europe. It, too, is unattractive at best, but its flowers are excellent for winter bouquets. The common name comes from the movement of the awns as the atmospheric humidity changes. It is an excellent grass flower to examine because all its parts are large enough to view with ease. These plants are really at their best with full sun, and the seeds will germinate within ten days.

Quaking Grass, or *Briza maxima* (HHA), will reach 2 to 3 feet tall. Native to southern Europe, quaking grass has been in cultivation as a garden ornament for well over two hundred years. The spikelets quiver and quake with every gentle breeze and look a lot like the popular cereal that was "shot from guns" on old radio commercials. In addition, its flowers are faintly striped with purple, making this a striking addition to any bouquet. The seeds will germinate in ten to fourteen days and are easily started in peat pots in early spring. The panicles should be picked before they open.

Little Quaking Grass, or *Briza minor* (HHA), grows 6 to 18 inches tall. If the adjective "cute" can be correctly applied to a grass, this one is it. This plant is an exact miniature of quaking grass. The same general rules for growth apply, except that heavy summer rains can quickly smash the plants. Show its flowers to people alongside its larger relative and tell them you've invented a secret shrinking process—they just might believe you.

Brome grass, or *Bromus macrostachys* (HA), was originally found in southern Europe but has many North American relatives, called chess or cheat grasses. While again, not really appropriate for an upfront position in the pot garden, as it grows 18 to 24 inches tall, the dried flowers retain all their character. They need full sun and should be sown outdoors in spring.

Brome grass, or *Bromus madritensis* (HA), which also grows 18 to 24 inches tall, is another member of the brome family, and asks for the same growing conditions as the previous example. It, too, is a beautiful addition to dried bouquets.

Job's tears, or *Coix lacryma-jobi* (HHA), is a close relative of the corns. Growing, 3 to 4 feet tall, Job's tears has the distinction of being one of the oldest ornamental grasses in cultivation. It's said this grass was grown for ornamental purposes in the fourteenth century. The seeds, which readily fall from the plant at maturity, are hard and white, streaked with gray or black, and very shiny. For years the seeds have been used for jewelry, especially rosaries, and the plants are often found growing wild in the southern states. The beads are the female flower and bear two feathery stigmas and two green male flowers above.

Job's tears will tolerate some shade and a damp spot in the garden. The leaves are a pleasant light green. In colder climates, start the seeds indoors in individual peat pots. Three to four weeks are required for germination. A form with variegated leaves, *C. lacryma-jobi* var. *zebrina*, is sometimes available if you search.

Love grass, *Eragrostis tef* (TA), was once called *Eragrostis abyssinica*, and in Ethiopia it's known as tef. One of the many love grasses cultivated in gardens, this 18- to 24-inch plant has been grown in India and Australia as a forage plant. In Africa, the seeds are ground for flour and used in making bread. Give the plants plenty of sun, and don't put them out until all danger of frost is past. An American species, *E. capillaris*, or lace grass, is a more open version of tef and is often found growing on the border between fields and woods in the Northeast. Others of this tribe are mentioned as perennials.

Hare's-tail grass, *Lagurus ovatus* (HA), grows 18 to 24 inches tall. Here's yet another native Mediterranean grass that's been in cultivation for years, and has been naturalized in parts of England. Hare's-tail grass is the only species in the genus. The name in Greek is *lagos*, a hare, and *oura*, a tail. It's lovely and produces a great many terminal spikes by the time of the killing frost. The foliage is light green, and the stems and leaves are soft with down. It is widely used in winter bouquets.

Besides being attractive, however, the flower heads do not shatter with age. It is also widely mistreated by people who feel an absolute necessity to improve on nature. They dye the seed heads electric pink, liver green, or malaria yellow, and then place them in plastic vases to be sold to weary drivers at interstate and thruway rest stops.

Golden top, or *Lamarkia aurea* (TA), is named after J. B. Lamarck, the naturalist who lost out to Darwin in the evolutionary science sweepstakes. Bursting up at 18 to 24 inches, golden top is truly a unique and beautiful grass. If I had to limit my choice of annual grasses to one, this might be it. When fresh, the one-sided panicles have a shimmering golden effect that turns silvery with age. By mid-summer, the plants are turning brown, so a second crop should be prepared. Be sure to pick them for bouquets before they dry, however, because the flowers shatter when mature. Golden top also occurs as a weed in the southwestern states.

Feather top grass, or *Pennisetum villosum* (HHA), will grow up to 2 to 3 feet tall. Although this grass from Ethiopia is a perennial in Zone 9, most catalogs list it as a half-hardy annual. Feather top is rather floppy in appearance, for the magnificent flowers become quite heavy. If picked before they open entirely, they can be dried for bouquets but will readily shatter at the slightest bump. They're beautiful when picked as fresh flowers and surrounded with garden phlox, coralbells, or astilbe. The seeds should be planted out-of-doors when all danger of frost is past.

Canary grass, or *Phalaris cananensis* (HA), also shoots up to 2 to 3 feet tall. Native to the Canary Islands and southern Europe, this grass is grown as birdseed for both wild and domesticated canaries. The flower heads are a variegated green and yellowish white at the top of long slender stems. While the plant itself is not attractive

The walled edge of my terrace is home to a number of potted plants and vegetables from early spring to mid-autumn. From left are Pennisetum *'Rubrum',* Bougainvillea *'Bridal Veil', a datura (*Datura *spp.), and ending with squash and tomatoes.*

enough to win a seat at the head of the pot garden, it is a good background choice. Since birdcage bottoms often get sent to landfills, canary grass is often spotted at the town dump.

Champagne grass, or *Rhynchelytrum repens* (HHA), is also known as *Tricholaena rosea*. Growing 3 to 4 feet, this is my second-favorite annual grass. It's another plant listed as a half-hardy annual in catalogs, while being a perennial in Zone 9. It blooms over a long season only to be cut down by frost, when the reddish pink plumes turn a soft silver. A great fresh-cut flower, it easily shatters with age. When gathering, pull the stems out of the leaf sheath instead of breaking them.

Foxtail millet, or *Setaria italica* (HA), is a striking 2- to 4-foot annual grass that really looks like the foxtails once tied on the rumble seats of an old Chevys during the 1930s. The dense panicles are often up to a foot in length and bow toward the earth with the weight of the seed grains. While the plants are tolerant to some lack of water, they perish quickly under drought conditions. First grown in ancient China in 2700 B.C., foxtail reached Europe during the Middle Ages, and entered the United States in 1849, where it has become an important fodder crop. The seed is harvested for bird feed. This is another grass that is a bit too ungainly for a formal garden, but, kept to the back of any arrangement, the panicles are striking additions. They are great as winter decorations and last as long as you have the patience to dust them.

Foxtail grass, or *Setaria lutescens* (HA), will grow 18 to 24 inches tall. In many catalogs it's still called *S. glauca* but regardless of the scientific name, foxtail grass was originally a common weed in Europe. After its introduction, it was also a common weed in America. The bristles on the panicles have a very striking yellow-orange color that remains after drying.

Wheat, or *Triticum aestivum* (HA), was previously known as *T. spelta*. The cultivation of this 3- to 4-foot tall cereal annual goes far back in time. It's extremely hardy but not good for flour, so today it's primarily grown for cattle feed. As an ornamental, the flowering stalks are very tall and the racemes most unusual with their regular order. A large group of these plants in a garden is a must.

Bearded wheat, or *Triticum turgidum* (HA), is shorter, growing only to 2 to 4 feet tall. The flour from bearded wheat, however, is known as durum and is popular for use in pasta recipes. It's very hardy and drought resistant, so it's grown in most arid regions of the world. The long awns are unlike any other grass inflorescence.

Variegated corn, or *Zea mays* var. *gracillima* 'Variegata' (TA), grows 3 to 4 feet tall. This is a relatively miniature corn and, unlike most annual grasses, is grown for its beautifully shaded leaves that are striped with green and pure white. The cobs never grow very large, and the silk just adds more interest to the plants. Corn is a rank feeder, so always plant in fertile soil, planning to add more fertilizer at monthly intervals; it also prefers plenty of water. Since corn is very sensitive to cold, and takes a goodly time for development, start plants indoors in individual peat pots, transplanting to bigger pots as they grow. Try putting variegated corn in 8-inch pots, and group a few for an effective outdoor-terrace decoration.

Z. mays var. *japonica* has the added distinction of a touch of red or pink with the variegations. There are other varieties of corn listed in the trade as rainbow corn, which produce ears of multi-colored kernels. Strawberry corn (var. *praecox*) grows roundish ears of pointed, red kernels that are said to make very good popcorn.

Wild rice, or *Zizania aquatica* (HA), is today an epicurean delight. It's also very, very expensive when purchased by the quarter-pound package. At 6 to 8 feet tall, it grows in the wild along inland marshes and at pond or lake edges, mainly in northern Minnesota and Wisconsin. This grain was a major food source of pre-modern Native Americans.

The plant itself is large and attractive in a waterside setting. Even a small pool may boast a few plants. Put them in pots with well-fertilized soil, covering the surface with gravel and submerging it at the pool's edge. If you're lucky enough to have a stream or pond in a sunny position, be sure to try a grouping of wild rice—if not for your table, at least for the visiting waterfowl.

The small, hanging spikelets on the bottom of the panicles are the male flowers, which eventually fall, leaving the rice-grains, or female spikelets, on the upper part.

There are many other annual ornamental grasses in addition to those I've described, including hair grass (*Aira elegans*), spike grass (*Desmazeria sicula*), dense silky bent grass (*Apera interrupta*), loose silky bent grass (*Apera spica-venti*), rabbit's-foot grass (*Polypogon monspeliensis*), and another love grass (*Eragrostis tenella*).

❧ SOME UNUSUAL ARRANGEMENTS

When I was a kid and addicted, like most kids in those days, to Plastic Man, the Green Lantern, and Wonder Woman, comic books also contained startling, wild, and totally tasteless advertisements with cartoon drawings that offered products from itching powder to x-ray binoculars. No doubt an advance indication of my horticultural interests, my favorite was an item called "Grow Hair on Cueball's Head." This last product was a large hollow white-clay head with a bald top peppered with tiny holes. You put grass seed on the head, kept the inside filled with water, and Cueball soon began to sprout a new crop of hair. (Only in later years was I introduced to the Chia Pet.)

While it's true that I always thought of the grass-growing head as a novelty of the 1940s, I have since learned that Cueball goes back even farther in time. It was created in the 1870s, back when the following excerpts about growing grasses on cones were written in *Window Gardening*, a popular gardening book of the era:

> Far prettier than many a pretentious and costly ornament is a simple bowl of grasses planted in pinecones, set in sand, in moss, or common soil. If grown in cones—procure them from the woods, and sprinkle with water; place the cones in sand or moss—and be sure they do not become dry—but water them sparingly at first, once a day, and set in a moderately warm place. Soon the seeds will sprout and the tiny spears protrude in every direction.
>
> Grass will sprout and grow in pinecones without any soil, but it serves to prevent the cone from closing too tightly when sprinkled, and also makes a more vigorous growth. The cones can be suspended in a window, either singly or in groups of three fastened together with thread or wire; or a rustic basket or stand can be procured, and filled with cones with different kinds of grass, growing in each cone. There are three thousand different species of grass in the world, and their study is a pleasing pursuit.
>
> A very charming effect can be produced by placing a wet sponge in a glass bowl, and sprinkling over it canary seed, grasses, and flax seeds; soon it will be covered with a thick growth of fresh bright green; it must be judiciously watered; if kept too dry it will wither away; if too wet it may damp off.
>
> Children and invalids can derive much pleasure from raising a grass garden; it is better to select the dwarf varieties, as the taller kinds require more nourishment.
>
> A tumbler garden may be made as follows: Fill a common tumbler or goblet with water, cut out a round of cotton batting, or of a soft thick flannel of just the size to cover the surface, and lay it gen-

tly upon the water, upon this scatter the seeds of grass, or flax . . . and gently set the tumbler away in a dark place. In a few days the seed will start . . . [and] begin to penetrate the cotton or flannel, slowly sending down their delicate white fibers to the bottom of the vessel, while the top will be covered with a little thicket of green. After the second day the vessel must be kept in a warm tight place, and two or three times a week carefully replenished with water by means of a teaspoon or syringe inserted beneath the flannel.

The devices for growing grasses can be extended *ad libitum*, and none are so poor that they cannot secure a tumbler or a saucer garden, which will prove a delight and joy to all beholders, while its care will be of the slightest.

❧ PERENNIAL GRASSES

Perennial grasses do beautifully in containers and can also be the high points of small gardens. Most of the imposing members of the family are not tropical, so they must have at least six weeks of rest in the winter at temperatures of 40°F (or lower), which can be easily accomplished by leaving the pots in a dry place such as a garage or storage shed. If the pots are shatterproof, they can be left outside in warmer areas, but in areas of USDA Zone 6 (or colder), make sure that, once frozen, they do not thaw. The following are just a few of the many species available today at garden centers, nurseries, and by catalog.

Lemon grass (*Cymbopodon citrates*) is a lemony-scented tropical often found at Chinese and Thai food stores. The base of each bunch of leaves resembles a bulb (but isn't), and is sliced and added to many oriental dishes. The plants grow about 5 feet tall but rarely flower in cultivation. Give it full sun.

Japanese sedge grass (*Hakonechlora macra* 'Aureola') is, surprisingly, a native of Japan. It's a mound-forming perennial grass that sports narrow bands of creamy yellow on arching bright green culms that truly resemble fountains without water. It's especially beautiful when growing in an attractive pot, and it's shade tolerant, too.

Sweet grass (*Hierochloe odorata*) is an upright perennial with slender, creeping rhizomes and not too many culms of a nondescript green. So why grow it? Because of the pleasant vanilla-like fragrance it gives off when you crush some leaves in your hand. It needs sun to semi-shade and moist soil, and it will survive as a houseplant in a bright window.

The miscanthus grasses (*Miscanthus* spp.) include a number of perfect grasses for pots, ranging from more than 10 feet tall to shorter versions that generally stay around 5 or 6 feet high. The species is considered a weedy threat, but its cultivars are generally sterile.

'Adagio' maiden grass (*M. sinensis* 'Adagio') is, as of today, one of the most beautiful of the small miscanthus grasses, forming a graceful 2-foot-high mound of tapered, narrow leaves. The green foliage turns reddish in the fall and is topped by 4-foot pink-tinted plumes. Full sun is best, and it's hardy in Zones 6 to 9.

Zebra grass (*M. s.* 'Zebrinus') forms a 6- to 8-foot fountain of graceful leaves sporting horizontal bars of a mellow yellow tone. It's hardy in Zones 6 to 9.

'Cosmopolitan' miscanthus (*M. s.* 'Cosmopolitan') may be one of the most beautiful variegated miscanthus grasses to date. At a height of 3 to 4 feet, the wide, striped leaves are beautiful to behold. It's hardy in Zones 6 to 9.

'Morning Light' (*M. s.* 'Morning Light') is a form of variegate maiden grass (*M. s.* 'Gracillimus'), found some years ago growing wild at the edge of a rural road in Japan. The narrow leaves have a center rib of white. It's hardy in Zones 5 to 9, and is one of the best container plants ever.

Variegated purple moor grass (*Molinea caerulea* 'Variegata'), has been a favorite of mine, and I often feature it in talks I give about finding plants that make great centerpieces in small gardens. It likes a moist soil, whether in the garden or in pots, and will not tolerate alkaline soil. The variegated form has leaves striped green and cream, with flower stems bearing horizontal bars of creamy white. It's hardy to Zone 4.

We acquired a *Zeugites americana* var. *mexicana* several years ago, but have been unable to identify it until now. It appeared to be a species of bamboo, but flowered so frequently that we were doubt-ful. It turns out to be a grass, as bamboo is, but of a different fam-ily—the Poaceae. The plant may reach 2 feet tall on very thin, weeping, or trailing culms. Its leaves are small, about a half-inch, broadly ovate, and, in this variety, white-striped. It prefers moisture and some shade, and is an unusual and attractive addition to the pond's edge in warm climates or in a greenhouse in cooler areas. It's hardy in Zones 9 and 10.

✤ BONSAI GRASSES

One of the most inspiring plant books I've ever owned was pur-chased by searching the Web after attending a lecture on bonsai hostas by Harry Abel of Smyrna, Georgia. The book, *Four Seasons of Bonsai* by Kyuzo Murata, is one of those books that can add years to a gardener's life. After seventy-some years of growing and training bonsai plants, and sixty years of those years as the official bonsai gardener to the Imperial Household of Japan, Mr. Murata is a genius.

Among the grasses appearing in his book are whistle grass, or gardener's-gators (*Phalaris arundinacea* var. *picta*), *shima-kusayoshi* in Japanese, which grows about 16 inches high in a shallow tray less than 8 inches wide, and does well in that tray for seven years.

An accompanying photo shows the plain species of *Phalaris arundinacea*, which is about 20 inches high in a slightly larger tray, this time at an age of twelve years.

Mr. Murata also grows the annual quaking grass (*Briza max-ima*), planting it late in the season and fertilizing sparingly, keeping the height at 7 inches in a small blue pot. He also cultivated the scouring rush (*Equisetum hyemale*) in a 5-inch-wide tray that holds more than thirty stems, at an age of two years in the photo. He uses coarse sand instead of soil, and copious amounts of water.

Japanese sedge grass (*Hakonechloa macra* 'Aureola'), *fuchiso* in Japan, is mentioned with the perennial grasses, but here it is again, this time some seventeen years old and about 10 inches high.

❧ SEDGES

Sedges are more primitive forms of grasses, but they still have their place in the garden.

Leather-leaf sedge (*Carex buchananii*) bears 2-foot very showy coppery leaves that provide a striking contrast in the landscape. Last year I saw a pair of black 14-inch-wide, oval-shaped pottery pots, sitting on the balustrade of the stone steps leading to the Moon Gate at Leith Hall in England, and each held one leather-leaf sedge. It's hardy to Zone 7.

Japanese sedge grass (*Carex morrowii*) ranks as one of the ten or twenty best perennial plants for small gardens and pots. The gracefully arched leaves are striped a creamy white and green. The flowers are not resplendent but are very welcome when they appear as small brush-like affairs in very early spring. It's hardy to Zone 6.

Great pendulous wood sedge (*Carex pendula*) grows between 2 and 3 feet tall, becoming a fountain of light green leaves topped with pendulous spikelets on thin arching stems. These plants prefer moist soil and some shade from the hot southern sun, and are hardy to Zone 5.

Plantain-leafed sedge (*Carex plantaginea*) gets its name from its slight similarity to a weed common to lawns, the plantain. But the sedge is far more beautiful, with its fresh green seersucker-striped leaves. It makes a great shady ground cover and is pretty in small pots. It's hardy to Zone 6.

❧ BAMBOOS

For me, bamboos conjure up visions of steamy jungles with orange orangutans crawling beneath masses of dark green leaves or Bette Davis as the femme fatale in the movie *The Letter.* But in today's international world of horticulture, bamboos have now achieved a prominent—if not exotic—place as desirable landscape plants and for growing, quite handily, in containers.

For many years bamboos were listed as giant grasses, and while there are similarities (both grasses and bamboos belong to the Graminae), bamboos are usually very large long-lived woody evergreens with stout stems (really culms) and well-developed (often far-ranging) root systems. Many bamboos are also monocarpic: They will die only a short time after flowering, and all clones of a particular species will often flower at the same time regardless of where they are in the world.

Most bamboos are very fast spreaders. Even in colder climates (such as Connecticut's), some species have been known to grow more than 10 feet in one month. The secret is its food reserves held in the roots and stems. That's why they're such popular foods in Asia.

There are two types of bamboos: the runners and the clumpers. Runners spread by sending out rhizomes at a depth of about a foot, although when hitting a natural (or artificial) barrier, they easily change direction. In one year, runners can spread so quickly that their progress can be measured in yards. In essence, clumpers grow in upon themselves, creating a non-invasive root clump. Their circle of growth enlarges too, but can be measured in inches. Runners make great ground covers, and clumpers are especially beautiful when grown as single specimens or in hedges.

Almost any bamboo, even runners, can be grown in a container. Some plants will continue to spread within them, eventually becoming pot-bound, but when well watered and supplied with fertilizer supplements they will continue to thrive.

Bamboos, however, do have one bad habit: They often shed leaves when grown in containers but plentiful watering will often help to alleviate this problem. Water is the crucial factor. Unless you are growing a water-loving bamboo, never over-water. But never let the roots dry out for any length of time, either.

Use a well-drained soil mix. During active growth, use half the amount suggested on the label of a high-nitrogen fertilizer. Provide at least a few hours of sun a day; the pots can go outdoors in the summertime. Black bamboo (*Phyllostachys nigra*) likes night temperatures near 50°F, but *P. aurea* and *P. bambusoides* can take higher temperatures. Just remember that with higher temperatures, more light is needed. Some bamboos that are commonly grown indoors, and are tolerant of lower light intensity fall under the *Pleioblastus* genus, *Sasaella masamuniana* 'Albostriata', and *Indocalamus tessellatus*.

⚘ CONTROLLING THE GROWTH OF BAMBOO

Want to try your hand at bamboo bonsai or simply modify the size of your plants? I called Albert H. Adelman at Burt Associates Bamboo and asked him how to control the size of potted bamboos.

"You can control the growth of any species," said Mr. Adelman, "by removing unwanted culms, cutting at soil level, cutting above a node, or root pruning. I've kept a *Sasella masamuniana* 'Albostriata' at about a 3-inch height, at home in a shallow bonsai container for three years by cutting the culms at nodes and feeding sparingly."

He went on to explain the best way to achieve growth control. "Shorten a bamboo by cutting just above a node. While many plants look butchered if their tops are cut off, a 'topped' bamboo usually holds its looks if the remaining topmost branch is left on the side where the culm is leaning. Some bamboos, particularly phyllostachys in pots, also look best, and mimic greater age, if the bottom third of the culm is bare of branches. Simply cut them off close to the culm. Also shorten the branches of potted phyllostachys to the second node of each branch. You'll get a spare look to the plant and expose and emphasize the culm. This technique is particularly effective if the culm has an interesting color or shape—and it emphasizes that bamboo quality. But if you prefer a shrubby look don't prune the branches.

"You can dwarf a bamboo simply by restricting its growth by growing it in the container. If fertilized, it will eventually completely fill a pot with root and rhizome. As with other bonsai, the stress of removing the plant from the container, removing some roots and replacing the soil will restrict the growth. Remove about one third of the roots."

Mr. Adelman went on to describe the growth process of a bamboo culm, where the length of a growing culm is biologically controlled at the base of the sheath covering the culm. "A classic method of interfering with elongation and shortening a culm, is to remove the culm sheath. As a result, not only is the internode shortened but it also bulges a bit, giving a bellied effect."

Mr. Adelman continued, "Removing part of the culm sheath can also result in twists and turns. But be warned that this is difficult to do without destroying the culm. Culms are very soft and tender at this time and easily damaged."

It can be tricky business to successfully remove the culm, but Mr. Adelman reassured me that with patience, it can be done. "Carefully cut the culm sheaths into sections or strips. Then remove the strips over the course of a day, removing no more than one sheath a day. One sheath every other day is better yet, as the procedure imposes considerable stress on the culm. Hurry it too much and you lose the culm. I use a tool called a Clip-it (used to cut clippings out of newspapers) for the delicate job of cutting the sheaths into strips. This technique is useful only if the culm is larger than about a quarter inch in diameter. Or if you have a touch considerably more delicate than mine.

"With few exceptions," Mr. Adelman said, "bamboos are not difficult. I treasured a 9-foot-high black bamboo (*P. nigra*) grown in a pot 11 inches wide and 7 inches deep. It over-wintered in our house, not a greenhouse, and sat on a patio in warm weather. It took three years to get to 9-feet from a plant in a 6-inch pot."

The following bamboos can grow in containers with ease. Many more can be found at Mr. Adelman's firm, Burt Associates Bamboo at the Website: www.bamboos.com.

B. multiplex 'Alophonse Karr' is a semi-tropical clumping bamboo with yellow culms sporting vertical green stripes. Outside it's hardy to 15°F, reaching a height of up to 30 feet. Indoors, near a sunny window, its height will stay at about 10 feet.

B. multiplex 'Whitestripe' is another semi-tropical clumper that bears green culms with occasional white stripes on both the culms and the leaves. Outside, it's hardy to 15°F, reaching a height of 30 feet. Indoors, with bright light, its height will stay at about 10 feet.

The square bamboo (*Chimonobambusa quadrangularis*) is named for the mature culms that are square rather than round. Its branches and leaves drape in a beautiful manner. Mr. Adelman notes that it's an excellent houseplant, reaching a height of 25 feet.

The marbled bamboo (*C. marmorea*) has marbled culms that are an attractive red color. It has a maximum height of 6 feet.

Chusquea coronalis, called the most beautiful bamboo in cultivation by the American Bamboo Society, is a semi-tropical clumper from Central America. Arching culms bear tiny leaves on branchlets that encircle the graceful branches. Outside, its maximum height is 20 feet, but it grows only 6 to 8 feet in a container.

Hibanobambusa tranquillans 'Shiroshima' is a running bamboo with large, strikingly variegated leaves in white and cream, reaching an indoor height of about 16 feet.

The Mexican weeping bamboo (*Otatea acuminata aztectorum*) is a semi-tropical clumping bamboo from Mexico and Central America. These plants bear a profusion of small leaves on arching culms. It's an excellent choice for out on your patio or indoors as a specimen plant.

Phylostachys nigra, or black bamboo, has shiny black culms about an inch thick and narrow green leaves up to 4 inches long. It's one beautiful bamboo. Outside, it's hardy to Zone 7, and, while reasonably at home in a smaller pot (about 8 inches across), plants do best in large tubs or containers.

Mr. Murata has a pot of this bamboo that has reached 22 inches high and is some sixty years old, growing in a 10-inch wide but very shallow pot. He writes that the bamboo's rhizomes will coil around in the pot's bottom, eventually pushing up the soil, so he recommends lifting the clump once a year and cutting the rhizomes back. He also suggests trimming the old leaves before the new leaves appear in the spring.

Pleioblastus chino murakamianus, a small-leafed bamboo, reaches a 4-foot height with some leaves that show a variety of variegation, and others that are all white.

The dwarf white-stripe bamboo (*P. variegatus*), on the other hand, bears green leaves with stark white variegations at a height of 3 feet. In the North it loses its leaves during the winter.

The dwarf fern-leaf bamboo (*P. disticha*) will be hardy outside to Zone 7. This is a small runner less than 3 feet in height, with 6-inch-long, bright green leaves on purple-tinted culms.

Pygmy bamboo, classed as *P. pygmaeus* or *Arundinaria pygmaea*, is one of the smallest of the bamboos, and makes an excellent garden ground cover (you can cut it with a mower if it gets out of bounds). But it's also very much at home in a pot. It likes full sun and moist, well-drained soil and is also hardy to Zone 7. It usually grows no higher than 10 inches. The variegated pygmy bamboo (*P. pygmaeus* 'Variegated') has cream- and white-striped leaves, and, because of its variegations, can take a location with open shade. Its height, however, will be less than 16 inches.

P. shibuyanus 'Tsuboi' is a small (2- to 3-foot) bamboo with unique variegation: The leaf's mid-vein is always white.

Three Outdoor Favorites

The following bamboos do not flourish indoors but in the small garden they are spectacular.

Kamuro-zasa bamboo (*Pleioblastus viridistriata* or *Arundinaria viridistriata*) is a true beauty in Zone 7. The leaves are hard to describe—their color often depends on the time of day and the heat of the summer (although its colors seem to fade when summer temperatures reach the high 80s). They have a velvety look when new and sport varying stripes of chartreuse and golden tones that meld together from a distance. In the South they really require some shade, and, while not fussy as to soil, need adequate water. The usually 30-inch-high culms should be cut down to ground level in early spring so new growth appears.

Sasa veitchii probably ranks as my number-one bamboo for both home and garden. Because of its late autumn leaf color it's sometimes called a variegated bamboo but it really isn't. True, its

One of the most decorative of all bamboos, especially for the small garden or large container, is the so-called Kuma bamboo grass or sometimes, "variegated bamboo" (Sasa veichii).

green leaves develop a light tan to off-white edge when cold weather appears, but that's just dead tissue, not a true color variation. During the summer it's an adequate bamboo but it shines in the winter garden, whether planted directly outdoors in the garden or in a pot upon the terrace. A slow spreader, it's hardy to Zone 6. There is a smaller variety known as 'Nana' or 'Minor' that stays about 3 feet tall.

My *Sasella masamuniana* 'Albostriata' has lived in a rounded handmade clay pot (about 1 foot wide and 1 foot high) for two years now. Its leaves are medium green striped with bold slashes of white, and endowed with a distinct Asian look. In my city garden it winters outdoors, against the side of the house, where it's protected from chill winds and occasional snows. New leaves emerge in early spring, and once the frost danger has passed, this bamboo spends the summer on the edge of a stone wall. It never begs for water, and when I'm away, I place about a third of a new kerosene lamp wick in the soil, with the remainder in a nearby glass of water. There is another cultivar called 'Aureostriata', its leaves dashed with yellow, which fades as summer temperatures rise.

✣ 12 ✣

SUCCULENTS AND HEAVY
METAL GARDENING

S UCCULENTS ARE THE PERFECT ANSWER FOR PEOPLE
who don't want to worry about watering their plants. Succulents will put up with a great deal of water deprivation.

For me, however, their best quality is not their high tolerance of
abuse, but the appearance of their flowers: Beautiful, bizarre, or
both, with unusual leaf structures that make them look like visitors
from another world.

Cacti and succulents are *xerophytes*, or plants that have adapted
to survival under conditions of limited water supply. Both groups
are called "succulent" because they have developed thick, fleshy,
stems or leaves designed to hold water. All cacti belong in one family, however, the Cactaceae. And these are the only plants that produce an *areole*, a special spot that generates spines. Therefore,
succulent is not a family name but applies to hundreds of different
plants from all over the world. If a plant has the ability to store
water in its leaves or stems, it's a succulent, regardless of its family.

The following plants are a few of the succulents I've grown in
containers.

✣ THE ORCHID OR POND-LILY CACTUS

This is wisely named after the fabled orchids, for the flowers of this
unusual member of the cactus family are among the most beautiful

found in nature. The genus *Epiphyllum* is from the Greek *epi*, upon, and *phyllos*, a leaf, because botanists at one time thought the flowers were borne on leaves. It turns out, however, that the leaves are actually flattened stems.

Although these plants are true cacti, they usually come from Brazil, Mexico, Costa Rica, and Guatemala—not the deserts one would usually imagine. They grow high up in the jungle canopy, where they find perfect drainage and receive the nutrients they need to survive, which are brought to their roots by tropical rains washing down the detritus caught in the tree bark. Their main branches are woody, with flat or thin green stems that have wavy margins. The typical cactus spines are missing on mature plants but are often present as bristles on seedlings or juvenile plants.

The older the plant, the more architectural it becomes, and the more blossoms that appear in early spring. Tiny buds appear between the scallops on the stems, buds that grow visibly larger every day until they suddenly open into truly breathtaking flowers, aglow with vibrant colors. The texture of the petals resembles that of glistening satin, and its glorious colors include white, yellow, red, scarlet, and red streaked with iridescent purple.

Among the many spectacular cultivars available are 'Argus' with its 5-inch blossoms of apricot with a mandarin rose center and yellow throat; 'Climax', with large off-white petals that have central stripes of light lavender, and outer petals that become a progressively darker amethyst that deepens to red; 'Fireball', a 7- to 9-inch-wide flower of satiny orange with overtones of pink, and a yellow-green throat with pink anthers and pistil; and 'Morocco', a flower that combines orchid, red, yellow, violet, and cream, and with two outer rows of petals that become progressively darker and have yellow bases.

Orchid cacti are adaptable plants. Temperatures can drop as low as 40°F during its dormancy in winter, without causing any damage. Freezing will kill them. While direct sun in summer can burn the stems, plants will do well in filtered sun to bright shade. Water them well during active growth, allow them to dry out during winter. When the stems begin to shrivel, however, water as fast as you can.

Perfect drainage is necessary and I use potting soil, peat moss, and sand, one-third each, putting the plants in hanging baskets lined with sphagnum moss. Fertilize once a month from April through September.

If possible, during the summer months, hang the cacti outdoors under a tree or on the front porch—mine summer under a sumac tree in the backyard. If the summer is unusually dry, or if the plants are sheltered from normal rains, you must water, letting the soil dry out between applications.

Propagation is by rooted cuttings set in barely damp soil.

✢ THE MONSTER AND THE GOLF BALL

The *Euphorbias,* or spurges, are some of the oddest plants in the Vegetable Kingdom. Numbering over 1,600 species, they are herbs, shrubs, or trees that contain a milky juice, bloom with strange flowers, and, in the shape they present to the world, boast bizarre configurations unlike any other plants. The genus is named in honor of Euphorbus, a Greek physician who attended King Juba of Mauritania, an ancient district in Africa.

The milky sap is potentially dangerous in many species including the Crown of Thorns, *Euphorbia milii;* snow-on-the-mountain, *E. marginata;* and the candelabra cactus, *E. lactea.* On the other hand, many people believe the Christmas poinsettia, *E. pulcherrima,* is poisonous. Although the sap can be an irritant to some susceptible persons, not one documented case involving a fatality has ever been reported. Native tribes in Africa often use this sap, which contains complex terpens, to poison arrow tips and to stupefy fish. *Hortus Third* suggests that many succulent euphorbias should not be planted along the edges of stocked pools since exudates from broken roots might prove fatal to a fish population.

The flowers are odd, too. In the poinsettia, for example, what look like bright red petals are actually specialized leaves, called bracts, that masquerade as petals. The true flowers are the tiny yellow balls clustered in the center of the bracts. If you look at them under a hand lens you'll see that some are pistillate, or female, and some are staminate, or male.

The two plants in my collection are *E. heptagonia*—what I call the monster, and other various references call the milk-barrel—and *E. obesa*, a truly odd plant called the golf ball, the living baseball, or the Turkish temple.

E. heptagonia—with *heptagonia,* meaning seven angles, referring to the ridges on the stem—comes from Cape Province of South Africa. In the desert it becomes a thorny, erect succulent shrub about 3 feet high. The stem is about 1¾-inch thick, turning silvery brown with age and bearing tiny linear leaves and light brown spines. The light green leaves are only found on the top of the growing stem and are less than ¼-inch long, while the spines—really flower stems that never bear blossoms—are ¾-inch in length. And when they do appear, the flowers are small greenish yellow orbs that soon dry to brownish balls.

It's not much but it's tough as nails and has been in the window garden for seven years. The golf ball bears the botanical name *E. obesa* and obese it is. The Turkish temple moniker refers to the onion-dome shape of the plant. The plants are small spineless globes about 5 inches high and termed *dioecious,* since male and female flowers are on different plants—the males being somewhat pear-shaped and the females a bit rounder. Its gray-green color is highlighted with rows of small knobs that resemble the stitching on a baseball and additional markings on its surface call to mind the curving decorations on the Chrysler Building in Manhattan. The leaves, when in evidence, are so small as to be easily missed.

Propagation for the golf ball is limited to seed. Female plants must be pollinated from separate male plants, and the capsules must be covered with a small piece of netting to prevent loss of seed. Propagate the monster during the warm months of the year using cuttings, but allow any wounds to dry. Then use a sand and gravel mix for potting and set them in a warm place.

Both plants require perfect drainage, so use clay pots. Use a mix of potting soil, peat moss, and composted manure at one-fifth each, and two-fifth in sand. Water only in the summer, letting soil dry completely before watering again. The monster wants temperatures above 50°F and the golf ball prefers 60°F. Both require sun but the golf ball prefers some shade from the noonday summer sun.

⚘ THE OX-TONGUE CACTUSES

Never having been licked by an ox's tongue, I can't be sure that this particular group of plants is properly named. But if those tongues look anything like I imagine them to be, most of these plants are spot on. All but one of the common names in current use refer to a tongue, including cow-tongue cactus, lawyer's-tongue, mother-in-law's-tongue, and, strangely, Dutch-wings. The genus is *Gasteria* and is named for the Latin *gaster*, or belly, referring to the swollen base of the flower tube. There are some fifty species of these succulents, all coming from South Africa. They are also closely allied to the aloes but are easily recognized because of the flower form. They are not cacti but are actually members of the lily family.

Its long fleshy but tough leaves grow in ranks of two, or some slowly spiral, eventually becoming rosettes. The leaves do resemble animal tongues, even including raised specks, or tubercles, that often cover the surface, much like taste buds. Some twenty species or cultivars are available from nurseries and would make a fine theme for a collection of unusual plants.

Gasterias are also excellent plants for people on the go since the thick leaves allow them to survive up to a month without water. For healthy growth, however, they should be watered well during the summer months then kept nearly waterless during its dormant winter period. Temperatures should be kept above 50°F, but keep strong sun to a minimum; too much causes the leaves to turn brown and lose much of their character. Partial shade is best. A good soil mix consists of potting soil, composted manure, peat moss, and sand, one-quarter each. Fertilize once in spring, summer, and fall.

A number of these plants are lumped under the name of *Gasteria maculata* (*maculata* means spotted). The leaves of these plants can grow to a length of 8 inches and about an inch wide. They are attractively speckled with raised off-white oval spots in an abstract pattern, and its pink flowers are ¾-inch long, blooming on scapes up to 3 feet high.

For those with limited space, look for *G. nigricans marmorata variegata*, a charming plant with fat and short leaves—less than an inch long—growing like little bow ties, each marked with dark brown and ivory stripes. Keep your eye out for *G.* 'Silver Stripes', a slightly larger hybrid that bears pebbles in green stripes on a gray-green background.

Propagation is by offsets. If they have few or no roots, they should be allowed to dry before being potted.

❦ THE DRUNKARD'S DREAM

The drunkard's dream, or dancing bones cactus, is one of five cacti species originally discovered in Brazil. First described in 1834, the genus is *Hatiora*, an anagram for Thomas Hariot, a sixteenth-century botanist. The species, *salicornioides*, means "like a *salicornia*," a small genus of plants found near the ocean that have thick jointed leafless stems and are commonly called glassworts.

The jointed stems are tan to green and strongly resemble small bottles, with smaller bottles growing from what would be the caps. Under strong light, tiny purple spots appear along the stems in no regular pattern. The typical cactus spines are reduced to minute patches of fuzz at the bottle cap position. Growing plants also resemble the stylistic skeletons and bones found on the confections featured in many religious holidays in Central and South America.

Its waxy yellow flowers open only in sunlight and are wheel-shaped when completely open, fading to an orange-salmon color. In the United States, plants bloom from January to March but occasionally last as late as April. The plant is supposed to set fruit: a small white translucent berry. But, I've never seen any.

Hatioras are epiphytes, or plants that use trees or other plants merely as a support without being parasitic. In 1915, Dr. J. N. Rose wrote the following while collecting in Rio de Janeiro:

> The plant grows on trunks of trees, its roots long and fibrous, [16 inches] long or more and wrapped about the trunk of the tree; at first [the plant] is erect, then spreading, and finally pendent.

Since hatioras hail from the Brazilian jungles, temperatures should always be kept above 60°F. The best soil mix offers perfect drainage, so use potting soil, peat moss, and composted manure at one-fifth each, and two-fifths of sand. Under the best of conditions, this soil mix should be kept evenly moist, which means watering as often as you can—remember where these plants originally grew. My plant spends the summer hanging under the sumac tree in the garden. I fertilize it once a month from April to September, and propagate by cuttings in spring.

✸ THE PEARLY MOONSTONES

Over the years, most of the plants in my various container gardens have been potted in old-fashioned clay pots, many of them picked up at garage sales, and the rest during end-of-the-year sales at nursery and garden centers. A few are in open-wire hanging baskets. Unless they are in self-watering pots of a very plain design, none are in plastic. In addition, I have a large collection of turn-of-the-century jardinières that pots can sit inside for a special show or for display either at the table or out on the terrace.

There are, however, exceptions. My plant known as pearly moonstones sits in a six-sided Chinese porcelain pot decorated with deep blue stylized birds and flowers that rests on a saucer with a light blue rim. The leaves of this plant so resemble carved jade that a pot of any less elegance would never do.

Moonstones belong to the genus *Pachyphytum*, which means "thick plant," and refers to the heavy stems and globular leaves of these succulents. The species is *oviferum* because the leaves are egg-like. They belong to the same family as the time-honored jade plant.

Originally from Mexico, these plants rarely reach above 6 inches, and ½-inch stems bearing the scars of old and abandoned leaves end in a cluster of tightly packed leaves, termed "glaucous" because they are covered with a pale gray-blue powder that is easily rubbed off. In the bright light of summer, leaf color intensifies and its surface glows with pink highlights. Older leaves eventually shrivel and fall off. When a stem bends over the soil, it also gives rise to aerial roots.

When the stems eventually become too tall and naked, it is time to start new plants—easily accomplished by cutting off the stems some 2 inches below the leaves and rooting the shorter piece. Individual leaves will also root.

Give plants all the sun you can for the best color. Temperatures should always be above 50°F. The best soil mix is potting soil, peat moss, and composted manure, one-fifth each and two-fifths sand. Water only when the soil is dry and let the plants rest in the winter months, watering only if the leaves show signs of shriveling.

✤ THE SANSEVIERIAS

For years, I thought that the name sansevieria meant "without evieria." I never bothered to look up evieria, assuming it to be a rare or under-used botanical term referring to seed structure or something of that ilk—and I knew that one day I'd take the time to track the meaning down and straighten it out. Well much to my chagrin, I just checked the *Dictionary of Gardening* and found that the name sansevieria was bequeathed in honor of Raimond de Sansgrio, the Prince of Sanseviero (1710–71). As to the reason for honoring the prince in this manner, I can find no reference.

Often called bowstring hemp—because the tough fibers making up its leathery leaves have been used for bowstrings, as well as hats, mats, and rope—the other common names are Devil's tongue, good-luck plant, hemp plant, and, to a few who have trouble with their wives' (or for that matter, husbands') mother, mother-in-law's tongue, a reference no doubt to the thick, flat, and pointed leaves found with most of the genus.

These stalwart plants are members of the lily family, a fact that is not at all in evidence until they bloom. Then the plants produce spidery night-blooming flowers, each with six pale green petals and long curving stamens, and exude a penetrating but sweet fragrance that quickly fills the room. Where the flower base meets the stem, they drip with crystal beads of sugary nectar that has a sharp undertaste.

More than seventy species and cultivars are now available. These include leaves that are spear-shaped and have either straight or fluted edges, are banded with various whites and silvers, endless greens, numerous yellows, or buff-colored blotches, and range in size from the very small to the very tall.

The most common species is *S. trifasciata*, usually called the snake plant, and often found growing in the windows of Mexican restaurants and Chinese laundries, where the combination of steam and heat pushes them through great spurts of growth. In fact, the leaves often reach a length bordering on 4 feet. Flowering can occur at almost any time.

Of the three that I've grown in containers, the strangest is *S. cylindrica patula*, an oddball plant with cylindrically curved and solid stems of dark green, with darker bands that verge on black and, as they grow, assume a fan shape.

The cutest is *S. trifasciata* 'Golden Hahnii', or the gilt-edged bird's nest, an East Indian clone that bears cup-shaped leaves dashed with wide, creamy yellow bands.

And for added color, there is *S. trifasciata* 'Laurentii', which has yellow bands on a dark green background, and was originally found growing in the wilds of Zaire.

Sansevierias are tender plants. They cannot take temperatures much below 50°F for any length of time, preferring days and nights between 60°F and 70°F.

As to light requirements, many people think that these succulent-like plants will do well in dark corners. Except for a few cultivars such as 'Nelsonii'—a slow-growing plant with dark green leaves that is specifically listed for room corners with poor light—most need full sun or, at best, partial shade offering diffused sunlight.

Use a soil mix of one-third potting soil, one-third peat moss, and one-third sharp sand, and add to each gallon of the mix, a teaspoon of super-phosphate, a dash of ground limestone, and two teaspoons of 5-10-5. From early spring to late fall, allow the soil to dry between watering. During the same time period, fertilize every three months. In winter, though, remember to use just enough water to keep the leaves from shriveling and never add plant food. Too much water under chilly temperatures with limited winter light spells a quick death for these plants. They do well when potbound so you need not bother repotting more frequently than every three years or so.

Propagate by dividing the plants any time of the year except in a northern winter, or else by leaf cuttings rooted in sand, using bottom heat. Don't use the cutting method for 'Laurentii', however, as the new plants will lose the yellow stripes and revert back to the species.

✤ THE STAPELIADS

An orange sun forms one fiery bubble in a flat and deep blue sky. The only signs of movement on the vast horizon are shimmering waves of heat rising in frantic whorls from the sea of sand that seems to stretch on forever. And it is hot—dry and hot.

At first glance all seems to be lifeless and bare: just the sand and stone enveloped in a deathly stillness. Then, in the shady crook of a large rock I spy a twisted bunch of thick green tapered stems all splotched with purple, and I hear the buzz of a lone fly. Looking again, I see a vivid orange and purple flower. Flower? What kind of flower looks more like tooled and wrinkled leather tattooed with strange colors rather than the jewel-like tones of a normal floral display? And the fly; why the fly? And too, the smell: ever so slight—of spoiled fruit or a bit of meat past its prime.

I watch the fly walk across a petal, crisscrossing the thickened ring standing slightly above and to the center of the pleated petals. Suddenly it disappears over the ring's edge, down into a dark crevasse where it buzzes all the louder, like a bee with honey.

Then the buzzing stops and the fly appears again. But now a bright yellow ball of pollen is stuck to one leg. It shakes the leg, trying to dislodge the added load, thinks better of it, and spirals up and around, descending to another nearby flower. What I've witnessed is the pollination of a blossom by a fly in a meadow of sand. For the desert is too hot and barren for a honeybee and too dry and dusty for the typical flower of the field.

Although the stems of the stapeliads—and stems they are, for the leaves are tiny or minuscule—have never been the hit of the houseplant world, the flowers certainly have. Bizarre, unique, and indelicate, they always elicit a response when displayed at flower shows and generate choruses of oh's and ah's when they accompany me on a lecture.

The genus is named after Johannes Bodaeus van Stapel, an Amsterdam physician who died in 1631. And there are hundreds of species belonging to a number of genera. But the most successful I've grown are the time-honored *Stapelia variegata,* or spotted toad flower; *S. longipes; S. cylista; S. nobilis; S. pasadenensis;* and *Edithcolea grandis. S. pasadenensis* can produce a flower greater than 6 inches in diameter and unlike other flowers, it is best kept outdoors when in bloom, since it can smell a lot like living near a large landfill.

Stapeliads are succulents, so the primary rule of care is to provide adequate drainage. I use a potting mix of one-third standard potting soil, one-third composted manure, and one-third sharp sand, with a liberal sprinkling of small charcoal chips and some bird gravel. I only fertilize every few weeks in the hottest part of the summer.

While most stapeliads will endure temperatures of 40°F, they do not respond favorably to such a chilly atmosphere. And if allowed to sit in even damp soil when the temperature falls that low, they will usually begin to rot. I withhold water from November to March, moving the plants to my study, where temperatures fluctuate between 50°F and 70°F.

Take cuttings off your plants in the late spring when the weather is on the warm side. The cutting is best removed from the joint of a parent stem then set aside for a few days until the cut or break is dry. Use pieces at least an inch long. Then, push cuttings into a dish or pot of warm, moist, clean sand to a depth of ½ to 1 inch. Roots will begin to appear in a few days.

Seeds should be sown when fresh, and any of the commercial "sow and grow" mixes can be used, but place the containers on heating cables. When seedlings appear, provide adequate ventilation and shade from the hot sun. In about three months the seedlings can be moved to 3-inch pots.

The only serious pest I've ever encountered with these plants is the mealybug. To eliminate this beast, use cotton swabs dipped in alcohol, and directly dab the insect's body. For severe infestations, sterilize the soil, washing stems and roots in denatured alcohol for a few minutes, then rinse in warm water before replanting.

⚜ HEAVY METAL GARDENING

It's amazing what you can use for a pot! From a plasterized gardener's shoe (great to hold a Gertrude Jekyll plant) to an old wheelbarrow to the top drawer of an abandoned dresser, there's nothing too good—or too mundane—to hold the right plant.

I've seen pots made of sewing machine parts, brilliantly colored plastic buckets, chipped tea pots, old silver-plate tea-service items, conch shells (well-washed to remove the salt), cake tins, little red wagons, broken baskets, and, yes, discarded rubber tires (but be sure and paint them a great color). Just match the container with the plant.

Obviously, if you're persnickety enough to iron the guest towels, then junk and junked containers are not up your alley—but you'd be amazed at what the careful placement of just one pot of bright orange geraniums looks like when a wire wastebasket becomes their summer home.

I'm not (directly) suggesting that you follow the lead of that great dadaist artist, Marcel Duchamp, who created the concept of "ready-mades"—found objects that merely need an artist's eye to single them out. By removing them from the mundane world, Duchamp, and others, created art. His greatest—and most controversial—find was a porcelain urinal, signed "R. Mutt" and entitled "Fountain" (it was just one step removed from a lavabo, often found on the walls of a monastery). Sometimes it's a good thing to let your imagination loose a bit. Duchamp, you might remember, was the artist who caused a scandal at New York's Armory Show of 1913, with his painting *Nude Descending a Staircase*, described by one critic as a wind blowing through a shingle factory!

✤ DRAINAGE, DRAINAGE, AND DRAINAGE

Whatever the container, you have to let the water run out of the bottom—or if you're creative, the sides. Therefore, you need to drill some drainage holes.

You can use a hammer and an awl to punch holes in various tin cans, but always place the object you're hitting on a solid foundation. Remember, when drilling into any hard material, use the right drill, the right bit, and let the tool do the job, not the brute strength of your mighty arm. Wood is usually fairly easy to drill, and you can use an old-fashioned brace-and-bit for holes. But with heavy, seasoned wood, an electric drill is better. When drilling into concrete, use a carbide-tipped concrete drill bit. For tile, use a glass/tile drill bit, and for ceramics, use a ceramic drill bit.

✤ MELLO'S METAL

There's an imaginary line connecting a garden in western North Carolina and a seaside garden on the English coast of Kent. One end is located in the old warehouse district of Asheville, close to the French Broad River, and the other is on the edge of the Atlantic Ocean, just outside the town of Dungeness, not too far from a very large nuclear power station. The first is the home of artist and gardener Christopher Mello, and the second is the garden and vacation home of film producer Derek Jarman. Both are excellent example's of what I call "heavy metal gardening."

Because it's next to the ocean, Jarman's garden used stone for walkways, but he excelled in adding strange and artful plants— plants that are always at home even when surrounded by sand and stone. To mark the pathways, he used tall pieces of driftwood, often topped with old tools, shards of scrap iron, or odd bits of ceramic found along the way.

Mello's garden, however, is one that only a city could hold: Instead of pathways made with time-worn stones, his paths are made of heavy sheets of metal or circular gears, some complete and some broken, that at one time were either the outer walls of large pieces of machinery or actually their inner workings.

Mello has a philosopher's beard and guarded eyes that look out on a less-than-perfect world. Instead of giving into the general ugliness that surrounds most of our public (and private) environments, however, he has created a new landscape that combines abandoned machine parts with plants perfectly wedded to their new homes.

"I was born a city-boy in West Asheville," said Mello, "but when I was ten, my dad bought some country property and I became a city-boy suddenly lost in the brambles. I remember one sunny afternoon, pushing aside a green curtain and coming upon a marvelous waterfall. That set the stage for my love of nature and the hope of bringing plants from the country to the city. Even today I clearly remember bringing ferns and horsetails back to our house in town."

His artist's eye is especially adept at finding scrap metal that combines a great shape with a time-worn texture, be it an old washing machine rotor, the cracked gear from a tractor, or the transmission from a 1939 Ford. If the piece is rusted enough, Mello chooses it for an eventual pot or sculpture.

"Today, I haunt scrap yards and junk heaps around the Carolinas, preferring those found in smaller towns. Why small towns? Well,

Christopher Mello of Asheville is a genius at melding unusual plants in unusual pots: Here are sedums (Sedum spp.) in an old iron pot.

the stuff moves too fast in the bigger cities, with collected metals quickly going to the smashers. In smaller places, the scrap stays around longer."

As to plants, he prefers succulents in general, and cacti in particular. Yet, any plant that has a primitive quality becomes grist for his particular mill.

"I began with hens-and-chickens, plants so tough they would survive an existence on a bare rock, giving them new ceramic or metal homes. Once I added just a little soil, they grew like wild things!"

He glances at a shallow pot planted with little, individual hens-and-chicks that he has set out in the shape of a slender snake circling about the confines of the pot's edge.

"I love the ancient feeling expressed by horsetails (*Equisetum hyemale*), because they remind me of the landscapes haunted by dinosaurs. In fact, you might say that my garden is a combination of Dr. Seuss and Edward Gorey."

After graduating from Haywood Tech with a degree from their School of Horticulture, Mello worked in the nurseries at the Biltmore Estate, then began arranging flowers for the main house, before finally deciding to go out on his own—although he still does occasional arrangements for the nearby Odyssey School, an institution devoted to the art of clay.

Walking through his garden, visitors find a fountain ruled by a very large, ceramic merman called "King Daddy Neptune." The king has the good fortune of looking out on a carefully jumbled collection of pots made of those incredible pieces of rusted iron, with cam-gears sprouting horsetails or pipe sections serving as a home for a fascinating mix of sedums and sempervivums.

Midway through the garden is a very large waterfall, only instead of being rock, this one is made of iron plates cut from the remains of the water tower that once looked down on this industrial area, back when the railroad was king and the various mills and small manufacturers made their homes along the river

Caring for a Mello creation is about as easy as gardening can be: Just provide plenty of sunlight and keep the pots away from too much rain. He's even been known to cover many parts of his garden with protective tarps if too much rain is expected. It's not hard to find Mello in the artists' district, which recently made its appearance on Asheville's Riverside Drive. There are lofts and studios springing up at every turn. And you'll find colorful artists and colorful plants there, around every corner.

⁂ 13 ⁂

WATER GARDENS

EVER SINCE I BECAME INTERESTED IN GARDENING I longed for water in the backyard. My first dreams were of a large flagstone terrace surrounded on three sides with ivy-covered stone walls: The wall on the left supporting awnings for afternoon shade; the center featuring an antique lavabo, set off on either side by climbing roses; and the right wall delineating an area for dining alfresco. The fourth side would be open to the woods and hills beyond.

In the center of my imaginary terrace is the pool (40 feet square), lined with blue tile, deep enough for a quick swim, and highlighted by a fountain with lead fishes on stone waves, squirting water high in the air. Scattered about would be tables and chairs designed by Edwin Lutyens—Gertrude Jekyll's partner, who created houses to match her gardens—and a number of large terracotta pots housing rare tropical plants.

Never underestimate the power of water in a garden. The sound of it, especially on a torrid day, is hypnotic. Its look, as lazy ripples widen where dazzling dragonflies have quickly trod, enchants the eye.

Needless to say, my dream never became a reality.

When my wife and I lived in upstate New York, however, after many years of planning and then a summer of actual work, we finally put in a pond. A number of uses were to be served: swimming, boating, a home for wildlife, stocking for fish, the aesthetic joy of water, and a home for a number of deepwater and shallow-water plants.

Back in the spring of 1984, when we finished the pond, we were introduced to new water sports and new wildlife. But by July we were still debating over which type of fish to introduce (pond owners get as excited over favorite fish as gardeners do over tomatoes), and we lost most of the water plants (except those in deep water) to our old friends the deer.

Then we moved to a house in Asheville with a garden by a lake. Unfortunately, the lake is too large to grow many water plants so we installed a small pond in one part of the present garden.

Using the PVC sheeting now on the market, your garden can feature a decent-sized pond for a very reasonable price. If you don't have time to properly install such a pool, you need only excavate a small hole and set within it one of the many free-form fiberglass jobs, or for a very small expenditure, fill a wooden or plastic tub with water and grow a cattail and a single exquisite water lily.

⚜ WHERE TO PUT THE POOL

For my garden pool I finally chose a level spot that would be in the sun from late morning on. It was also close to the terrace, so we could sit comfortably and yet be able to watch the water and its reflections. An electrical outlet was also installed nearby in case I wanted to add lights sometime in the future.

Next I consulted the catalogs to see what size of vinyl lining was available. I found that a 10-by-10-foot liner of extra thick (20 mil.) plastic would make a pool just under 6-by-6-feet, about 18 inches deep. One simple rule of thumb for estimating how much liner to buy: Add to your maximum width twice the depth, plus 2 feet, to allow a 1-foot overlap on each side. Do the same for the length. I chose battleship gray for the liner's color, which does not make the brash statement that a turquoise or blue liner would.

To make your pool, first dig a hole 18 inches deep. If you plan on a large pool, use a garden hose to lay out its shape. Also use a line and line-level to make sure your excavation is level; now is the time to be careful. Remove all the rocks, pebbles, or other debris, putting a ½-inch layer of sand on the bottom and working it up the sides to fill any holes left by removed stones. If you have especially rocky soil—as we do—add a layer of .002-inch commercial building polyethylene over the sand, before you lay the liner.

Drape the liner into the hole, placing bricks or stones on its sides to hold it down. Now start filling it with tap water. As the pool fills, occasionally remove the stones, allowing the liner to fit tightly into the hole. After the pool is full, trim the liner to a 6-inch overhang and cover that with a layer of fieldstone slabs. If you want a very formal look, you can lay stone paving on a bed of mortar. If you intend to put fish in the pool, let the water settle for a week before they join the swim. Use a siphon to empty the pool. If you use cement, try to keep it out of the pool—it's deadly to fish.

❧ PLANTING THE WATER GARDEN

Instead of throwing soil directly into the pool, put water lilies and other aquatic plants into individual pots. The mix should consist of three parts of good topsoil—and in this case a heavy clay soil is fine—and one part of well-rotted cow manure. Cover the soil after planting with a 1-inch layer of clean gravel to prevent it from riling up the water, and then saturate the pot and earth before setting it into the pool.

Never plant the tropical lilies in water under 70°F. They will not snap out of dormancy. Individual plants also require a specific water depth but you can easily adjust this by placing the pots on bricks or stones.

Keep tight control over the number of plants! A pool will only hold so much and retain its healthy state. A 6-by 6-foot pool has a surface area of 36 square feet and will hold three or four small to medium water lilies and one or two other water plants, plus those that will grow along the pool's outer edge.

In the North, you can treat tropical lilies as annuals, replacing them every gardening season or bringing them into a greenhouse pool. In the South, where winters are Zone 10 and temperatures rarely fall below 30°F, they can be left out all year.

Store hardy lilies over winter in a cool basement where temperatures hold between 40°F to 50°F. In the fall before a hard freeze, lift the lily pots from the pool, drain well, and store them, leaves and all, by covering with damp peat moss so they will not dry out over the winter. In the spring empty the rhizome from the pot, clean them off, remove any suckers—small, yellow leaves—and repot as you did the year before. Hardy lilies can only be left outside in a pond so deep that the ice line is above the tuber and the pot. Tropical water plants, on the other hand, can be held over in the greenhouse, sun porch, or an unheated garage.

❧ PLANTS FOR A WATER GARDEN

The following plants are meant either for the pool itself or for around its edge. Ground should be damp at all times, and the plants, unless otherwise noted are hardy to Zone 5.

Marsh marigold or cowslip (*Calhan palustris*) blooms in early spring with bright yellow flowers on 1- to 2-foot stems with heart-shaped leaves. They like boggy conditions with plenty of humus and should never dry out. They go dormant in midsummer and can be over-planted with a crop of annual summer forget-me-nots (*Anchusa capensis*) or, if the garden is permanent, biennial forget-me-nots (*Myosotis sylvatica*). Propagate from seed or by division in spring.

Water canna (*Canna* spp. hybrids) is a tropical hybrid of the typical bedding canna meant for planting in water up to 6 inches deep. They are 4-feet high and blossom either in red or yellow with orange spots. They can also grow around the edge of the pond.

Fraser's Sedge (*Cymophyllus fraseri*) is a family of a plant that's often called *Carex fraseri* in old catalogs. It requires damp soil with a good deal of humus and a spot with filtered shade, either from an overhead tree or larger plants in the vicinity. The evergreen, strap-like leaves are usually 12 inches long with white flower spikes on 20-inch stems in early spring. While hardy in Zone 6, it will survive in Zone 5 if given a good winter mulch. Propagate by division in spring but only with mature plants.

The white turtlehead (*Chelone glabra*) is aptly named, for when viewed from the side its flower looks just like a turtle. Blossoms are on 2- to 3-foot stalks and appear in late summer to early fall. Plants like wet feet so they will do well on the edge of the pond or pool (deer relish them). Propagate from seed or by division in spring.

Swamp pink (*Helonias bullata*) is a very rare American flower of great beauty, usually only available from seed. It is another family of one, with tufted evergreen leaves growing 1 foot long. In spring a 2-foot branch will appear, topped with a very dense raceme of fragrant pink flowers. It prefers a swamp or bog and likes wet feet. Propagate from seed or division in spring.

Rose mallows (*Hibiscus moscheutos* subsp. *palustris*) are graced with summer-long 4-inch-wide blossoms of pink or white, resembling tropical hibiscus. They like a wet place in full sun and will reach 7 feet in a good spot. Eventually they'll fill a large area, so allow for a 2- to 3-foot spread. Propagate by seed or division after the shoots emerge in spring.

Red iris (*Iris fulva*) will grow to 2 feet in wet soil that has a water depth of 6 inches. The mid-spring flowering period is short, but the leaves are very attractive all summer long. With winter mulching, they are hardy in Zone 5. Divide in late summer.

Siberian iris (*Iris siberica*) forms huge clumps in damp soil or in water up to 4 inches deep. Purple flowers on 3-foot stems stand above sharply pointed leaves that would be grown in gardens even without flowers. Propagate by dividing the clumps in early fall.

Cardinal flowers (*Lobelia cardinalis*) are among the most beautiful of American flowers. Brilliant red blossoms march up 3-foot stems in late summer. In nature they often grow along the bank of a stream, with some shade in midday from overhanging branches, a winter mulch of leaves, and plenty of water at the roots. If your cli-

A small preformed fiberglass pool is home to a number of wild grasses and sedges (planted in pots). In summer, additional pots of various flowers are added, here a dark-flowered iris (Iris spp.).

mate is colder than Zone 6, be sure to use a winter mulch and don't let plants go into winter with dry soil. Propagate from seed.

Great blue lobelia (*Lobelia siphilitica*) resembles the cardinal flower except that the flowers are not quite as graceful and of a light blue color. These plants are a bit hardier and seed more freely in the garden. The species name refers to the alleged efficacy of blue lobelia in curing syphilis (which it didn't do).

Lotuses (*Nelumbo nucifera*) are grandiose flowers. Their blossoms exude a rich fragrance, standing with the leaves above the water on stout stems. When blooming is over, the seedpods remain. Colors are white, rose, pink, yellow, and red. The American lotus (*N. lutea*) has yellow petals and is only slightly less impressive than its tropical kin. Treat it as a hardy lily. Leaves often grow to 2 feet across and are quite unusual, in that they shed water as if they were the back of a duck.

You must have space for both of these plants. Tubers are placed in a tub 20 inches in diameter or larger and kept with 6 to 12 inches of water above the soil. They must have six hours of sun a day.

Day-blooming water lily (*Nymphaea odorata*) has fragrant white or pink petals and is hardy, with leaves up to 10 inches across. This tuber may be placed in a 6-inch pot for a small pond. Propagate by separating roots in spring when they become crowded.

Hardy water lilies (*Nymphaea* spp.) come in varying sizes that spread from less than 6 square feet to more than 12. Colors are white, pink, yellow, and red, in a bewildering number of cultivars. A few varieties will bloom in partial shade, but all require at least three hours of direct sun every day. The flowers open during the day and close at night. Propagation is by dividing the tubers.

Victoria water lilies (*Victoria amazonica*) were discovered in 1837 in British Guiana. Seeds packed in wet clay and flowers preserved in alcohol were brought back to England in 1846. The first flower appeared in 1849 and was presented to Queen Victoria, who must have loved it. Blossoms measure 16 inches across and have the pleasant smell of sweet pineapple. Petals appear white on their first day, turning to rose early in the second morning, then rapidly changing to red, before finally dying some forty-eight hours later as crimson. Each flower is surrounded in the water by leaves 5 to 6 feet in diameter, with edges turned up and so buoyant from air-filled veins beneath, that they will usually support a child's weight—and have been known to float two hundred pounds.

This water lily is not for the small pond—it can cover an area up to 30 feet across. The species usually grown is *V. Cruziana*, which can take lower water temperatures than the queen's. Roots must be started in 70°F water, and you must make sure all of the water is warm. If any part of the plant hits colder water, it goes into dormancy. I tried it in our pond and never got more than two leaves because of the cold springs along the bottom. Plants cost around $40 but if you have the place for it, the Victoria has a great entertainment value.

❧ WATER IN A TUB

Every season or so used barrels (generally cut in half) are on sale in garden centers and discount stores. Usually measuring about 2 feet across and 17 inches high, they make great little water gardens. I knew that keeping the water pure in these casks might be a problem, but since I had no intention of adding fish, they seemed clean enough. They can also be lined with heavy plastic, carefully stapled to the inside top of the cask. Or a readily available plastic tub, 19-inches in diameter and 9 inches deep could be set inside the barrel after using some concrete blocks to line up the edges.

Some years ago I remembered reading an article in *Flower and Garden* which reported that Joseph Dayton had successfully planted water lilies in two 12-gallon sauerkraut crocks (18 inches wide by 24 inches deep). The lilies were planted in 8-inch clay pots, and they bloomed, each plant bearing four to six flowers. I decided to try it for myself, bought a tub, washed it out carefully, and let it sit in the sun the next few days.

I then ordered one white pygmy water lily, one spike rush, and one dwarf papyrus from a water garden nursery for spring delivery. I kept the number of plants low, acknowledging that with a tub this size it is best to underplant.

Upon arrival in mid-May, the water lily went into an 8-inch plastic pot, the type with many openings on the bottom. The other two plants went into 6-inch clay pots. Either plastic or clay pots can be used. I used three-quarters heavy garden soil and one-quarter composted manure. The soil was topped with a layer of pea gravel to prevent escaping dirt from muddying the water. Each pot was then plunged into a pail of water to completely soak the soil.

After being put in its permanent place on the terrace, the tub was filled to within 4 inches of its top with water from the hose, and was left to sit for a day. The next morning I placed the water lily on the tub bottom. The spike rush and the papyrus were then placed on bricks so that the water level was raised about 5 inches above their dirt when the tub was full. I topped off the water.

The tub sat on the terrace where it received sun most of the day. (You have to add water to a tub garden every week or so to replace any that evaporates.) And the little water garden was a success. The lilies bloomed, the spike rush grew into a healthy fountain of green tipped with brown non-flowering buds, and the dwarf papyrus shot up 2½-foot stems topped with a fan of leaves.

Once autumn arrives and temperatures start to fall, the water garden should be emptied until the following spring. Hardy water lilies will survive outside if the water above them never freezes solid. But in a tub exposed to the elements this will be the natural order of things.

If you wish, the lilies can be kept over the winter in a cool basement (45°F to 50°F). The roots should be stored in moist sand and need not be kept in water. The papyrus can be a happy houseplant if kept warm (62°F to 80°F) in maximum light and moist soil. As to the spike rush, I've never wintered one over.

✢ PLANTS FOR THE TUB GARDEN

There are a number of pygmy water lilies on the market today. They are all cultivars of *Nymphaea pygmaea* so I will just list them by their cultivar names. 'Yellow Pygmy', 'White Pygmy', and 'Joanne Pring' (with 2-inch, dark pink flowers) all need full sun. 'Helvola' has flowers the size of a 50-cent piece and needs at least five hours of sun to bloom.

N. colorata has blossoms colored a wisteria blue and needs three to five hours of sun to bloom. *N. nucifera* 'Momo Botan' is a rose-colored lotus that will live and bloom in a tub with six hours of sun.

All the pygmy water lilies should have 4 to 6 inches of water above the tops of their pots, which should each be of the 8-inch variety.

The following water and bog plants will all do well in 6-inch pots, using the same soil mix as the water lilies.

Water arum (*Calla palustris*) has small white flowers over dark green, spear-like leaves. It needs 6 inches of water and at least six hours of sun.

Dwarf papyrus (*Cyperus haspans*) sends up 2½-foot stems when grown in 6 inches of water. They need full sun.

The water poppy (*Hydrocleys nymphoides*) bears 2-inch, three-petaled yellow flowers just above the water's surface. Its leaves are 3 inches wide. It requires three hours of sun to bloom and 4 to 12 inches of water.

Spike rush (*Eleocharis montevidensis*) bears 2-foot quill-like leaves and needs three hours of sun to succeed.

Water snowflake (*Nymphoides cristatum*) has ¾-inch white flowers and heart-shaped leaves, and needs three hours of full sun to bloom. It requires 4 to 10 inches of water.

Four-leaf water clover (*Marsilea malica*) grows 3-inch leaves like perfect clovers floating on the water. It needs three hours of sun and 4 to 10 inches of water.

Sweet flag (*Acorus calamus*) prefers full sun and needs 6 inches of water to succeed. The leaves have a sweet smell when crushed and are the source of the drug calamus.

Horsetail (*Equisetum hyemale*) is a primitive plant and looks it. The jointed stems will grow up to 3 feet tall, and the plant is happy in full to partial sun in up to 6 inches of water. This plant has a striking, architectural beauty all its own.

Gardener's garters (*Phalaris arundinacea* var. *picta*) has been grown as an ornamental grass for centuries. But few gardeners know that it will also do well in water. Leave 3 inches between the gravel on top of the pot and the water's surface.

Blue flag irises (*Iris versicolor*) will grow to 24 inches high and bear lovely flowers in early summer. It needs full to partial sun and up to 6 inches of water.

❧ BOG GARDENS

Bog plants like water but not to any great depth, preferring constantly moist conditions. Such conditions are easy to maintain when using containers.

Potted bog gardens can range from huge, specimen plants such as the gunneras (*Gunnera manicata*), a rhubarb-like plant from Chile, with leaves up to 3 feet across, to a small pot full of a clump of horsetails (*Equisetum hyemale*).

The only container caveat is that it be watertight. And, if you plan to leave your garden outside during the winter, it must be frost-proof. If you have a favorite container that has a drainage hole, it's easily fixed with a rubber plug cut to size or by gluing a piece of crockery over the hole using one of the silicon-based sealers found at hardware stores.

Wooden tubs are great, but once dry, the boards shrink. To guarantee a waterproof situation, before planting, line the barrel using heavy plastic sheeting or a piece of pond liner (again available from garden centers and purchased by the foot).

Remember to site your bog garden before beginning work— once the pots are full of soil, plants, and water, larger ones will be almost impossible to move.

❧ PREPARING A BOG CONTAINER

Fill your chosen container to three-quarters of its depth with good potting soil or packaged garden soil. If you have some decent compost it never hurts to mix it with your purchased soil.

Set your plants and fill the soil around them, keeping a depth of 2 inches between the soil surface and the pot's top edge. Carefully water until it's moist from top to bottom. For a rich mulch, add a layer of gravel (available in bags at garden centers). This helps to retain the moisture and prevents the soil from drying out.

For plants that like damp feet, but dislike standing water, check the list above. But you can also choose most of the sedges and rushes, including the spiral rush (*Juncus effusus* var. *spiralis*), or the Japanese butter-bur (*Petasites japonicus* var. *giganteus*), and most of the ligularias (*Ligularia* spp.), as well as the cattails.

14

GROWING FRUITS IN
CONTAINERS

O NE OF THE GREAT THINGS ABOUT GARDENING IN
containers is the number of plant types you can actually
grow in your house, on your porch, or in the backyard. If you
think you're limited to just plants covered in previous chapters, however, think again. An amazing number of fruit-producing plant
species thrive in a wide range of containers. The following are just a
few of the many choices on the market today.

ALPINE STRAWBERRIES

It should be no surprise that strawberries belong to the rose family,
especially when one considers the marvelous fragrance of its fruits.
If you've never had the opportunity to wander a sunny field in early
summer and collect ripe wild strawberries, to be eaten with sweet
cream, you've missed one of life's great pleasures.

The Alpine strawberry (*Fragaria vesca* 'Alpine') thrives in good
soil and, when grown in pots (not in strawberry jars, as they do not
produce runners), it's easy to provide the soil they need. And since
in their natural habitat they grow in fields, they really like a bit of
shade rather than full sun, and that's especially important in the
South.

The easiest way to raise these plants is from seed using one of
the new hybrids such as 'Mignonette' or 'Sarian'. Sow the seed in

early spring and once the seedlings can be easily pulled, plant them out in a frost-free environment or in flats for the coldframe or greenhouse. They will bloom and bear fruit that summer.

You can also grow plants that can be potted in the fall, before frost threatens, and bring them indoors to a cool greenhouse, where the pots can go outside the following spring, and you will have fruit by early June.

✤ AVOCADO OR ALLIGATOR PEAR

Amazingly enough, in the Southeast I've never found an avocado plant offered by any nursery that sells fruits and vegetables. The only source is to buy an alligator pear at the local supermarket, eat the fruit for lunch, and keep the pit for germination. The botanical name is *Persea americana*, named after a tree of Ancient Egypt and Persia, but the avocado originally came from Central America. The fruit has high nutritional value.

After lunch, wash a pit in warm water to remove as much of the surrounding skin as possible. You will often find the pit has already split in preparation of producing a root and soon a stem.

Fill a whisky-type glass with tepid water. Dry the pit, and, at about a third of the way up from the base—the larger flat end—force the first of four toothpicks half its length into the pit. Space the toothpicks equally around the circumference. Now put the toothpicked pit on the rim of the glass, letting about a half-inch of water cover the pit's base.

Stow the glass in a warm place, away from direct sunlight, and keep the water level up at all times. Usually within a week or so, a root-tip will begin to emerge from the bottom of the pit. (If the water becomes cloudy and the pit begins to decay, throw it out and begin again).

Soon, the pit splits entirely and a green shoot sprouts with tiny leaves at the tip. Now comes the hard part. In order to check the soon-to-be-rapid growth of the plant, and to ensure plentiful branching, you should cut off the growing tip when the stem reaches a height of 6 inches, leaving about 3 inches of stem when you are finished. Within a week or so, a shoot will appear.

Pot the pit when the glass is full of roots and about two weeks after you have cut back the main stem. The pot should be clay and measure 8 inches across the top. Cover the drainage hole with a shard or stone and fill with a mix of good potting soil, composted manure, peat moss, and sand, one-quarter each. Position the pit so its tip is even with the top of the pot and add soil until only the pit's top-half is exposed.

When the stem reaches a height of 16 inches, add a ⅝-inch wooden dowel to the pot for future support for the developing trunk.

Give your tree as much sun as possible, watering well as soon as the soil begins to dry. Keep temperatures above 50°F and fertilize every three months whenever the tree is in active growth.

When the tree reaches 6 feet (and it will), move it into a bigger pot. The next best home is a wooden redwood tub, the kind with brass stays.

If the humidity is low in your home or apartment, spritz the leaves with a mister, preferably every day during the summer. Leaves often brown around the edges because of a lack of moisture in the air. Watch out for spider mites—they are partial to avocado leaves.

Avocados grown for produce come from specific varieties developed for improved fruit and are usually reproduced by grafting. If grown from a pit, there is no guarantee that your tree will bear decent fruit, or for that matter, even bear fruit at all. It takes about seven years for a tree to flower.

⇥ BANANAS

Bananas are amazing plants. How many fruits have a theme song about not storing them in a refrigerator? And how many fruits have a trunk that isn't a trunk but is, instead, a fruiting stem or pseudostem? Not many.

Those fleshy banana stems are wrapped with huge leaves that can grow up to 25 feet in a year or less. Each pseudostem produces one flower cluster, which results in bananas, then dies. Under the ground, however, the roots and their rhizome will produce new plants the following year.

I have a banana that I grow for its leaves and its statuesque beauty, but you can, with patience, grow fruit. The one banana to select is the Cavendish, or canary, banana (*Musa cavendishii*). It's a dwarf among the bananas, but with 4-foot long leaves and a trunk that can grow to a foot in diameter at the base, it's not a midget either.

To grow this banana in a hothouse you will need a space of at least 8 by 8 feet, with 10-foot headroom. Growing plants need full exposure to sunlight and cannot abide being cold. For your tree to bear fruit you will need 65°F by night and around 80°F during the day. If temperatures are right you should expect your first banana crop in ten to fifteen months.

Bananas send up suckers, and in the beginning only one sucker at a time should be allowed to live and bear fruit. After your first crop, you can let a second sucker grow.

Water well because in hot temperatures those huge leaves lose a great deal of moisture through transpiration. And with all that water, you must also fertilize it at least once a week. And if temperatures fall while fruits are ripening, the flavor will be tarnished.

Flowers appear at the top of the trunk. Its many buds will turn down or reflex up on emerging so that the floral base will be on top. As fruits develop, the flower bud continues to produce male flowers. Since they are useless, however, they should be removed. Each bunch of fruit is made up of several so-called hands, which sport the "fingers," or bananas.

I'll admit that a large Cavendish banana often requires a change of scenery so don't forget the 'Dwarf Cavendish', which only reaches 6 feet but produces tasty 5-inch sweet yellow fruits. And if that's too big, look for the 'Super Dwarf Cavendish' a small plant that tops out at 4 feet but still produces fruit and is at home in an 8-inch container—it's hardy to Zone 8 and above.

There is also a species called the Japanese Fibre Banana (*Musa basjoo*) that's sold as "the world's cold hardiest banana." It is hardy to

-3°F planted in the open ground and, with protective mulching, down to -20°F. From southern Japan, this banana is commonly grown for the fiber in its leaves, rather than its fruit, which is small and seedy, but still edible.

⚜ BLUEBERRIES

Growing blueberries in pots for both decoration and for fruit was not possible until recently. A new blueberry cultivar was developed by hybridizing a native southern species (*Vaccinium darrowi*) with a northern highbush species (*V. corymbosum*). Needing only two hundred to three hundred hours of 45°F temperatures, these new bushes can grow as far south as central Florida and still produce excellent fruit. 'Sunshine Blue' is a dense, rounded, semi-dwarf blueberry growing between 3 and 4 feet high, with silvery leaves that remain evergreen through the winter and bearing pink flowers in the spring. As if that weren't enough, it's self-pollinating (you need only one), is tolerant to a higher pH than the average blueberry (which dotes on acidic soil), and bears dime-sized, dark-blue berries that have a great flavor. It only needs one hundred and fifty hours of chilling and is still hardy as far north as Chicago (below Zone 5, however, container plants must be protected by trenching or kept in a warmer environment). Provide a good, humusy soil, and remember blueberries need moist, but not wet, soil. Finally, remember when pruning that berries are produced on the previous year's wood, so too much cutting will mean no fruit for the coming season.

⚜ COFFEE PLANT

You won't be able to one-up Juan Valdez by having your own coffee tree, but it certainly will be a great conversation piece at dinner parties.

There are some sixty species of coffee but the one usually grown for the coffee bean is *Coffea arabica*. Originating in the province of Kaffa in Ethiopia (hence its name), the first Arab record of coffee dates from the fifteenth century. After a long and often romantic history (not to mention skullduggery of the highest order) coffee is now one of the world's most popular beverages.

Unless you live in an area without winter freezes, your coffee tree will spend half the year outside and the other half in a safe place where the temperature stays above freezing, which is fine, because most coffee trees top out at 5 or 6 feet when grown in pots. Although coffee plants are more resistant to frost than many other tropicals, the cold prevents new shoots from developing and slows everything down.

Ideal temperatures are between 65°F and 70°F and, as the TV commercials tell us, coffee plants are more tolerant of a cool summer than high temperatures.

The best soil mix consists of a good garden loam, peat moss, and sand, one-third each. Coffee plants want an evenly moist soil, not wet or boggy, so it's suggested that you water from below.

Its fragrant white waxy flowers open in spring and summer against a backdrop of shiny green leaves. Upon maturing, they produce red, pulpy berries that house the coffee bean within.

✑ A FEW GOURDS

A tunnel of gourds can be made in the backyard or on the terrace by constructing a framework of white bendable plumber's plastic piping or by purchasing a portable trellis strung with plastic netting. Various gourds can be grown in pots, and by midsummer the tunnel is a cool, green place to sip a glass of good wine, protected from the summer sun above.

The soil should be housed in 10-inch (or larger) plastic pots and should consist of good potting or landscape soil mixed with one-third composted cow or sheep manure. Water well and fertilize once a month while the gourds are in active growth.

The wax gourd (*Benincasa hispida*) is a native of tropical Asia, named after Count Benincasa, an Italian botanist who died in 1596. Its vines are strong, with 6-inch rounded leaves that reach 10 to 12 feet in length. Its 3-inch flowers are yellow, and its cylindrical fruits are about 10 inches long and about 2 inches wide. They are whitish with a waxy covering, which gives the plant its common name.

Queen Anne's pocket melon (*Cucumis melo*) is a smaller vine growing no larger than 6 feet and bearing smaller fruit. Its flowers are yellow and about ¾-inch wide, and its rounded leaves are 3. inches wide. The oval fruits are green at first but turn to yellow stripes on a brown background when ripe. The best reason to grow this vine is the sweet perfume of its ripened fruit. It's said that Good Queen Anne would carry this melon in her reticule as she walked the palace, inhaling its fragrance now and then to be revived from odors permeating the halls.

The fig-leaf, or Malabar, gourd (*Cucurbita ficifolia*) is a giant among vines. Here is an ornamental to be used only for screening an entire barn from view. Its large leaves (*ficifolia* means fig-leafed) look like their namesakes, at a healthy 9 inches wide. Liberty Hyde Bailey in his book *The Garden of Gourds* called the fig-leaf gourd the most vigorous species he ever grew. Measuring the length of the main stem and branches of one plant, it totaled 825 feet—and this in Ithaca, New York.

Its fruits are almost round, about 6 inches in diameter and beautifully marked with streaks of white on a dark green background.

The bottle gourds, bushel basket gourds, and powder horn or penguin gourds are all variations within one species (*Lagenaria siceraria*). Their nocturnal flowers are large, sometimes measuring up to 5 inches across, with white paper-thin sweet-smelling petals. Vines can reach up to 25 feet in a good growing season, and leaves can measure a foot across. I've grown a powder horn of a light, pastel green that hangs 15 inches off the vine twining the tunnel overhead.

Summer squash (*Cucurbita pepo* 'Zucchini'), the hybrid zucchini, grows beautifully in a 14-inch pot. After forty-five days the cultivar 'Gold Rush' will produce hordes of bright yellow fruits (they are especially delicious served raw and cut up for salads). Plant three seeds in a 3-inch peat pot. Remove two and set the strongest plant in a large pot. Use a good commercial potting soil and add about a quarter-weight of sharp sand. Don't forget plenty of water, especially when summer temperatures climb. Apply a liquid fertilizer every ten days or so, when the plant is bearing fruit.

⚜ MANGO

Almost everyone has grown an avocado in his or her day, but have you ever thought of starting a mango tree? With today's supersonic delivery systems, fresh mangoes are often found at the local supermarket, right between the pomegranates and the kumquats—and you can always ask someone from Florida to send a pit up north.

Being a vegetarian, my wife is one of those determined people who are always on the lookout for new fruits to bring to the table. A few years ago the local co-op was featuring some ripe mangoes and Jean bought five to use in desserts. They were about 6 inches long with a reddish skin speckled with black, and had sweet and juicy light orange flesh and a large flat seed.

The seeds wound up in the compost heap. That should have been that, especially since it was January, and even in western North Carolina, nights were cold. So it was with great surprise that I saw a green shoot rising from a bed of kitchen scraps a few weeks later. Upon investigation I found it to be a mango seedling, its germination prompted by the internal heat of the compost heap.

Mangifera indica (from *mango*, the Hindu name for the fruit, and *fero*, to bear) is believed to have first appeared somewhere in eastern Asia, where it's been under cultivation for more than 4,000 years. Somewhere between 632 A.D. and 640 A.D., the Chinese traveler Wen T'sang brought the tree to the outside world; by the 1700s, mangoes were grown under glass by most of the nobility of Europe. In 1850, *Curtis's Botanical Magazine* described one English nobleman's attempt to cultivate the fruit:

> The mango is recorded as having been grown in the hothouses of this country at least 160 years ago but it is only within the last 20 years that it has come to the notice as a fruit capable of being brought to perfection in England. The first and we believe the most successful attempt was made by the Earl of Powis in his garden at

Walcot where he had a lofty hothouse 400 feet long and between 30
and 40 feet wide constructed for the cultivation of the mango.

Obviously our local mangoes—at least in the colder areas of the
country—will not be grown for fruit but merely as a fascinating
houseplant. The seeds (or pits) are rather perishable and will not tolerate much drying. Kept at temperatures below 50°F, they do not
germinate well, so don't attempt it if the fruit has been refrigerated
for long periods of time.

But if you do try to grow a mango, wash the pit well of pulp, and
plant it no more than 1-inch deep in sterile potting soil or any commercial grow-mix medium. Store the pit in a warm place (the
warmer the better), trying to maintain at least 70°F. (That first plant
germinated in the heat of a compost heap, where temperatures in
excess of 120°F are common.)

When seedlings are 6 inches tall, transplant to a 6-inch pot,
using a mix of good potting soil, composted manure, and clean
sand, one-third each.

During the summer months, provide plenty of water, but let the
soil dry out between waterings from September to March. In about
three years from germination, you can force the tree to blossom by
following the same watering schedule. A dry atmosphere with plenty
of sunlight is the key to flowering. Fertilize every month during the
summer. Provide as much sun as possible and always keep the mango
warm with temperatures above 50°F.

As the tree grows, pot on to larger containers. You will find that
the mango is more attractive in form than the avocado, and its leaves
do not brown as easily.

❧ THE MONSTERA OR SWISS CHEESE PLANT

Every year TV shows dedicated to decorating (not to mention slick
magazines), tell us to throw out the old and bring in the new.
According to these purveyors of fashion, many once-popular horticultural trends are now as passé as snoods for women, swim-tops

for men, and iceberg lettuce in salads (although this last pronounce-ment has never reached the chefs at many of America's fast-food joints).

During the 1950s, every home attempting a stab at style had an orange, yellow, or red fiberglass tub with a rounded bottom, held aloft by a polished brass ring set with polished brass legs, which con-tained a monstera (*Monstera deliciosa*), trained to climb up a cedar slab or a wooden fence post. (Other common names include hurri-cane plant, Mexican breadfruit, and the fruit-salad plant).

In the tropics these plants climb to the very tops of trees, mak-ing a gigantic tapestry of overlapping leaves, with each leaf exhibit-ing large holes and deeply lobed cutouts (supposedly to protect the leaves from complete destruction by hurricane-force winds).

Flowers resemble pale Jack-in-the-pulpits, with a greenish yel-low spadix marked like a honeycomb and enclosed in a waxy white spathe. Over a period of some fourteen months, the spadix grows to the size of an ear of corn, turns yellow, and loses the scales covering its surface, winding up as a fruit with a pineapple-banana odor and a sweet taste.

Use a compost of one-quarter each peat, leaf mould, clean gar-den loam, and sand. Water freely during the summer, and keep at a temperature of 55°F to 65°F, under partial shade or filtered sun dur-ing summer months.

⚜ THE TREE TOMATO

This particular plant has the same questionable cachet of many oth-ers appearing in the pages of the *National Enquirer* or similar tabloids found in the checkout lanes of the local supermarket. You know the kind I mean: papers that blare headlines like: "Grandmother Lives in Basement for Three Weeks on Tiny Fungus!" or "Gardener Grows Potatoes and Tomatoes on the Same Plant!" or "I Was an Earwig for the FBI!" For the tree tomato has often appeared in advertising that never shows the plant's photograph, but only a rather crudely colored drawing of a giant tree festooned with bright red fruit that completely dwarfs the people standing beneath its branches. A caption announces the amazing news that this plant can feed a family of four all winter long with its delectable harvests.

Cyphomandra betacea, or the tree tomato (*Cyphomandra* is from the Greek for "humped man" and refers to shape of its anthers), belongs to the same family as the garden-variety tomato and the potato. It's a soft-wooded bush that grows to a height of 10 to 12 feet in the wild, but it's considerably smaller in the confines of the home. A fast-growing plant, it's been cultivated for centuries in Central and South America for its edible fruit. Outside of botanical gardens and a few knowledgeable growers in this country, however, cyphomandras are relatively unknown. James Tweedie (1775–1862), a botanist who trekked through Argentina up to Peru, introduced it to the world—and he also discovered pampas grass (*Cortaderia selloana*) and the original ancestor of the bedding petunia, *Petunia violacea.*

Either start your tomato tree from seed or purchase a small specimen from a plant supplier. It will need a good soil, well laced with organic matter or composted manure, and should be repotted annually until it is at home in a large pot or wooden tub. I use potting soil, peat moss, and composted manure, one-third each, and fertilize over the summer months every three weeks. If it gets too rangy, prune it in April or May.

Its fragrant flowers are purple and green, appearing in the spring, although in the right conditions, it will flower most of the year. Flowers are followed by orange-red egg-shaped fruits, about 3 inches long and rich in pectin, with light orange pulp and black seeds. Until mature they taste decidedly flat, and ripe fruit—although it can be eaten raw—is best used in jams and preserves, or for stewing.

Water well most of the year, holding back only in mid-winter months when light levels are low. Give tree tomatoes plenty of sunlight and keep the temperature above 50°F—although plants will survive an occasional dip to just above freezing without enjoying it.

Plants do better in low humidity, so watch out for spider mites because they find the leaves a delightful place to dine.

﹡ 15 ﹡

BULBS AND OTHER
TUBEROUS PLANTS

OR YEARS I GAVE AN ILLUSTRATED LECTURE ON
bulbs and never noticed the audience's mystification when I
compared a bulb to a portmanteau, a comparison I made
because both carry supplies: for the bulb: leaves, roots, and flowers;
for the traveler: clothing, toiletries, and shoes. I've changed "portmanteau" to "suitcase" but somehow the new comparison lacks that
touch of class.

Still, a bulb is basically a storage container. It's an underground
stem wrapped in a series of leaves that look like scales, forming a
rounded shape that, if cut lengthwise, shows embryonic leaves, a
stem, and a flower—all ready to bloom when the right time comes
around. Lilies, daffodils, and onions are all bulbs. Today most nurseries include corms, tubers, and rhizomes in the bulb group.
Structurally different than bulbs, they still contain everything needed
to keep the plant growing during the early weeks of development.

Corms are a series of underground stems wrapped in a round
or pear-shaped package, usually flat on both top and bottom.
Crocuses and gladiolus are examples of corms. Tubers, which are
modified underground stems, are swollen with stored food.
Daylilies, dahlias, tuberous begonias, and potatoes are all tubers.
Rhizomes, also underground storage systems, are horizontal perennial stems that bear roots and upright stems. Calla lilies and iris
grow from rhizomes.

The marvelous thing about bulbous plants is their ability to carry an initial food supply. If you buy top-quality plants from reliable sources, they will usually all bloom the first year (what happens the second season, however, depends on the gardener). Bulbs are very easy to plant. You can carry an entire garden in a paper bag while you mull over your pot collection. When dormant, they are far easier to move than most garden plants. And they are easy to propagate—the majority, from tulips to daffodils to lilies, readily adapt to pot culture.

✳ BULB CULTURE

There are two major requirements for growing bulbs. The first is good drainage, since most bulbs will not tolerate wet soil. The second is friable soil. Hard, dense soil can actually cause bulbs to pop right out of the ground, propelled by their strong root systems. If you have heavy, clay soil be sure to incorporate plenty of organic matter when planting bulbs.

Most bulbs are dormant part of the year. Their leaves turn yellow, dry up, and finally disappear. To cover any bare spots left in the garden by dormant bulbs, bring in geraniums as bedding annuals.

Just as a small percentage of the commercial world is greedy, there are greedy souls in the world of gardening. Instead of propagating new plants in nurseries, unscrupulous collectors go out into the wild, dig up native bulbs, and then sell them to unsuspecting gardeners. Too many bulbs are now rare or have disappeared entirely from their natural habitat. Prevent further loss by purchasing only nursery-propagated bulbs. Look for a notice in catalogs or on garden center packaging.

✳ FAVORITE BULBS FOR THE GARDEN

Use bulbs as you would perennial plants, choosing between containers or just sticking them in the border wherever color, texture, or form would be welcome. Once planted, some bulbs are permanent fixtures; others are tender. They will not survive a freeze and must be dug up in the fall or have their pots moved to the potting shed or greenhouse during winter. Over the years I have developed some favorites, and their descriptions follow. It is an idiosyncratic selection. Unless noted, these bulbs are hardy in Zone 4.

Peacock orchids (*Acidanthera bicolor*) once belonged to the *Acidanthera* genus, but the name recently changed to *Gladiolus callianthus*. Whatever the name, though, they are close relatives of the glads but infinitely more attractive. Their star-shaped flowers are creamy white with a dark maroon center and are pollinated at night by moths attracted to their sweet fragrance. They stand about 2 feet high and, north of Zone 7, you can jump-start their season by planting each corm in a 3-inch peat pot. I put a large grouping of peacock orchids in the middle of a blue porcelain pot surrounded by geraniums and variegated ivies that drip off the pot's edge.

Lily-of-the-Nile (*Agapanthus africanus*) has attractive strap-like leaves rising from thick rhizomes. They are really great plants for decorative pots, and I've had the same pot full of these beauties for four years. Its flowers are blue or white and bloom for at least a month or longer with dozens of individual flowers making a globular cluster on a long, straight stem. 'Peter Pan' is a dwarf cultivar with sky-blue flowers, which rarely tops 16 inches. Leave these plants outdoors only where the ground never freezes.

Stars-of-Persia (*Allium christophii*) produce 8-inch, round balls of many small metallic-pink star-shaped flowers with green centers. Its dried seed heads are attractive, but the wide leaves look very untidy after the plants bloom, so place the bulbs behind other flowers. *A. karataviense* has no common name but does have beautiful strap-like leaves that enfold burgeoning balls of starry, greenish white flowers. These bulbs do well when forced in a pot for late winter blooming.

Italian arum (*Arum italicum*) is a tuberous plant that produces unusual flowers resembling ghostly Jack-in-the-pulpits, hidden behind arrowhead-shaped leaves. By late summer, both its flowers and leaves are gone, but in the fall, 1-foot-high stalks are topped with

The walled edge of a small garden is great for a pot of bulbs, here the lily-of-the-Nile (Agapanthus *spp.*), *with a host of variegated Solomon's-seal* (Polygonatum *spp.*) *blooming below.*

lipstick-red berries. Then, in late fall or early spring—depending on your climate—the new leaves appear. This elegant plant looks great in front of a stone wall. Cultivars include 'Pictum', with dark green leaves marbled with veins of a light yellow-green. In the South, Italian arum needs partial shade.

Caladium x *hortulanum* is the botanical name for the fancy-leaved caladiums. These tropical tubers are grown for their colorful leaves, which range from white veined with green to pink edged with red to endless combinations of maroon, silver, fuchsia, and creamy to dead white. The flowers are interesting but resemble unattractive relatives of the Jack-in-the-pulpit. Plant heights vary from 9 inches to 2 feet and they make great edgings or are wonderful when massed in floral beds. Before planting, make sure the soil temperature is 70°F. The larger the tuber, the greater number of leaves you will have. Caladiums need partial shade up North and deeper shade in the South. I've lined our stone pathways and steps with the brighter colors—they guide us through our garden at night.

Autumn crocus (*Colchicum* spp.) are cormous herbs that belong to the lily family. They're marketed in a number of lavender or mauve variations, but the one I like best is *Colchicum* 'Waterlily'. This hybrid was registered before 1927, and in my opinion, nothing better has appeared on the market since. The mauve-colored double blossoms, which appear in early October, look much like the blossoms of showy aquatic plants. Its none-too-attractive leaves show up in spring. The plants naturalize well and should be planted in large groups. For pots it's best to set them in containers while they are dormant for blooming in the fall, then plant the corms out in the garden so the leaves can appear in spring and build up strength. Then the cycle can begin again. Or, even if the bare corms are placed in a sunny window, without soil or moisture, they will bloom within a few weeks.

The crinum or spider lilies (*Crinum* spp.) are spectacular members of the amaryllis family. *C.* x *powellii* 'Album' is one of the best and is hardy in Zone 6. The bulbs are very large—often more than 4 inches wide—and produce long, medium green strap-like leaves followed in summer by 3-foot-tall stalks topped with trumpet-shaped blossoms. They have a very sweet fragrance especially at night. Plant the bulbs at least 9 inches deep so only the tops of the necks are exposed. These plants like lots of sun, even in the South. They do beautifully in pots but remember to let roots get crowded before you repot.

Crocosmia spp. are corms that produce many blooms on arching 2- to 4-foot stems that appear in mid- to late summer when days are really warm. They are hardy in Zone 7 if planted in a sheltered spot; we have a large batch against the west wall of our house. The best is *C.* 'Lucifer', well named for its brilliant red flowers. In colder areas, dig up the corms after frost browns the leaves and store them in a bag of peat moss at 50°F.

Crocus includes dozens of species and cultivars, all easy to plant and dependable bloomers. My favorites for welcoming spring are *C. chrysanthus* 'Princess Beatrix', a clear lobelia blue with a golden yellow base, and *C. sieberi* 'Firefly', bearing flowers that open with rich lilac petals, each with a yellow base. Both bloom as the snows recede.

The saffron crocus (*Crocus sativus*) is a true autumn-blooming crocus. They bloom in late fall and are followed by grass-like leaves that last well into the winter. Corms require a moist, rich soil that does not dry in summer and is laced with well-rotted manure. Plant at least 5 to 7 inches deep; replant every three or four years. In my experience, saffron crocuses are not reliably hardy north of Zone 6. The bright orange flower stigmas of these flowers are used in a number of medical treatments and are also gathered and dried for an aromatic food coloring.

The cyclamen (*Cyclamen persicum*), or, as it's sometimes called, the desert cyclamen or Persian Violet, has been a beloved pot plant since before the time of Queen Victoria. Beginning in the late nineteenth century hybridizers began working with this species and changed their dainty, sweetly scented reflexed flowers of white flushed with pink into the large, blousy blossoms traditionally given to Mom on Mother's Day. Two of the best species are *C. coum* and *C. hederifolium* (also known as *C. neapolitanum*). The first plant blooms in late fall and early winter, when purple-magenta flowers appear on 3-inch stems held atop shiny green leaves. The second plant bears pink flowers in late summer and continues blooming into autumn; the lovely green leaves are marbled with silver. Both cyclamens need well-drained soil rich in organic matter and a place in the shade. Because both species are hardy only to Zone 6, I grow all my cyclamen in pots. Unlike other tuberous plants, cyclamens grow larger every year, producing ever greater numbers of flowers.

Winter aconite (*Eranthis hyemalis*) pushes its buttercup blossoms up through the snow to face the cold air of very early spring. Each 1-inch-wide flower has six waxy yellow sepals (the petals have evolved into nectar-secreting areas within the flower) and bunches will bloom on 4-inch stems, carpeting an area with gold. These bulbs need full sun, but can be planted under deciduous trees, since the foliage fades away by early summer. The tubers are usually shipped in early fall and will be especially florific if soaked in tepid water for twenty-four hours before planting. Winter aconites can be moved or divided even when they are in full bloom and that's the time to put them in pots for a delightful spring display. If happy outside, they naturalize with ease.

The guinea-hen flower (*Fritillaria meleagris*) produces bell-shaped blossoms drooping on delicate stems. Its petals bear checker-board patterns ('Artemis' sports a square pattern of purple and green; and 'Poseidon' has gleaming white petals marked with purple checks). Their exotic appeal is outdone only by *F. michailovskyi*, a new species that has bell-shaped blossoms of burnished mahogany tipped with gold.

Snowdrops (*Galanthus* spp.) bloom a bit earlier than crocuses but produce blossoms for weeks. Like aconites, they require a shady spot with good woodsy well-drained soil. Blooming plants can actually be dug up and put into pots. When their bloom is over, set them outside once again. Plant new bulbs in the fall, but when time-honored plants become crowded, dig them up and divide them in the late winter or early spring. This procedure does not harm snowdrops at all. Roots form in August, however, so digging them up at that time can be fatal.

There are many snowdrop cultivars, including 'Flore Pleno', which has more and larger flowers than the species, and 'S. Arnott', a new snowdrop on the scene that reaches a height of 10 inches. All of the species except *G. nivens* are sometimes harvested in the wild, so be sure you know your supplier.

Galtonia candicans, or the summer hyacinth, struggled in our northern garden but has done beautifully in North Carolina. If you garden in Zone 6, be sure to include this plant in your summer border. Forty-inch stems bear twenty to thirty fragrant, bell-shaped flowers of white, with a touch of green at the base. The flowers look like spring hyacinths but are, to my mind, far more attractive. If snow cover is scarce in your area, and you don't have the time to mulch heavily, plant the bulbs in open-mesh bags and dig them up for storage over the winter.

The daylilies (*Hemerocallis* spp.) have long been popular warhorses of the garden, more than 7,000 cultivars have been created since the late 1800s. And some 3,000 cultivars are still available today—with new varieties appearing every year. These perennial tubers bear clumps of narrow, sword-shaped leaves that are often evergreen where winters are warm. The stout floral stalks bear six-petaled, lily-like flowers in all colors except pure white or blue. Depending on the type, daylilies bloom any time from late spring to autumn.

H. fulva, the common tawny daylily, came to Europe from Asia in the Middle Ages. Self-sterile, they're known today as the cultivar 'Europa'. All of the daylilies that line the back roads of America are descendants of *H. fulva*; they were not spread by seed but by roots (or pieces of them) pushed about by plows and bulldozers—or just thrown out with the rest of the garden trash.

Daylilies are virtually carefree. They can hold dry, rocky banks together or grow with perfect ease in moist soil by a lake or stream. They have no major problems with disease, harbor few—if any—insect pests, and are reliably hardy throughout the country. Plants may be left in one place for many years, but once blooming declines and plants become overgrown, it's time to divide. You can transplant

Daylily cultivars (Hemerocallis *spp.*) *number in the thousands with a fantastic range of colors.*

whenever you like, but the best time is in early spring before growth hits its stride.

To plant daylilies, dig a hole, making a small mound of dirt at the bottom; spread the tuberous roots around the mound. Although tough, daylilies respond to this treatment and settle in to be prolific bloomers.

Daylilies are well suited for beds, borders, and rock gardens, as well as edging walkways and carpeting slopes where other plants rarely succeed. There are literally hundreds of new introductions of daylily cultivars every year. Check the source lists for nurseries that specialize in these flowers.

H. citrina blooms in summer and bears arching 40-inch leaves and fragrant, yellow blossoms on 4-foot stems that open in the early evening and through noon of the following day. *H. fulva*, mentioned above, is too rough for today's formal gardens. *H. lilioasphodelus*, or lemon lily, has fragrant blossoms that appear in late May and early June. A dwarf species, *H. minor*, has yellow fragrant flowers and grass-like leaves that reach a height of 18 inches.

For pots and for small gardens no cultivar is as fine as 'Stella d'Oro', with 2-foot-long leaves and golden yellow flowers that bloom throughout the season. There are also many new miniature daylilies that usually stop at 2 feet and bloom for six weeks in the North and twelve weeks in the South. Look for 'Mayan Gold', whose golden yellow flowers sport a green throat, and 'Pardon Me', which has bright red flowers.

And for pots, remember the beauty of 'Happy Returns', a reblooming plant with sweetly fragrant flowers of a clear yellow. Or look for 'Black Eyed Stella', with 3¾-inch blossoms on 20-inch stems that bloom throughout the summer months.

Too fleeting in bloom for most container gardens (although if you don't mind the work of repotting, they look great for a few weeks), the tall bearded iris (*Iris* x *germanica*) is the iris most people think of when they hear the genus name. Its fan-like leaves are gray-green, and its flowers come in a multitude of color combinations. It's hardy to Zone 4, and some varieties bloom in both the spring and fall. The tall irises are more than 2 feet high; intermediates are between 16 and 27 inches; standards are between 8 and 16 inches; and miniatures are smaller than 8 inches. Perhaps the best introduction to the seemingly unlimited colors available is to order a mix from a nursery special offer.

The autumn snowdrop (*Leucojum autumnale*) is one of the few flowers to appear in the fall, so this is a favorite. Louise Beebe Wilder called it a "rare, little autumn-flowering bulbous plant [from] Portugal, Morocco, and the Ionian Isles." Be sure to plant them—in groups of at least a dozen—in front of a low rock wall or a sunny border. Otherwise, the nodding white flowers, so characteristic of the snowdrops, will be lost to view.

Muscari botryoides, or grape hyacinth, looks like a bunch of grapes hanging upside down. It blooms in mid-spring and comes in bright blue, pale blue, or white. *M. comosum* 'Plumosum', or feather hyacinth, was introduced from the Mediterranean in 1612. The name derives from its petals, which are fringed as though cut with a tiny scissors.

The genus *Narcissus* includes daffodils, narcissuses, and jonquils. Daffodils have flowers with wide trumpets (or cups), narcissus flowers have short trumpets, and jonquils have the shortest trumpets and the sweetest scent. There is a multitude of *Narcissus* species and cultivars, ranging from dainty (for example, the captivating *N. triandrus* 'Hawera') to very large (*N.* 'King Alfred', for instance). The time of bloom is very important: some bloom in early April and at the month's end; others are still pushing up flowers well into mid-May.

Tulipa includes far more beautiful and unusual flowers than most gardeners would believe. There are always the familiar tulips, with brightly colored, waxy petals found in parks and formal gardens, but those bulbs must be replanted every year or so and are a great deal of effort for so small a return. Wild or species tulips, however, multiply and naturalize on their own. These diminutive relatives are at home in the rock garden, as edging for a small formal garden, or even planted between paving stones. They require full sun (partial sun in the South), good soil that is laced with organic matter, and perfect drainage.

Among the species you should try is *Tulipa eichleri*, with showy lipstick-red petals and bright yellow centers, or *T. vvendenskyi* 'Tangerine Beauty' whose petals are an even more brilliant scarlet-red—and the leaves are not only rippled at the edges but also bear maroon adornments. For a beauty smaller than 4 inches, try *T. pulchella* 'Persian Pearl'. Its delicate petals are magenta-rose with a greenish tint; inside they are cyclamen-purple, dashed with buttercup-yellow at the base.

T. tarda is a 4-inch-high wild tulip from central Asia. It bears white-petaled flowers with hints of bronzed green above a yellow base. Its bulbs need a hot, dry place during the summer months in order to bloom well the following spring. This is one species of tulip that should be in every alpine garden.

Zephyranthes candida is commonly called the swamp lily of La Plata, or the zephyr lily. The first name is derived from a South American region; the second refers to the west wind (the bulbs were discovered in the New World). This perennial bulbous plant has 10-inch rush-like leaves surrounding lovely, pure white star-like flowers that open in late August and continue to bloom until October. Zephyr lilies require a fairly rich soil, with plenty of organic matter mixed in. During the summer months, give them plenty of water.

Z. drummondii and *Z. pedunculata* are perfectly made for the evening garden, since they both bloom in the cool night air. The first bears white lily-like blossoms on foot-high stems. The second has 3-inch-long pink flowers on 5-inch scapes. Both species have a sweet fragrance.

LILIES IN POTS

One of the most elegant additions to a small garden is a large pot overflowing with blooming lilies; few perennials take to pot culture with the ease of these magnificent flowers. Once in containers, they can be moved around the terrace or garden, bringing glorious color

The perfect backdrop for jewel-toned lilies, Abeliophyllum distichum *produces lovely white, sweet-smelling flowers before the leaves appear.*

to hitherto dark corners. Later, when the flowers fade, you can move the containers to a less conspicuous spot.

In every garden, we've always included *Abeliophyllum distichum.* A member of the olive family, it is called the white forsythia because its white four-petaled, honey-sweet flowers resemble those of the forsythia. After its early spring bloom is through, the layered foliage of this bush provides a dark green background for a series of jewel-toned lilies.

In amongst the thicket I always plant a number of Japanese gold-banded lilies (*L. auratum*). In late summer, their tall, arching stems bear dozens of pure white fragrant flowers, each banded with gold that radiates from the flower's center. Stamens drenched with rich chocolate-red pollen set off every petal. 'Platyphyllum' has 10-inch flowers with waxy white petals dotted with crimson specks as though a toothbrush loaded with pigment has been splashed across each golden band. 'Opala' bears pure white flowers.

But before the heat of late summer arrives, I also place pots of lilies at the base of the bush. For bloom in June and July, I include Asiatic lilies, offered in a wide range of bright colors, including maroon, yellow, orange, deep pink, and white, plus pastels such as cream, pale peach, coral, and light pink. Some nurseries feature nat-uralizing mixes; try planting some directly in the garden and the rest in pots. Especially attractive, *L.* 'Admiration', has creamy white blossoms with maroon spots on 20-inch stems. It's splendid on a moonlit night.

L. canadense, an American native, is also lovely in containers. Commonly called Canada lily, it bears orange-yellow to red flowers in late June.

In July and August, both the early orientals and the Aurelian hybrids bloom. Jan de Graaff, one of the greatest lily hybridizers of all time, created the Aurelian strain, including the spectacular 'Moonlight Strain' and 'Golden Splendor'.

'Casa Blanca', an oriental lily, blooms in early August and fea-tures fragrant 10-inch flowers with pure white petals and burnt red anthers. They blossom atop 5-foot stems. Another oriental lily,

'Strawberry Shortcake', bears 6-inch, sweetly fragrant flowers the shade of ripe strawberries edged with cream. Only 24 inches high, this dwarf hybrid is perfect for pots. 'Little Pink' is another short variety, perfect for edging the border or in pots.

Lilies that bloom in August and September include the various hybrids of *L. auratum* and the magnificent *L. formosanum*. This second species bears 6-inch-long, sweetly fragrant white blossoms atop 4- to 6-foot-tall stems. It hails from Taiwan, yet is hardy in this country as far north as Zone 5, if protected with mulch. Because it blooms so late, it requires special protection in the North from early frost. In addition, this species is susceptible to a virus infection called lily mosaic, so do not plant it with other lilies. 'Little Snow White' is a cultivar with large solitary, paired, or multiple flowers on 9-inch stems. If grown from seed sown in September, this lily will bloom the following summer. It is especially well suited for pots.

In general, buy or order your lily bulbs as early in the spring as possible. If they arrive and you aren't prepared, store them in a cool place, such as the refrigerator. In spring, our refrigerator often has seed packets in the butter compartment, seed flats in the freezer, and bulbs in the crisper.

I use straight-edged black plastic pots for lily bulbs. When the buds have developed to the point of showing color, I remove the pots from the bed and place them in decorative containers.

Use large pots that are at least 15 inches deep and wide enough to hold about a cubic foot of soil. The bulbs must be planted deeply, since many lily stems bear roots above the level of the bulb. Also, lilies need a good deal of soil, since they are heavy feeders.

Although many garden writers claim that soil drains perfectly when there is nothing in the bottom of the pot except a small hole, I've found healthier root growth if, when potting up, you pack at least an inch of pebbles or broken pottery in the bottom. Use a mix of good potting soil, sand, and composted manure or shredded leaves, and add a dash of lime.

Put about 2 inches of soil mix in the bottom of the pot, then set the bulb (or bulbs) in place—for small bulbs use a 3- to an 8-inch pot, and then fill the pots to within a half-inch of the top. Gently firm the soil.

Water well and place the pots directly in the soil of a protected nursery bed. They will need at least six, but preferably eight, hours of sunlight a day. Water well and feed with liquid fertilizer once a month.

After the bulbs have stopped blooming, move the pots back to the nursery bed to allow the foliage to ripen. Either plant the bulbs out in the garden or store them in a deep cold frame or another cold, protected place for the winter.

For a special touch, plant some crocus bulbs around the edges of the lily pots. The early season blossoms will provide welcome color before the lilies appear.

✢ FORCING BULBS FOR OFF-SEASON BLOOM

Nothing can warm a cold winter's heart more than a window full of blooming bulbs. Whether narcissuses, tulips, daffodils, or hyacinths, the fragrance and sprightly aspect of these flowers will lift your spirits and put a real spring in your step.

Among the bulbs that can be forced well in pots are crocus, 'Paperwhite' narcissus (*Narcissus Tazetta* 'Paperwhite'), *N.* 'Tête-à-Tête', *Hyacinthus* 'Anna Marie', lily-of-the-valley (*Convallaria majalis*), and white calla lilies (*Zantedeschia aethiopica*).

Hardy Bulbs That Need a Chill

These instructions will get you started with tulips, narcissuses, hyacinths, and crocus. Special directions for tender bulbs and lilies-of-the-valley will follow. The only requirement you will need for forcing hardy bulbs to bloom early in the season is a cool room, cellar, or garage that maintains a temperature between 45°F to 50°F. If you have no objections to a bit of grit in the fridge, it's a great place to root bulbs, since temperatures usually run about 40°F to 45°F near the crisper.

Use 6-inch clay pots—plastic pots are too lightweight, and they prevent the passage of air into the soil—planting between three to six bulbs per pot. For hyacinths, be sure to plant in seasoned clay pots—never new ones. For some unknown reason (at least to me), new pots and hyacinths do not mix.

For soil, equal parts potting soil, sharp sand, and shredded peat moss, plus a little composted cow (or sheep) manure works well. Crock the drain hole and fill two-thirds of the pot with the planting mix. Tamp it down, then set the bulbs carefully on the medium about an inch apart. Do not twist the bulbs—it can easily damage the basal plate and interfere with root formation. Fill the spaces around the bulbs, leaving just the tips of their noses uncovered.

Now soak the pots in a bucket of tepid water (or use the sink) until the mix is thoroughly wet. As you immerse each pot, hold your hand over the mix, lest it rise up and out. Next, drain the pots. The mix should be wet but not dripping.

Put the bulbs in a box or cover them with sheets of newspaper or cardboard—anything to prevent light from reaching the soil surface. Move the bulbs to an area where the temperature is cool and constant. It should take about eight to twelve weeks for the bulbs to develop root systems. Check to see that roots are peeping through the drainage holes. If you don't have an appropriately cool spot indoors, place the potted bulbs outdoors in a cold frame or a pit, covering them over with leaves and straw. Remember, if left outdoors, the bulbs must not be allowed to freeze. If they do, they will not bloom.

Nothing in life is perfect, but if you follow the above instructions, your tulips should root within twelve to fourteen weeks, the narcissus between ten and twelve weeks, and the hyacinths and crocus between six and ten weeks.

Once the roots form, bring the pots indoors to a cool window (around 60°F), away from any artificial heat. When the new shoots turn green and are about 4 to 6 inches high, move the pots to a sunny window for blooming. Never let the medium dry out.

After flowers fade, cut their stems off close to the bulbs. Keep watering the hardy bulbs, allowing leaves to mature and die naturally, then transplant to the garden in the spring for future blooming.

Tulips are not as easy to force as other hardy bulbs but I've always had good luck with *Tulipa fosterana* 'Red Emperor'. When planting these bulbs, use six to a pot, placing the flat side toward the edge of the container. This flat side is the spot where the first leaf will emerge, growing gracefully over the edge instead of toward the center.

Spring-flowering crocus, grape hyacinths (*Muscari armeniacum*), star of Bethlehem (*Ornighogalum umbellatum*), and *Iris reticulata* are all easy plants to flower in the winter.

Pre-cooled Bulbs

Many nurseries now offer pre-cooled, hardy bulbs specially prepared for early bloom. Such bulbs should be planted immediately upon receipt and can go directly into a favorite dish or container, stored between four and six weeks at 50°F for some root development, then brought into a warm room for immediate bloom.

Tender Bulbs

So-called 'Paperwhite' narcissus, 'Soleil d'Or', and Chinese sacred lilies (*Narcissus tazetta* var. *orientalis*), are the usual varieties of tender narcissus bulbs offered in the trade. They usually come pre-planted, or you can pot them up in your own container with a bowl at least 3 inches high. Pebbles, gravel, or pre-packaged bulb mixes will keep the bulbs stable. Fill the container with 2 inches of mix and add water until the mix is thoroughly wet. Place the bulbs on top and surround them with more stones to keep them in place, leaving the top half of the bulb in the open. Place the bulbs in a cool (45°F to 50°F), dark well-ventilated spot until the emerging leaves reach about 3 inches tall. Rooting time is between two and three weeks for 'Paperwhite' and four to five weeks for 'Soleil d'Or' and the sacred lilies. Move the container to a lighted area for three or four days so the plants do not lean, and keep watering. Discard these bulbs after blooming.

Lily-of-the-Valley

When ordering bulbs, don't forget to include some prepared lily-of-the-valley pips. They're usually available in a special mix, and all you add is water. You can, however, save a bit of money and often get containers that are more attractive by buying the pips and planting them yourself. They can be potted in almost any mix that holds water, but the basic mix given for the hardy bulbs is fine. The roots are planted in 3-inch pots with the buds just above the surface. Water thoroughly and place them in a dark, well-ventilated spot for about two weeks. When flower stems are well developed bring the plants into more light.

16

SUPPLIERS FOR SEEDS, PLANTS, AND SUPPLIES

SEEDS:

B & T WORLD SEEDS, Route des Marchandes, Paguignan, 34210
Olonzac, France. Phone: +33 (0) 4 68 91 29 63.
Web site: www.b-and-t-world-seeds.com.
A simply staggering collection of seeds from around the world.

CHILTERN SEEDS, Bortree Stile, Ulverston, Cumbria LA12 7PB,
England. Phone: +44 (0) 1229 581137.
Web site: www.chilternseeds.co.uk.
*An amazing selection of seeds from around the world—one that
grows year by year.*

THE FRAGRANT PATH, PO Box 328, Fort Calhoun, NE 68023. *Large
selection of rare and unusual plants from seed.*

SEEDS OF ITALY, 260 West Hendon Broadway, London NW9 6BE,
England. Phone: +44 (0) 20 8930 2516.
Web site: www.seedsofitaly.sagenet.co.uk.
*Seeds of Italy were founded in 1783 by the current owner's great-
great-great-great-great-grandfather, who sold seeds from his horse-
drawn cart.*

SOUTHERN EXPOSURE SEED EXCHANGE, PO Box 460, Mineral, VA
23117. Phone: (540) 894–9480.
Web site: www.southernexposure.com.
Unusual vegetable and flower seeds.

✺ PLANTS:

DIGGING DOG NURSERY, PO Box 471, Albion, CA 95410.
Phone: (707) 937–1130.
Web site: www.diggingdog.com.
Another esoteric catalog with many fascinating plants.

DUTCH GARDENS, PO Box 2037, Lakewood, NJ 08701.
Web site: www.dutchgarderns.com.
A large selection of bulbs and plants imported from Europe.

FORESTFARM, 990 Tetherow Road, Williams, OR 97544-9599.
Phone: (541) 846–6963.
Web site: www.forestfarm.com.
*An incredible nursery with a tremendous selection of plants and
great packaging for shipping.*

GIRARD NURSERIES, PO Box 428, 6839 North Ridge East, Geneva,
OH 44041. Phone: (440) 466–2881.
Web site: www.girardnurseries.com.
Rhododendrons, conifers, and shrubs.

GOODNESS GROWS, 332 Elberton Road, PO Box 311, Lexington, GA
30648. Phone: (706) 743–5055.
Web site: www.goodnessgrows.com.
A marvelous selection of perennials.

LOGEE'S GREENHOUSES, 141 North Street, Danielson, NC 06239-1939.
Phone: 1–888–330–8038.
Web site: www.logees.com.
*An amazing collection of tropicals, including begonias, geraniums,
and fruits.*

McClure & Zimmerman, 335 South High Street, Randolf, WI
53956. Phone: 1–800–883–6998.
Web site: www.mzbulb.com.
A wide selection of bulbs that are shipped for the spring and fall seasons.

New England Bamboo Company, 5 Granite Street, Rockport, MA
01966. Phone: (978) 546–3581.
Web site: www.newengbamboo.com.
A varied selection of specialty bamboos.

Native Sons, Inc., 379 West El Campo Road, Arroyo Grande, CA
93420. Phone: (805) 481–5996.
Web site: www.nativeson.com/home2.html.
A nursery for perennials, grasses, and shrubs that flourish in a climate defined by moderate winter rainfall and warm dry summers.

Niche Gardens, 1111 Dawson Road, Chapel Hill, NC 27516.
Phone: (919) 967–0078.
Web site: www.nichegdn.com.
An eclectic collection of native plants including ornamental grasses.

Plant Delights Nursery, Inc., 9241 Sauls Road, Raleigh, NC
27603. Phone: (919) 772–4794.
Web site: wwwplantdelights.com.
Another fine collection of perennials.

Roslyn Nursery, 211 Burrs Lane, Dix Hills, NY 11746.
Phone: (631) 643–9347.
Web site: www.roslynnursery.com.
Shrubs, including rhododendrons and conifers, plus perennials.

Roycroft Daylily Nursery, 942 White Hall Avenue, Georgetown,
SC 29440. Phone: (843) 527–1533.
Web site: www.roycroftdaylilies.com.
A complete selection of daylilies.

Southern Exposure, 35 Minor at Rusk, Beaumont, TX 77702-
2414. Phone: (409) 835–0644.
Tropicals for home and gardens.

TRANS-PACIFIC NURSERY, 16065 Oldsville Road, McMinnville, OR
97128. Fax: (503) 843–4214.
Web site: www.worldplants.com.
Their Web site is an introduction to plants you never knew existed.

TRENNOLL NURSERY, 3 West Page Avenue, PO Box 125, Trenton, OH
45067. Phone: (513) 988–6121.
Rock plants and many small evergreens.

WILKERSON MILL GARDENS, 9595 Wilkerson Mill Road, Palmetto,
GA 30268. Phone: (770) 463–2400.
Web site: www.hydrangea.com.
*Elizabeth Dean runs a marvelous nursery with a glowing collection
of perennials and a special collection of hydrangeas.*

❧ SUPPLIES:

BONSAI BY THE MONASTERY, 2625 Highway 212 SW, Conyers, GA
30094-4044. Phone: 1–800–778–POTS (7687).
Web site: www.bonsaimonk.com.
Everything you will ever need for bonsai.

CHARLEY'S GREENHOUSE & GARDEN, 17979 Star Route 536, Mount
Vernon, WA 98273-3269. Phone: 1–800–322–4707.
Web site: www.charleysgreenhouse.com.
Everything you'll ever need for your greenhouse.

WALT NICKE COMPANY, PO Box 433, 36 McLeod Lane, Topsfield
MA 01983. Phone: (978) 887–3388.
Web site: www.gardentalk.com.
The original garden supplier of tools and equipment.

✤ BIBLIOGRAPHY

Bailey, L. H. (Liberty Hyde). *The Garden of Gourds.* New York: Macmillan, 1937.

———. *Hortus Third : A Concise Dictionary of Plants Cultivated in the United States and Canada.* New York: Macmillan, 1976.

Brunfels, Otto. *Herbarum Vivae Eicone.* 1530–1536.

Elbert, George A., and Virginie F. Elbert. *Foliage Plants for Decorating Indoors.* Portland OR: Timber Press, 1989.

Gerard, John. *Herball, or, Generall Historie of Plantes.* London: John Norton, 1597.

Graf, Alfred Byrd. *Exotic Plant Manual.* Rutherford, NJ: Roehrs Co., 1970.

Huysmans J.-K. *À Rebours.* Paris: C. Charpentier, 1905.

Indoor Gardening. Brooklyn: Brooklyn Botanic Garden, 1987.

Jekyll, Gertrude. *Colour Schemes for the Flower Garden.* London: Country Life, Ltd, 1925.

Jervis, Roy N. *Aglaonema Growers Notebook.* South Miami: International Aroid Society, 1980.

Lloyd, Christopher. *The Adventurous Gardener.* New York: Random House, 1985.

Marshall, Nina L. *Mosses and Lichens.* New York: Doubleday & Company, 1907.

Murata, Kyuzo. *Four Seasons of Bonsai.* New York: Kodansha International, 1991.

Pizzetti, I. and H. Cocker. *Flowers: A Guide for Your Garden.* New York: Harry N. Abrams, 1968.

Robinson, William. *The English Flower Garden.* London: J. Murray, 1906.

White, Mary Grant. *Pots and Pot Gardens.* London: Abelard-Schuman, 1969.

Williams, Henry T. ed. *Window Gardening.* New York: Ladies Floral Cabinet Company, 1871.

Wright, Richardson. *The Story of Gardening.* New York: Dodd, Mead & Company, 1934.

❧ INDEX

Note: Page numbers in **boldface** refer to illustrations.

A

À rebours, 40–41
Abel, Harry, 81–87, 156
Abelia chinensis, 103
Abeliophyllum distichum,
219, 220
Abies balsamea 'Nana,' 125
Abutilon, 33–34
Acacia retinodes, 34–35
Acalypha hispida, 36–37
Acer, 87–88
  A. japonicum, 103
  A. palmatum, 87, 125
  'Beni schichihenge,' **126**
  dissectum atropurpurum,
    87–88
Acidanthera bicolor, 209
Acorus calamus, 192
'Adagio' maiden grass
  (*Miscanthus sinensis*
  'Adagio,' 155
Adelman, Albert H., 159–161
The Adventurous Gardener,
  44
Aegopodium podagraria, 90
  'Variegatum,' 90
African gardenia *(Mitrio-*
  stigma axillare), 47
African hemp *(Sparmannia*
  africana), 76–77
Against the Grain, 40–41
Agapanthus africanus, 209,
  210
Aglaonema Growers
  Notebook, 61
Aglaonema modestum, 60–62
Agrostis nebulosa, 146–147
air plant *(Kalanchoe pin-*
  nata), 50
Aira elegans, 152
Alchemilla, 91
Allegheny spurge
  (Pachysandra procum-
  bens), 96
alligator pear or avocado
  (Persea americana),
  196–197
Allium christophii, 209
alpine gardens, 115–132

plants for, 125–132
scree beds, 117–120
Alpine strawberry (Fragaria
  vesca 'Alpine'), 195
Amaranthus 'Tricolor
  Perfecta,' 59
amaryllis, blue *(Worsleya*
  raynerii), 39
Amaryllis belladonna, 37–38
amaryllis *(Hippeastrum)*,
  37–40
  procreation of., 39–40
Amorphophyllus rivieri, 52
Anchusa capensis, 186
Andreaea petrophila, 112
Androsace villosa, 125
angel wings *(Caladium*
  bicolor), 66–68
Anthurium, 41–42
Apera, 152
aphids, 26–27
Aquilegia, 127
aralia, false *(Disygotheca ele-*
  gantissima), 68–69
Aralia laciniata, 68–69
Aristolochia, 134–135
Artemesia schmidtiana var.
  nana, 127
artificial light, 14
Arum italicum, 209–211
Arundinaria, 162
Arundinaria viridistriata,
  109–110
Asarum, 91
Asia, 202
Aspidistra elatior, 10, 62–63
Athyrium filix-fernina, 91
Aucuba japonica, 103
autumn crocus *(Colchicum*
  spp.), 211
autumn snowdrop *(Leu-*
  cojum autumnale), 217
Avena, 147
avocado *(Persea americana)*,
  196–197

B

balloon flower *(Platycoden*
  grandiflorus 'Mariesii'),
  131

bamboo, 157–164
controlling growth, 159–160
bamboo spiderwort
  (Murdannia actifolia var-
  iegata), 78–79
bamboos.com (Burt
  Associates Bamboo),
  159–160
Bambusa, 160–161
banana *(Musa)*, 197–199
barberry, Japanese *(Berberis*
  thunbergii), 103–104
barrenworts *(Epimedium)*,
  93
Bartramia pomiformis, 112
Beaucarnea recurvata, 63–64
  var. *intermedia*, 64
beefsteak begonia *(B. x ery-*
  throphylla), 43
Bégon, Michel, 42
Begonia, 42–45, **43**
  'Red Dragon,' **104**
Bénét's Reader's
  Encyclopedia, 77
Benincasa hispida, 200–201
Berberis
  B. thunbergii, 103–104
  'Golden-nugget,' **104**
Bergenia cordifolia, 92
  'Purpurea,' 31
bibliography, 231–232
birthwort *(Aristoochia)*,
  134–135
bishop's-hats *(Epimedium)*,
  93
black bamboo
  (Phyllostachys nigra),
  158–159, 160, 161
black mondo grass
  (Ophiopogon planiscapus
  'Arabicus'), 130
Bletilla striata, 127
blue flagg iris *(Iris versi-*
  color), 192
blueberries *(Vaccinium)*,
  199
bog gardens, 193–194
bonsai
  containers, 82–83
  grasses, 156

233